"Throw the book away"

ALSO BY AMIE A. DOUGHTY

*Folktales Retold: A Critical Overview of
Stories Updated for Children* (McFarland, 2006)

"Throw the book away"

Reading versus Experience in Children's Fantasy

AMIE A. DOUGHTY

McFarland & Company, Inc., Publishers
Jefferson, North Carolina, and London

LIBRARY OF CONGRESS CATALOGUING-IN-PUBLICATION DATA

Doughty, Amie A., 1970–
　　Throw the book away : reading versus experience in children's fantasy / Amie A. Doughty.
　　　　p.　　cm.
　　Includes bibliographical references and index.

　　ISBN 978-0-7864-4982-8
　　softcover : acid free paper ∞

　　1. Children's literature—History and criticism.　2. Children—Books and reading.　3. Fantasy literature—History and criticism. I. Title.
PN1009.A1D667　2013
809'.89282—dc23　　　　　　　　　　　　　　　2013013759

BRITISH LIBRARY CATALOGUING DATA ARE AVAILABLE

© 2013 Amie A. Doughty. All rights reserved

No part of this book may be reproduced or transmitted in any form or by any means, electronic or mechanical, including photocopying or recording, or by any information storage and retrieval system, without permission in writing from the publisher.

On the cover: girl reading, fairy, forest scene and background (iStockphoto/Thinkstock); elf (Hemera/Thinkstock)

Manufactured in the United States of America

McFarland & Company, Inc., Publishers
　Box 611, Jefferson, North Carolina 28640
　　www.mcfarlandpub.com

For Nathan, Eden, Anna,
Alaina, Laurel and Clark

Table of Contents

Acknowledgments ix
Preface 1
Introduction 5

Part I. Overviews

    1. Children's Literature, Fantasy and Metafiction 9
    2. Books as Artifacts of Power 27
    3. Interacting with Books 50
    4. The Writer-Character in Children's Fantasy 64
    5. Books and Storytelling in Film 81

Part II. Specific Series

    6. *Harry Potter*, Book Learning, Adolescent Scribbling
       and Self-Reliance 111
    7. *Inkheart* and the Rejection of Literacy 140
    8. Living Characters and Life Behind the
       Scenes in *The Sylvie Cycle* 155

Conclusion 167
Chapter Notes 169
Bibliography 175
Index 195

Acknowledgments

This book would not exist without the encouragement and support of many people. First, I would like to thank both Charlotte Amaro and Bianca Tredennick for their feedback on several chapters as well as for their cheerleading. I would also like to acknowledge the editorial help of Christy Jaromack, who passed her eagle eye over Chapter 6. Other family, friends, and colleagues from SUNY Oneonta and beyond have also offered encouragement and support through the long process of completing this book, and I want to thank them for their support.

Chapters 2 and 4 were presented in an earlier form at Northeast Popular Culture Association conferences. Chapter 4 was also presented at SUNY Oneonta for Parnassus, the English Club. Chapter 3, 6, 7, and 8 were all presented in early versions at National Popular Culture Association/American Culture Association conferences. All of the chapters presented underwent significant revisions for the final book.

Preface

Children's literature critics such as Perry Nodelman, Charles Sarland, and John Stephens point frequently to how most people expect children's literature to have a purpose, to contain a didactic element that upholds the current ideology of the culture for which the book is published. Other critics such as Alison Lurie have pointed to children's books that stand the passage of time as subversive in some way or another — even if that subversion is less apparent over time (Lurie points to Jo from *Little Women*, whose actions in the novel were quite radical at the time of publication but do not seem radical to contemporary readers). The reality of children's literature, as Nodelman and others indicate, is that even subversive texts contain messages that are not subversive. There is a balance in children's literature between didacticism and subversion regardless of genre rather than an opposition.

Given the intended audience of children's literature, it is hardly surprising that many adults want to encourage literacy through the presentation of books, readers, and reading in stories for children. Books represent adult authority in children's literature. The avid reader is the most common type of reader seen in children's literature, though both the ambivalent and the reluctant reader may also appear. Because children are learning to read and to value literacy as they develop, adults might expect the message of these texts to be that reading and books are wonderful and that everyone should read more. Indeed, this message can be found in some of children's literature, particularly in realistic fiction, where books are merely books. However, children's fantasy fiction often presents books and reading in ways that reflect the fantastic nature of the texts, and the view of books, readers, and reading in these fantasies often differs from realistic fiction.

There are several ways in which books, readers, and reading can be incorporated prominently in children's fantasy fiction. The most common way in which books are used is as artifacts of power. Books can be used as portals, as in Herbie Brennan's *Faerie Wars*; they can be used to manipulate other characters, as in Eoin Colfer's *Artemis Fowl*; they can be used to comfort characters separated from home, or to give them advice, as in Gail Carson Levine's *Ella Enchanted*; and they can be used as magical guides, as in Garth Nix's *Abhorsen* trilogy. Books can even contain forbidden knowledge and pose a danger to those who possess them. Such is the case in Tony DiTerlizzi and Holly Black's *The Spiderwick Chronicles* and Rachel Caine's *The Morganville Vampires* series. In J.K. Rowling's *Harry Potter* series, books are seemingly useful tools for the young characters' education — the primary setting is Hogwarts School of Witchcraft and Wizardry, after all — yet in several of the novels in the series, books are a threat to the main characters, as with Riddle's diary in *Harry Potter and the Chamber of Secrets*. In other novels in the series, notably *Harry Potter and the Order of the Phoenix* and *Harry Potter and the Half-Blood Prince*, over-reliance on books comes under fire, and students are forced to rethink the importance of book learning. The main characters in *Harry Potter* are forced to negotiate the world of adults through their books, classes, and the media. If they do not examine these elements critically, they are placed in danger.

While books as artifacts of power are the most common uses of books in children's fantasy fiction, other novels in the genre use books in a much more fantastic way. In these fantasy novels, characters emerge from or enter into fictional works within the novel and interact with the main characters. These interactive types of fantasies focus to a large extent on the creation of stories and what motivates characters. In some cases, as with Tony Abbott's *Cracked Classics* series, reluctant readers are forced to follow a classic story such as *Treasure Island* along with the book's characters and gain an appreciation for the story, if not ultimately for reading. In other books, such as Lauren Child's *Beware of Storybook Wolves*, characters emerge from the fictional text to interact with the main character until they are somehow returned to their fictional home. In Cornelia Funke's *Inkheart* series, there is a combination of entering and exiting the focal fictional text of the series, *Inkheart*, and much of the drama revolves around how much power writers and readers can have over fictional characters. Though this series begins in a way that should seemingly reveal the importance of reading and of books, by the end, the importance of both comes into question with the main characters' rejection of the literate world in favor of a fictional one in which reading is a rare skill and books belong only to the very wealthy and powerful.

Still other children's fantasy fiction focuses on writer-characters creating texts. Rick Riordan's *Percy Jackson & the Olympians* and *The Kane Chronicles* series both present young narrators whose narrative technique closes the gap between the fantastic events of the series and reality. Dav Pilkey's *Captain Underpants* series, by contrast, revolves around two troublesome boys who write their own comic book called *Captain Underpants*, but the events they write about in the comic come alive in their world. The structure of this narrative serves to underscore the fictional nature of the series. In Roderick Townley's *The Sylvie Cycle*, the focus of the series is Sylvie, the main character in a fictional book called *The Great Good Thing*. This trilogy is unique in that it is presented almost entirely from the perspective of fictional characters who know that they are characters in a book. Though there is some interaction with "real" characters, the focus of the book is how fictional characters cope with life in little-used books, on the Internet, and in space, and how the way in which they are "written" affects their actions when the book is closed.

While there is some criticism of books and readers in children's literature, notably articles by Joe Sutliff Sanders and Claudia Nelson, little examination has been made of how books, readers, and reading are presented in children's fantasy fiction. Instead, critics examine fantasy as a genre or metafiction, or they discuss reading children's literature (rather than the portrayal of reading in children's literature), but they do not focus on books, readers, and reading in the manner approached here. The goal of this book is to explore how books, readers, and reading are presented in children's and young adult fantasy fiction. From books as artifacts of power to interactive books to writer-characters, these fantasy texts do not fully embrace books, and the young characters frequently learn that actions and experience are as important, if not more important, than reading. Despite the association between adult authority and books in children's literature — perhaps even because of the association — books are often left behind as the youthful main characters begin to learn self-sufficiency.

Introduction

The picture "Mr. Linden's Library" from Chris Van Allsburg's picture book *The Mysteries of Harris Burdick*, which is a collection of unusual pictures each with a caption and a brief description, shows a young girl asleep in her bed. Beside her lies an open book from which a creeping vine has begun to escape, just starting to touch her arm. The picture's caption reads, "He had warned her about the book. Now it was too late." Though the "he" of the caption is not clarified, presumably "he" is "Mr. Linden," the adult who has apparently loaned the girl the book. The girl, then, is caught between two authorities: Mr. Linden the librarian and the author of this book. By trusting the book's authority over Mr. Linden's authority as librarian (and thus as an expert on books), the girl has endangered herself. The implication behind this image and its caption is that reading this book — or at least leaving it open and unattended — is dangerous. This danger can be overcome by listening to adults.

The role of authority figures is critical in much of children's literature. It is not unusual for child protagonists to question or disregard authority figures — teachers, parents, other adults with whom they come in contact. Sometimes these child characters even mock the authority figures, subverting their authority. Such is the case with Tom in *The Adventures of Tom Sawyer*, with Pippi in *Pippi Longstocking*, and with Harry, Ron and Hermione (among many other young characters) in the *Harry Potter* series. But subversion is not the sole focus of these books. No matter how enjoyable it is for the character (and the reader) to question, disregard, or mock authority, this subversion often comes with consequences, and the characters generally pay the price for disregarding those in charge — no matter how dislikable these adult authority figures may appear. The characters learn lessons about life from their actions, and most characters demonstrate some kind of growth as a result of the lessons. These lessons may be overt and clearly articulated, as is frequently seen in fables and folktales, but most children's literature from the Golden Age of children's literature to the present embeds the lesson within an entertaining story.

Critics of children's literature point toward the lessons as part of the expectations of children's literature because the young readers for whom the adult authors write are in their formative years. Books form part of children's education and help to indoctrinate children into their society by showing appropriate behavior even as it entertains them. Authors such as Charles Sarland, Perry Nodelman, and John Stephens, who look at children's literature and ideology, emphasize how ideology is embedded in children's literature, something that further explains why didacticism is part of most children's literature regardless of how entertaining the stories are. This didacticism exists regardless of genre.

Also common in children's literature regardless of genre are depictions of schooling and education, from day schools to boarding schools to other educational activities. These depictions can serve to underscore the educational component of children's literature by setting the stories in places of learning. Alongside this educational focus come books, readers, and reading. Though not all children's literature featuring books is set in a school, like the educational systems, these books are tied to adults and their authority. In realistic fiction, books are books—they may enthrall their readers, excite them, or even alienate them, but books serve the same purpose that they serve in the real world.

Fantasy fiction for children, however, expands the role of books. While mundane books like those in realistic fiction dominate children's fantasy, other types of books also appear. Some books act as artifacts of power. They may possess magical properties, acting as portals or changing their text with each use, as in *Faerie Wars*, *Ella Enchanted*, and *The Secrets of the Immortal Nicholas Flamel* series. They may also be non-magical but dangerous because of their content, such as the books in *The Spiderwick Chronicles* and *Libyrinth*. Other books, like the one represented in "Mr. Linden's Library," may have an interactive quality to them. The level of this interaction can vary. Though Van Allsburg depicts flora rather than a character emerging from the book, other books, such as Lauren Child's picturebook *Beware of Storybook Wolves*, contain characters who emerge from fictional books within the stories. Other children's books present the opposite, sending the characters of a book into the book they're reading, as with Tony Abbott's *Cracked Classics* series and Lauren Children's *Who's Afraid of the Big Bad Book?*, the sequel to *Beware of Storybook Wolves*. Still other children's books combine the two modes of interaction. Such is the case with Cornelia Funke's *Inkheart* series.

Other children's fantasy presents writer-characters who are responsible for shaping the stories of which they are a part. These children's fantasies are heavily metafictional and, rather than focusing on outside books, focus on themselves as artifacts. The narrative mode of these books affects how the fantasy/reality distinction is either exposed or erased. Narratives in which an adult is clearly shaping the story, as in *The Name of This Book Is Secret* or in which the focus is parody as in the *Captain Underpants* series expose the fictional nature of the texts. On the other hand, consonant first person narratives like those in the *Percy Jackson & the Olympians* series and *The Kane Chronicles* tend to erase the line between fantasy and reality.

With all of these modes of presenting books, reading, and writing in children's fantasy, the question becomes "What do these children's fantasies have to say about books and reading?" Because reading is something adults want to encourage in children — if only to sell more books, though ideologically to emphasize the importance of education and literacy — the expected message is, to use Claudia Nelson's argument, "Read!" (228). Reading matters and child readers should see protagonists embracing books and reading, surely.

This book examines the various ways in which books, readers, and reading are portrayed in children's fantasy fiction. Part I offers background information on key ideas and then explores different roles that books, readers, and reading can take in children's fantasy. Chapter 1, "Children's Literature, Fantasy, and Metafiction," examines the three main areas covered in this book — children's literature, fantasy fiction, and metafiction. It explores the role of didacticism and subversion in each area and ties books to adult authority. Chapter 2, "Books as Artifacts of Power," explores children's fantasy in which books act as artifacts of power. It examines how main characters interact with and utilize books. Some of the texts examined include the *Septimus Heap* series, *The Spiderwick Chronicles*, *The Secrets of the Immortal Nicholas Flamel* series, and *The Morganville Vampires* series. Most of these series focus on the importance of balancing reading and action so that the young protagonists start to become independent.

Chapter 3, "Interacting with Books," looks at children's books such as *The Neverending Story*, *Cracked Classics*, and *Malice*, in which the young main characters interact with fictional characters. Sometimes this interaction occurs when fictional characters emerge from the books the main characters read, though more often the main characters enter into the fictional books. Messages about books and reading in these fantasy books are quite mixed, and the importance of books and reading is often undermined in some way. However, other messages are presented in a more overt manner than in other fantasies discussed. Chapter 4, "The Writer-Character in Children's Fantasy," focuses on writer-characters in such works as Rick Riordan's *Percy Jackson & the Olympians* and *The Kane Chronicles* series and Dav Pilkey's *Captain Underpants* series. It explores the way in which different narrative techniques affect the relationship between realism and fantasy, as well as the role of parody in these metafictional fantasies. Chapter 5, "Books and Storytelling in Film," explores how films and television series aimed at children and young adults parallel the modes of incorporating books and reading in children's and young adult fantasy discussed in chapters 2, 3, and 4. Films and television programs such as those in chapters 2 and 3 operate similarly to their written counterparts. However, the writer-character (or storyteller-character) in films functions quite differently than those discussed in Chapter 4.

Part II turns to in-depth examinations of three series of books. Chapter 6, "*Harry Potter*, Book Learning, Adolescent Scribbling and Self-Reliance," focuses on J.K. Rowling's *Harry Potter* series, in which books act similarly to those in Chapter 2. In *Harry Potter*, the three main characters must learn to negotiate the adult-controlled realms of books, education, and media to become self-reliant. At the same time, adolescent writers explore their worlds through their own writing, which often foreshadows their later place in adult society.

Chapter 7, "*Inkheart* and the Rejection of Literacy," delves into Cornelia Funke's *Inkheart* series, which resembles the books discussed in Chapter 3. This series more than any other explored in this book seems to reject literacy through the way in which Funke presents avid readers and how she concludes the series. It also breaks with traditional children's literature that presents a home/away/home structure.

Finally, Chapter 8, "Living Characters and Life Behind the Scenes in *The Sylvie Cycle*," explores Roderick Townley's *The Sylvie Cycle*, a series that Farah Mendlesohn calls an "irregular" in relation to her fantasy schema because it does not fit neatly into any of her categories. It similarly does not fit any type of book-focused children's fantasy discussed here. The series revolves around the life of characters in a book both during "performances" of the story for readers and during times when they wait for new readers to open the book. The series, like most of those discussed in this book, does not focus on the importance on reading; instead, the importance of action and of doing "great good things" dominates the series.

Despite the importance of teaching children to engage in reading, books, readers, and reading in children's fantasy fiction are secondary to action. The ultimate message of the majority of these book-dominated fantasies is that the adult authority represented by the books must be questioned and that the young main characters must experience the world on their own to succeed.

PART I. OVERVIEWS

1

Children's Literature, Fantasy and Metafiction

In the Preface to the second edition of her collection *From Instruction to Delight: An Anthology of Children's Literature to 1850*, Patricia Demers notes that

> prior to the middle of the eighteenth century, ... the emphasis [in children's literature] fell heavily and deliberately on instruction — so much so that before 1744 there were, properly speaking, no children's books. In that year, John Newbery produced *A Little Pretty Pocket-Book*, which heralded the beginning of *delight* and, along with the ubiquitous chapbooks, ushered in a new era in children's reading [xv, emphasis in original].

The focus on instruction in early children's literature reflects the priority given to educating children over entertaining them. By the Golden Age of children's literature (mid–1800s to early 1900s), however, the view of children was shifting and books produced for children reflect this shift. As Demers and other children's literature critics have noted, even before the Golden Age, the attitude was changing. Diane M. Barone, in *Children's Literature in the Classroom: Engaging Lifelong Readers*, notes that in Charles Perrault's time (1628–1703), "children read books for enjoyment rather than just to learn a lesson, although the lessons were embedded in many fairytales" (10). Perrault's fairy tales, written for upper class women more than for children, each contain a moral at the end to make clear the lesson from the tales. This embedding of lessons was not limited to folktales, and Barone notes that in the 1800s and early 1900s, "didactic books although still present, did not dominate. Many authors and illustrators created works for children that were expected to result in joy rather than just lessons learned" (11). This balance between didacticism and entertainment remains a hallmark of much children's literature regardless of genre, and Barone even notes that a current trend in children's literature, particularly in books written by celebrities, is "a return to didacticism" in a heavier manner than the more balanced books (16), a move that she does not like.

Many critics of children's literature attribute the didactic nature of children's literature to the unique position that it occupies as a genre. Peter Hunt, for example, in his introduction to *Understanding Children's Literature: Key Essays from the Second Edition of the International Companion Encyclopedia of Children's Literature*, notes,

> Children's books are different from adults' books: they are written for a different audience, with different skills, different needs, and different ways of reading; equally, children experience texts in ways which are often unknowable, but which many of us strongly suspect to be very complex. If we judge children's books (even if we do it unconsciously) by the same value system as we use for adult books — in comparison with which they are bound *by definition* to emerge as *lesser* — then we give ourselves unnecessary problems [3, emphasis in original].

Children's literature is "lesser" when compared to adult literature because adult literature is considered the norm while children's literature is an offshoot of adult literature — it is marked to use the term introduced by Nikolai Trubetzkoy and Roman Jakobson to describe phonological elements and later expanded to describe artistic trends by Jakobson.[1] And though comparing children's literature to adult literature may lead to "unexpected problems," it is nearly impossible not to compare them. Critics such as Jack Zipes even question if children's literature is a valid label. In *Sticks and Stones: The Troublesome Success of Children's Literature from Slovenly Peter to Harry Potter*, Zipes makes the bold pronouncement that "children's literature does not exist. If we take the genitive case literally and seriously, and if we assume ownership and possession are involved when we say 'children's literature' or the literature of children, then there is no such thing as children's literature..." (39–40). Children's literature is nonexistent because "most of the readers, writers, agents, editors, critics, and publishers of children's literature are adults, as are the distributors and owners of bookstores" (40). Because children play such a small part in children's literature, in other words, the label is inaccurate. Though his view is extreme, it is not singular, and it demonstrates the role that adults play in the shaping of children's literature. Barone notes that "clearly, children's books are different from adults' books in that they are written for a specific audience — children — by adults. They are influenced by what cultures believe about children and thus change with the times" (8). She continues this idea, saying, "Children's books ... are written with the current view of childhood in mind and include topics that authors perceive as relevant to them" (8). Children themselves have little say in their reading materials. They are introduced to books by adults who choose them based on any number of criteria: what they enjoyed as children; what they think children should read — often classics and award winners; what fits the curriculum; what other adults recommend. Though children are not voiceless in choosing children's literature, their voice is generally small compared to adults, and they remain reliant upon what adults choose to publish, purchase, and distribute for their reading materials even on the occasions when they make the final choice of what to read — something that does not happen often.

Further, as John Stephens notes in *Language and Ideology in Children's Fiction*, ideology plays a significant role in children's literature:

> Children's fiction belongs firmly within the domain of cultural practices which exist for the purpose of socializing the target audience. Childhood is seen as the crucial formative period in the life of a human being, the time for basic education about the nature of the world, how to live in it, how to relate to other people, what to believe, what and how to think and in general, the intention is to render the world intelligible [8].

Because adults believe children need to be taught how to be successful members of society, the literature published for children is traditionally imbued with the "proper" social expectations — and characters deviating from expected societal norms are either punished or have their behavior modified, sometimes both. Even an anti-hero such as Artemis Fowl, for example, though he commits criminal acts, has redeemable characteristics in the end — notably his desire to see his mother healthy. As Perry Nodelman notes in *The Hidden Adult: Defining Children's Literature*, "What adults most frequently believe children need from their literature is education" (157). The information meant to educate children may be overtly or covertly presented, as Charles Sarland indicates in "Critical Tradition and Ideological Positioning." Using Peter Hollindale's ideas as a reference point, Sarland discusses "three levels of ideology" in children's literature:

1. the "overt, often proselytising or didactic level";
2. the "more passive level" in which "views of the worlds are put into characters' mouths or otherwise incorporated into the narrative with no overt ironic distancing"; and
3. an "underlying climate of belief" (39).

The first level is often associated with older texts in children's literature, including fables, while the other two can be readily seen in entertaining children's literature. If the message is imbedded, the literature is assumed to be better because it is more likely to engage child readers. All three levels are didactic, though the first level is often rejected by recent critics of children's literature. As Nodelman notes, "It has been fashionable for the last hundred or more years for commentators to express dislike of 'didactic' children's books.

But the often proclaimed distaste for the didactic is usually actually just dismay about the *obviously* didactic, on the assumption that, ideally, children's literature ought to teach without seeming to do so" (157–8, emphasis in original).

Didacticism is *expected* in children's literature, even if it is masked by entertaining stories, and as Hugh Crago indicates in "Healing Texts: Bibliotherapy and Psychology," "there are few examples of successful and popular literature which do not offer both delight and 'instruction' in some form or other" (183). Continuing this line of thought, Sarland notes,

> The very expression "children's literature," for instance, brings with it a whole set of value judgements which have been variously espoused, attacked, defended and counterattacked over the years. In addition, discussion of children's fiction ... has always been characterised by arguments about its purposes. These purposes, or in some cases these denials of purpose, stem from the particular characteristics of its intended readership and are invariably a product of the views held within the adult population about children and young people themselves and about their place in society [30].

The purpose-driven nature of children's literature differentiates it from adult literature. Though adult literature can and does sometimes contain messages, it is not *expected*. Adults, because they are viewed as mature and finished with their education — because they have "grown up" — are not subject to the same message-driven literature as children.

Given the role of adults in all aspects of children's literature, children's books can be associated directly with adult authority. As David Rudd in "Theorising and Theories: How Does Children's Literature Exist?" says, "The fact that children are seen *not* to have a stake in this [writing their literature] is, once again, a product of the way children's literature (in its texts and its criticism) has become institutionalised, such that — ironically — only commercially published work is seen to count; or, to put it another way, only adults are seen to 'authorise' proper children's literature" (19, emphasis in original). Part of Rudd's article focuses on the fact the children do indeed write and tell stories but that these stories are not validated the way in which published adult-generated literature for children is. Adults have power over children at all levels, including the books they read: teachers/schools choose the literature assigned in classes; parents, caregivers, and other adults often choose much of the literature children read at home. The power is not all-inclusive, of course, for children have ways of gaining access to "forbidden" texts, but the majority of children's literature comes from adults. As a result, according to Nodelman, "the texts assume the rights of adults to wield power and influence over children" (78). Adult authority, textual or otherwise, is a key aspect of

1. Children's Literature, Fantasy and Metafiction

children's literature. Hunt, like Sarland, comments that "in the judgement of children's books, then, *for* is often the key word. Books are not just 'good,' but 'good *for*.' Children's books are used for different purposes at different times — for more things than most books are" ("Introduction" 10, emphasis in original). Children's literature serves a purpose — or should according to many adults. Still, Nodelman comments, "Children's literature is not so much what children read as what producers hope children will read" (4). This child reader is in fact a construct, an ideal figure in the mind of the author (and publisher and other adults involved in the production of children's literature). The reality is much harder to pinpoint and has generated extensive discussion.

Children's literature often focuses around the education of children. British boarding school stories from Thomas Hughes's *Tom Brown's School Days*, to Rudyard Kipling's *Stalky & Co.*, to Anthony Horowitz's *Groosham Grange* to J.K. Rowling's *Harry Potter* series, have long been popular publications. Similarly, in the United States, children's fiction largely, though not exclusively, realistic, may focus on schooling in whole or in part. Such is the case of *The Adventures of Tom Sawyer*, many of the later *Little House* books, many of Judy Blume's novels including *Tales of a Fourth-Grade Nothing*, Beverly Cleary's *Ramona* books, Barbara Park's *Junie B. Jones* series, and countless other books for children. This focus is not surprising for two main reasons: school is a focal point for most children, who spend most of their waking hours there, and adults associate learning, schooling, with childhood, making school a logical setting for and focus of children's literature. And schooling, like books and reading, is associated with adult authority.

Given that one of the goals of educating children is to make them effective — and hopefully engaged — readers, it might also be expected that children's literature, again regardless of genre, that contains references to books, readers, and reading would promote and validate active, engaged reading. Surely characters who demonstrate positive responses to schooling and to the practice of reading are the ones adults want children to model. And characters who are initially reluctant readers can be taught to enjoy reading and schooling, demonstrating to their young readers that they too can learn to love reading. Sarland comments that "the assumption is that readers 'identify with' the protagonists, and thus take on their particular value positions. Readers are thus ideologically constructed by their identification with the character" (42). However, he points out that reader identification varies both in terms of character and in intensity (43). Indeed characters such as Laura Ingalls do seem to enjoy schooling. Yet some of the most popular characters in children's literature, from Tom Sawyer to Pippi Longstocking to the characters in Shel

Silverstein's poems to Harry Potter, often eschew book learning and reading in favor of less accepted activities, many of which involve skipping school. This rejection of school is highly subversive (though quite common).

Indeed, despite the many arguments about the impact of adults on children's literature, some critics argue that children's literature often contains a subversive element. Alison Lurie, in her book *Don't Tell the Grown-Ups: The Subversive Power of Children's Literature*, argues that the children's literature that has had the greatest lasting impact — books such as *The Adventures of Tom Sawyer, Alice's Adventures in Wonderland, Little Women*— contains at its core a subversive element: "Most of the great works of juvenile literature are subversive in one way or another" (4). At its heart, subversiveness is a rebellion against authority, and, for children, the highest authority is often the adult figures in their lives, particularly parents/caregivers and teachers. If indeed subversion in children's literature is, in part, a rejection of adult authority, then it stands to reason that books and reading may be rejected in children's literature, and indeed this seems to be the case in many pieces of children's literature. However, even in subversive children's literature, a message, a thread of didacticism, may appear. Both Hunt and Nodelman temper Lurie's view on subversion, pointing out its limits in an adult-dominated genre. Hunt comments, "History, as constructed, generally shows us (obviously enough) that adults can and do control the production of children's literature — however subversive the child's reading might be.... Censorship permeates the process, operating both before and after the texts are produced" ("Introduction" 5). Nodelman points out, in response to Lurie's ideas about subversiveness, "if it does this [attack conventional adult wisdom] ... it can only be because its adult writers wish to be free from and attack the conventions of other adults. It is a rebellion by some adults against other adults under the banner of something here identified as childhood" (182). Nodelman then presents the idea that subversion and "non-subversion" exist side by side in children's literature and that subversion is limited by society (publishers and, more importantly, buyers) (182–3). The balanced view of subversiveness and didacticism makes sense given the nature of children's literature and the role of adults in the genre.

Fantasy Fiction and Children's Literature

Like children's literature, fantasy fiction is a marked genre. The history and definition of fantasy can vary widely among critics of the genre. For example, some critics such as Richard Mathews place the origins of fantasy with some of the oldest texts in the world — *The Epic of Gilgamesh* (ca. 2000 B.C.E.),

The Odyssey (ca. 750 B.C.E.), and *The Mahabharata* (ca. 400 B.C.E.)—while other critics declare that fantasy as a genre does not exist until it is separate from folk literatures, usually in the 18th or 19th century. Literary fantasy, the focus of most criticism about fantasy, certainly comes to life much later than its folk origins. Though Mathews in *Fantasy: The Liberation of Imagination* points out that "there are no pure genres, and fantasy is no exception" (5), nevertheless there are some defining attributes of fantasy, generally contrasting it with its dominant counterpart, realistic fiction. Pamela S. Gates, Susan B. Steffel, and Francis J. Molson in *Fantasy Literature for Children and Young Adults* say, "Any book for children or young adults is fantasy if at least one element in it cannot exist in the world as we know it" (8). Lucie Armitt in *Fantasy Fiction: An Introduction* names two characteristics of fantasies: "They deal in the unknowableness of life" and "[convey] 'a world not necessarily known through the senses or lived experience'" (8). Mathews's definition is similar: "Although it is difficult to define literary fantasy precisely, most critics agree it is a type of fiction that evokes wonder, mystery, or magic—a sense of possibility beyond the ordinary, material, rationally predictable world in which we live" (1). He continues, saying, "Fantasy as a distinct literary genre ... may best be thought of as a fiction that elicits wonder through elements of the supernatural or impossible. It consciously breaks free from mundane reality" (2). The connection among all of these definitions is the unknown or impossible element of the stories. Not all critics agree on the core of fantasy, however. Armitt believes that "the utopian impulse—the desire to go 'beyond'—underlies all fantasy writing, even, paradoxically, of the darkest kind" (113). She believes this because she sees fantasy as looking toward (and beyond) a horizon that is unreachable—the "no place" that constitutes the literal meaning of *utopia* (113). Mathews, on the other hand, disagrees with this view and in fact thinks utopian fiction is separate from fantasy because "it usually sticks closer to the 'realistic' rules" (5). For the purposes of this book, fantasy will be defined as any piece of literature that contains something that could not happen in the real world. Some fantasies will bear a great similarity to realistic fiction barring one or two elements that are unrealistic (e.g., *The Name of This Book Is Secret*), while other fantasies may be set in completely different worlds and/or contain many elements that separate them from reality (e.g., the *Septimus Heap* series).

Regardless of the definition, fantasy is viewed by society, like children's literature, as marked. It is, to use Hunt's term regarding children's literature, seen as *lesser* than realistic fiction. Fantasy critics even today will often spend time trying to demonstrate the validity and value of fantasy as a genre before entering into analyses of specific texts. Armitt, in her defense of fantasy, claims that all fiction writing is "fantasy" (2), though not in the sense that she ultimately defines literary fantasy. And Mathews indicates that fantasy was part of a "dialectic" with realism when realism was a new concept and notes that fantasy is an older genre than realism (2). Wendy Mass and Stuart P. Levine in their essay "What Is Fantasy?" spend quite a bit of time defending fantasy fiction. Similar to Armitt and Mathews, they argue that "Upon closer examination ... fantasy literature has no more an element of escapism than any other work of fiction. In fact, good fantasy literature is often based around notions of exploring social, political, personal, and even spiritual issues" (19). They continue, noting,

> Today, as entire window displays are dedicated to authors such as J.K. Rowling and Robert Jordan, some critics question the value of such literature. Although many see it as a valuable category of fiction, worthy of the popular acclaim it has received, others see it as simple, mindless fluff. Some detractors have even gone as far as condemning the genre as harmful to the healthy development of young minds [23].

This final sentence ties back to the discussion of children's literature and, to use Sarland's term, the *purpose* of the literature. Fantasy, as separate from reality and associated with escapism, comes under fire for not having the right purpose for children because adults frequently assume fantasy does not contain messages for its readers. In response to the detractors of fantasy, Mass and Levine indicate that "proponents of the genre argue that not only isn't fantasy literature dangerous, but is essential to the stimulation of a person's imagination and creativity. Children often learn the roots of how to think 'outside the box' by being exposed to literature that has no boundaries" (24). Like the opponents, then, the proponents of fantasy argue for its *purpose* for children. Despite its marked nature, fantasy is an increasingly popular genre of fiction for all levels of readers, particularly in the young adult market, thanks to the popularity of *Twilight* and *The Hunger Games*, and in the children's market, thanks to *Harry Potter*.

Beyond defending fantasy as a genre, a focus of many fantasy critics is how to subcategorize fantasy, though not all critics believe fantasy needs to be subcategorized. For example, Armitt comments, "I have long deemed the desire to subclassify fantasy into different boxes to be anathema to the texts' innate creativity" (114). She comments of criticism that subcategorizes fantasy, "This is not criticism, it is travesty" (193). Though her point is interesting, Armitt seems to be shortsighted, for subcategorizing fantasy — no matter how — allows for a better understanding of fantasy fiction. The most common types of categories are represented by Mass and Levine. They reference high fantasy (often called quest fantasy or hero fantasy), time slip fantasy, animal fantasy, and humorous fantasy (14–5). Certainly high fantasy, represented most often by J.R.R. Tolkien's *Lord of the Rings*, is a common subgenre of fantasy. Other subgenres can be harder to decide upon, with some critics focusing only upon low fantasy in contrast to high fantasy and others, like Mass and Levine, Gates, Steffel and Molson, and Susan Lehr creating more subcategories. Farah Mendlesohn, in her book *Rhetorics of Fantasy*, approaches the topic differently, saying that she is working "across the more commercial definitions of fantasy, as well as the categories of children's and adults' fantasy, dark fantasy, and light and comic fantasy" (xv). She has devised four categories of fantasy:

> The portal-quest, the immersive, the intrusive, and the liminal. These categories are determined by the means by which the fantastic enters the narrated world. In the portal-quest, we are invited through into the fantastic; in the intrusion fantasy, the fantastic enters the fictional world; in the liminal fantasy, the magic hovers in the corner of our eye; while in the immersive fantasy we are allowed no escape [xiv].

The most important of her categories for the purposes of this book is the intrusion fantasy, though the portal-quest and immersive fantasies also appear in smaller amounts.

Because of the importance of intrusion fantasies to the book, this subgenre will be discussed in more detail. Nicole M. Didicher, in her article "The Children in the Story: Metafiction in *Mary Poppins in the Park*," also uses the term *intrusion fantasy* for the type of fantasy she is exploring, noting that in this type of fantasy, "the fantasy elements intrude into a recognizable and realistic fictional world" (137). Her definition is similar to Mendlesohn's though not the same. Mendlesohn explains that "in intrusion fantasy the fantastic is the bringer of chaos" (xxi). The fantastic sets the events of the story into motion. However, "the intrusion fantasy is not necessarily unpleasant, but it has as its base the assumption that normality is organized, and that when the fantastic retreats the world, while not necessarily unchanged, returns to predictability — at least until the next element of the fantastic intrudes" (xxii). In intrusion fantasies, then, the fantastic is not necessarily a permanent part of the world. If it does remain permanent — as it does in the *Harry Potter* series — subsequent books in the series are usually immersive fantasies rather than intrusion fantasies, though as Mendlesohn notes (see below), immersive fantasies can contain intrusion fantasies. Further, "because the base level is the normal world, intrusion fantasies maintain stylistic realism and rely heavily on explanation" (xxii). This explanation is necessary for the characters to grasp the intrusion elements (and to explain them to the reader). Thus, in *Harry Potter and the Sorcerer's Stone*, much attention is given to explaining to Harry what the different aspects of the wizarding world are, initially by Hagrid when he delivers Harry's acceptance letter to Hogwarts and then takes him school supply shopping in Diagon Alley, and then later by classmates and professors. In addition, "intrusion fantasy, although usually associated with 'real world' fantasy, can be set within the immersive" (xxii). This happens when new fantasy elements upset the balance of a fantasy world. For example, as the *Harry Potter* series progresses, the Horcruxes that Voldemort has created intrude in the familiar fantasy world to which Harry (and the reader) has become accustomed. Finally, Mendlesohn notes that "the trajectory of the intrusion fantasy is straightforward: the world is ruptured by the intrusion, which disrupts normality and has to be negotiated with or defeated, sent back whence it came, or controlled" (115). In *Harry Potter*, Voldemort's intrusion on the wizarding world is defeated — his Horcruxes are all destroyed — and, as the Epilogue demonstrates, the wizarding world is back to normal. This type of resolution works well with children's literature, which usually has clear closure.[2]

The relationship between children's literature and fantasy is quite close despite some critics' opposition to fantasy for children. Mass and Levine note that "some critics see the link between children's literature and adult fantasy as one of the firm underpinnings of the modern fantasy genre" (20). Mathews too connects children's literature to fantasy: "Children's literature has proven to be an enduring influence on adult fantasy" (17). Some of the earliest fantasy fiction is for children — George MacDonald's *The Princess and the Goblin* and Lewis Carroll's *Alice's Adventures in Wonderland*, as well as folktales that have become almost synonymous with children's literature despite their broader origins thanks to Andrew Lang's colored fairy books. These same books are some of the most enduring pieces of children's literature. Other critics, by contrast, try to distance children's and adult fantasy. Armitt, for example, while acknowledging that "some of the most influential fantasy narratives *were* written for children," emphasizes the separation between children's and adult fantasy literature because adult fantasy literature is not "childlike" (3, emphasis in original). Armitt seems to fear that allying children's and adult fantasy will make fantasy fiction more marked, though her sense of what constitutes children's literature is questionable. The texts she references as influential fantasy narratives — *Alice's Adventures in Wonderland, The Wind in the Willows, The Hobbit, The Chronicles of Narnia* — are not inherently "childlike," though they may possess elements of play in them and their main characters are young (or young-seeming). Similarly, contemporary fantasy fiction for children also often has a serious if not dark undertone to it. *Harry Potter*, despite its youthful protagonist, deals with weighty issues such as the death of a parent (or classmate), fate versus free will, and classism and racism. Like many who do not study children's literature, Armitt is making broad assumptions about what constitutes that literature. Similarly negative reactions to fantasy fiction often come from those who have not studied it but assume they know how it works.

Regardless of the attitude of critics toward children's literature, fantasy remains an important element of children's literature, and in fact fantasy for children is often seen as a place where overt didacticism wanes. Gates, Steffel, and Molson refer to 19th century literary fantasies by Hans Christian Andersen and Lewis Carroll, which "departed from the cultural renditions [folktales] by removing some of the levels of didacticism" (4). They further note that "heroic-ethical fantasy is didactic in the best sense of the word and not moralistic or proselytizing: It teaches, it challenges, and, never to be overlooked, it entertains" (132). This comment ties back to Stephens, Hunt, and others on the current desire of adults to balance didacticism and entertainment. Fantasy for children evolved with the shift from purely didactic books to those for entertainment. However, as Maria Nikolajeva indicates in her article "The Development of Children's Fantasy,"

> at its best, fantasy for children provides moral and spiritual guidance for young people, addressing an audience that has not yet any firm distinction between reality and imagination; that does not dismiss magical worlds and events as implausible; that has strong potential for secondary belief. The best examples of classical fantasy for children use the fantastic form as a narrative device, as a metaphor for reality [60].

As with other genres of children's literature, fantasy fiction retains a didactic element. Though Nikolajeva's article focuses on children's fantasy from its origins to the mid-twentieth century, children's fantasy from that point to the present also retains a didactic or moralistic feature. In her article "Modern Children's Fantasy," Catherine Butler points out that changes in social mores have led to some changes in children's fantasy; however, the moralistic feature remains. Butler indicates that "contemporary children's lack of independence militates in favor of fantasies set entirely in secondary worlds, or in which real-world protagonists are decisively removed from their familiar surroundings and transported to another time or reality" (225). This shift of reality allows child characters the freedom to explore magical realms without the level of adult interference that they would encounter in a real-world-based fantasy.

Despite the didactic element, fantasy for children comes under attack by adults, as shown above in Mass and Levine's discussion of attitudes toward children's fantasy. Even proponents of fantasy temper their praise of fantasy at times. Jeanne Murray Walker, for example, explores how fantasy just as often encourages children to follow the status quo as question it in her article "Fantasy Allows Children to Question the Status Quo":

> But far from isolating children or encouraging them to escape from their social responsibilities, "high fantasy" unites people into groups and reinforces the values around which those groups cohere.... [I]f fantasy presents any danger, it is the danger of preparing the reader for obedient, uncritical participation in a comforting, authoritarian system. But the best children's fantasies encourage questioning of commonly held cultural values rather than mere conformity to them [69].

This comment hearkens back to Nodelman and Stephens's arguments about the role of subversion and ideology in children's literature. Ideologically, according to Walker, "fantasy instructs its readers in the norms and truths of an identifiable social community. It portrays those truths as the standard by which adulthood is measured. And adulthood is the valued goal; unlike some other kinds of fiction, fantasy does not pretend to present a snapshot of the world that is value-neutral" (73). Like Stephens and Nodelman, Walker's focus is on how many fantasy texts underscore certain ideological beliefs for their readers. Fantasy encourages conformity, she argues, through its presentation of good and evil: "Good wins. What does that mean? In most popular fantasies, good is nothing more than us, our group, people who dress like us and eat what we eat.... Good equals us equals the successful questor. This formulation powerfully urges readers to conform; any reader who dissents dies, either as the unsuccessful questor or as the evil enemy" (74). However, Walker distinguishes between "good" or "quality" fantasy and popular fantasy: "The best fantasy, novels like *A Wizard of Earthsea* and *The Lion, the Witch, and the Wardrobe*, presents complex and clearly defined values, not vacant symbols of the powerful versus the powerless" (74). Thus, though for Walker fantasy fiction can encourage conformity, it does not unilaterally do so. The way in which she distinguishes between "good" and "quality" literature and popular (or pulp) fantasy is through the complexity of the presentation of good versus evil.[3] Walker applauds "quality" fantasy but clearly does not approve of popular fantasy because it does not have the proper complexity to demonstrate the importance of questioning the status quo.

Tamora Pierce, in her article "Fantasy Books for Adolescents Inspire and Empower," is less ambivalent about the value of fantasy for children and young adults: "These stories appear to have little to do with reality, but they do provide readers with the impetus to challenge the way things are, something YAs respond to wholeheartedly" (64). Pierce herself is a celebrated children's fantasy author — *The Lioness Quartet, The Immortals* series — and thus arguing based on her goals as a writer. It is clear from all this discussion of fantasy for children that, despite its association with entertainment, children's fantasy contains messages. It is didactic like its realistic counterpart. Like Walker, Pierce believes that children's and young adult fantasy can encourage independent thinking. Further, fantasy empowers children: "In the real world, kids have little say. This is a given; it is the nature of childhood. In fantasy, however short, fat, unbeautiful, weak, dreamy, or unlearned individuals may be, they find a realm in which those things are negated by strength" (65). Though as a marked genre within a marked genre fantasy for children comes under great scrutiny, it is also largely celebrated as a positive genre.

Metafiction and Children's Literature

Like children's literature and fantasy fiction, metafiction is a marked type of writing, though given its association with the literary elite, it is not as marked as it was in the mid–1900s. Patricia Waugh, in her seminal book *Metafiction: The Theory and Practice of Self-Conscious Fiction*, defines metafiction:

> *Metafiction* is a term given to fictional writing which self-consciously and systematically draws attention to its status as an artefact in order to pose questions about the relationship between fiction and reality. In providing a critique of their own methods of construction, such writings not only examine the fundamental structures of narrative fiction, they also explore the possible fictionality of the world outside the literary fictional text [2].

Her definition, along with definitions of metafiction by Linda Hutcheon, Brian Stonehill, and many other critics, focuses on the self-consciousness of metafiction and its tendency to shine a light on what constitutes fiction. The effect of this tendency breaks the illusion of reality that is a hallmark of the dominant realistic fiction. As Anita Moss notes in "Varieties of Children's Metafiction," "By its very nature metafiction underscores the distance between actuality and fiction, between nature and art" (90).

Metafiction is a marked genre despite its long history — different critics point to *Don Quixote* and *Tristram Shandy* as some of the earliest novelistic uses of metafiction, and indicate that meta devices were used in other forms of literature prior to the novel. Though metafiction has been evident in the novel, in fiction, since its beginning, the 19th century saw a backlash against metafiction and a favoring of realism, and realism became the dominant form for the novel. As a result, much of the early criticism about metafiction, like criticism of fantasy, attempts to justify the value of metafiction, often by tying metafiction to realistic fiction. Waugh, for example, believes that "metafiction is a tendency or function inherent in *all* novels" (5, emphasis in original).

Linda Hutcheon similarly notes in *Narcissistic Narrative: The Metafictional Paradox*, "*All* literature could be said to be 'escape' literature: readers as well as authors want to create worlds as real as, but other than, the world that is .... In fact, all reading (whether of novels, history or science) is a kind of 'escape' in that it involves a temporary transfer of consciousness from the reader's empirical surroundings to things imagined rather than perceived" (76–7, emphasis in original). Similarly, Maria Nikolajeva comments in *Children's Literature Comes of Age: Toward a New Aesthetic*, "A realistic story is also arranged, manipulated. A realistic novel is no more real than a fantasy novel. It is also an illusion" (205). All of these critics, by tying metafiction to the dominant realism are attempting to justify its worth. Brian Stonehill in *The Self-Conscious Novel: Artifice in Fiction from Joyce to Pynchon* is the most positive and least defensive about the connection between metafiction and realistic fiction: "All *fictions* require us to suspend our disbelief. The realistic novel does so covertly, as it endeavors to pass itself off as real life. But *self-depicting* fictions, by acknowledging the limitations of their own imitations, invite us to suspend our disbelief not only willingly but wittingly" (15, emphasis in original). For Stonehill, then, metafiction makes the reader more engaged ("witting") than realistic fiction, and this fact makes metafiction a valuable form of fiction. His observations about metafiction lead to his conclusion that "it would be more accurate to conceive of a *spectrum* of fictional modes, composed of varying *degrees* of self-consciousness" (15, emphasis in original). Here, like Waugh, Hutcheon, and Nikolajeva, Stonehill ties metafiction to realism.

Metafiction is associated with literary fiction. Stonehill discusses its place in the literary elite, noting, "There is a strong tinge of élitism to the self-conscious novel, a sense that those who do not share a certain body of knowledge are excluded from its implied audience" (7). This "body of knowledge" is intertextuality, and the well-read are often more likely to grasp the intertextual references of metafiction than non-readers. Given the elite quality of metafiction and its goal to alienate readers by throwing realism into question, it should be no surprise that metafiction (and postmodernism more generally) has come to children's literature later than to adult fiction, or that it has remained a marginalized form. Geoff Moss in "Metafiction and the Poetics of Children's Literature" examines the debate over the suitability of children's metafiction. Detractors of children's metafiction share similar concerns about the lack of realism and the elitism of metafiction that early critics of adult metafiction felt. Critics also believe metafiction is too difficult for children, who are just learning what literature is and how it works, to comprehend (50). Those in favor of metafiction for children, by contrast, argue that children are more than able to cope with the non-realistic devices inherent to metafiction and that they do not require simplified texts. Moss ultimately believes that metafiction is suitable for children for three reasons:

> Firstly, because children do have an interest in these kinds of texts — certain kinds of readers find them fascinating. Secondly, because such texts may well have the function of providing an active criticism of more mainstream texts, of defining the limits of poetics and finally because children's literature, like any form of literature will inevitably build on, toy with and perhaps even destroy conventional forms as it develops [52].

Like many children's literature critics, Moss here focuses on the *purpose* of metafiction for children in addition to the "interest" some may have in it, hearkening back once more to Sarland's comment about children's literature as purposeful.

Both Sylvia Pantaleo, who has written extensively about children's metafiction and its place in the classroom, and Bette P. Goldstone also argue in favor of children's metafiction. Pantaleo in "Young Children Engage with the Metafictive in Picture Books" notes that "through their experiences with picture books with metafictive devices, children will grow in their abilities as readers; their metafictive awareness will assist them as they encounter similar devices in other printed texts, movies, television programs, video games and other digital texts" (31). And Goldstone in "Whaz Up with Our Books? Changing Picture Book Codes and Teaching Implications" comments, "Postmodern children's stories are more closely aligned to hypertext than they are to traditional picture books" and concludes that "the question then is not, 'Is postmodernism appropriate for children's literature?' but rather 'How can these books be used successfully in classrooms?'" (367). Even more than Moss, Pantaleo and Goldstone focus on the practical value of children's metafiction and its place in educating children who will need to negotiate the array of media in their world.

On a structural level, the form metafiction takes in children's literature is often less extreme, less distancing, than adult metafiction. Ann Grieve in "Metafictional Play in Children's Fiction" notes that "children's books also have a strong ideological function and, historically, exert social control, functioning as part of an education apparatus — a means of teaching and influencing children" (5), paralleling the discussion of didacticism and ideology in children's literature earlier. As a result of the purpose of children's literature, "the forms and language of metafiction in children's books are not normally so far removed from realism as to be entirely beyond the young readers' knowledge of narrative or modes of communication" (6). Grieve argues that "metafiction for children functions by preserving a balance between the innovatory and the familiar, so that the reader can make predictions and construct coherence" (6). The balance of form parallels the balance between entertainment and didacticism discussed earlier. Nikolajeva also notes how metafiction functions in children's literature — "Metafictional levels in books for young readers exist within two separate semiotic systems or groups of artistic codes: that of the adult and that of the child" (*Aesthetic* 192) — and, because the adult is a more sophisticated and experienced reader, "metafictional elements will more often be found within the adult code" (192). For Nikolajeva, then, metafiction is more accessible for adults than for children. Despite its less extreme form, metafiction for children has similar distancing effects for children as it does for adults. And because it breaks away from the more dominant, realistic narrative mode, children's metafiction is subversive. Stonehill comments, "There is something palpably subversive about a self-conscious novel, despite the distinguished tradition which it itself enjoys" (8). Though Stonehill is talking about adult metafiction, his comments on subversion apply well to children's literature, hearkening back to Lurie's comments, though as Nodelman observes, the subversion is tempered some by audience, just as the degree of metafiction is tempered.

Metafiction also aligns with fantasy fiction. Peter Bramwell in "Fantasy, Psychoanalysis and Adolescence: Magic and Maturation in Fantasy" argues, "Fantasy lends itself to self-conscious narration, alerting the reader to the artifice of fiction and alternate ways of telling" (144). Stephens sees a similar connection between fantasy and metafiction: "Because fantasy readily fractures illusions of verisimilitude, it is predisposed towards self-conscious display of its textual strategies, and hence towards metafiction" (288). And Jules Zanger in "Fantasy Literature Both Reflects and Defies Reality" notes that "Fantasy ... always exists in a symbiotic relationship with reality and its conventionalized representation, depending on it for its existence and at the same time commenting upon it, criticizing it, and illuminating it" (36). Because both fantasy and metafiction challenge realistic fiction, it seems natural that they can work well together, though not all fantasy fiction is metafictional, nor does all metafiction contain a fantastic element. Because the focus of this book is on books, readers, and reading in children's fantasy, however, metafictional elements do appear in many texts, particularly those discussed in Chapter 4.

Joe Sutliff Sanders's article "The Critical Reader in Children's Metafiction" explores metafiction in children's literature and critiques popular arguments labeling children's metafiction "anti-didactic." His argument bears extensive examination because it is related to how books and readers are presented in children's metafiction, particularly in China Miéville's novel *Un Lun Dun*. Early in his article, Sanders comments that in its "ongoing effort to distance itself from didacticism, children's literature scholarship embraces the subversive potential of metafiction enthusiastically" (350). Sanders feels that critics of metafictional children's literature overstate the anti-didacticism of the literature and that, in fact, "children's literature featuring readers and their books at best provides a muddled form of subversion" (349). His choice of children's literature to analyze is very specific:

> The mode of metafiction I address is that sort of metafiction that documents the relationship between books and their readers. In this mode, the relationship between reader and text is generally ennobling for the imagined reader; it is an uncomplicated, benign relationship that implicitly argues that whatever else might need subverting, the reader-book bond is sacrosanct. If metafiction succeeds in creating moments in which the child is jolted by the self-referential stance of the fiction being read, children's metafiction that portrays a relationship between readers and books then immediately papers over any discomfort by promising that books are safe, that they are to be trusted [351].

Sanders explores the relationship between readers and their books briefly in *The Book Thief, The Absolutely True Diary of a Part-Time Indian*, and *Mrs. Frisby and the Rats of NIMH* before turning his attention to *Un Lun Dun*. These analyses reveal that "any discomfort inspired by metafiction is blunted by the solace and empowerment that come from relationships with books" (351). Sanders's analysis of *Un Lun Dun* reveals that though readers and books ultimately maintain a relationship, it is not an unquestioning relationship: "The first step in deconstructing the conventional relationship between readers and their books is destroying the assumption that books can be trusted without question" (356). This questioning, however, "must not be of a reader out of a comfortable position, but of books out of a privileged space in which critical readings are not necessary" (356). Despite no longer privileging books, "readers are not called upon to reject books" (359). Sanders demonstrates through his analysis of *Un Lun Dun* how the main character Deeba is able to maintain a relationship with the sentient book with which she interacts despite having to learn to be critical of it. Books remain friendly, but not unquestioned, and Sanders argues, "previous arguments also contend that metafiction is good because it is anti-didactic, but surely stories telling readers to trust the authority of books is at *least* didactic—we might even call it propagandistic" (352, emphasis in original). Since books are a type of adult authority, his comment about didacticism certainly makes sense. The message supports current ideology about books as desirable (and often authoritative) products for society, though calling the stories "propagandistic" seems extreme given his argument that books must not be "trusted without question." Questioning authority, as mentioned above, is generally a sign of subversion. Like Nodelman, Stephens, and Grieve, Sanders is stressing the role that children's literature plays to educate children in the ways of society and thus limits — if not fully discounts — the role of subversion and "anti-didacticism" in children's metafiction.

This argument, supplemented as it is in Sanders's article by close analysis of a single novel and with brief references to several other children's and young adult novels, is problematic. While his choice of children's texts does indeed show a positive relationship between books and readers, even if that relationship is occasionally fraught with problems, in fact most children's novels do not present a positive relationship between readers and books — and certainly not an "ennobling" and "sacrosanct" relationship. In particular, as the remainder of this book will demonstrate, children's fantasy in which books and reading play a prominent role often rejects books, leaving them behind in favor of action, thereby subverting adult authority — at least as it is related to books. Sanders's argument, along with those presented by Nodelman and other critics, that metafictional books are not anti-didactic does seems accurate; however, how that didacticism presents itself is not usually in the relationship of characters to their books. Instead, it is located in various other places, to be discussed in each of the subsequent chapters.

2

Books as Artifacts of Power

Children's and young adult fantasy fiction, like much of children's and young adult literature, often presents young characters learning their place in the world. This learning may involve formal education, book learning, or experiential learning or a combination of the two. While the majority of children's and young adult fantasy that incorporates books presents those books as tools much like books in realistic fiction, many pieces of children's and young adult fantasy place more importance on books. Books can be imbued with magical powers that make them appear sentient and they can be dangerous items that allow characters to manipulate other characters and/or the world around them. Though Joe Sutliff Sanders argues that the relationship of books and readers is "sacrosanct," in fact, the young protagonists of these fantasy novels often learn to be wary of books, reading, and writing and to favor experience and action, over reading. This wariness often represents a wariness of adult authority, as represented by books, which, as discussed in Chapter 1, frequently have a didactic element. By not relying solely on books, reading, and writing, children learn to succeed on their own outside the shadow of adults and how to balance book learning and action.

Gail Carson Levine's novel *Ella Enchanted*, a revision of "Cinderella," incorporates a magical book as a means of keeping Ella, the narrator, apprised of others' actions. Shortly before her father sends her to finishing school, Ella is given a book by her fairy godmother (and the family cook) Mandy. Though she initially believes it to be a book of fairy tales, she soon learns that the untitled book has magical properties. When she opens it on the ride to boarding school, she discovers "an illustration of Mandy," a picture of Prince Charmont, a map of her country Frell, and a picture of her father's coach (55–7). These images are followed by a revised version of the folktale "The Shoemaker and the Elves." Her traveling companion, and eventual stepsister, Hattie, who has discovered that Ella must obey all direct orders, demands the book when she sees Ella's interest in it, and Ella fears that Hattie will keep it. However, the magical properties of the book alter the content when Hattie looks at it, showing dry treatises on the Centaur Tick and Gnomish Mining (57). Hattie returns the book to Ella.

Throughout the novel, Ella uses her book as a means of keeping close to her family and friends, as well as learning what Hattie and her other stepsister Olive are doing. Though it does not always show her what she wants — at one point she longs for a map from her finishing school to the land of the giants — the book does offer her comfort at the times of her greatest distress. In particular, when she has been forced to reject Prince Char's suit and they are no long exchanging letters, she uses it to keep track of his actions. Once the main story is resolved and Ella and Char marry, she reveals that they use the book to keep track of their children when she and Char are away from the castle. It represents her late mother and her godmother Mandy, as well as the protection of their adult authority.

Ella is a reader from the start of *Ella Enchanted*, and her book serves as a comfort. She retreats to her book in times of distress, as she retreats to the library in her new family's home when she wants to escape notice. Ella's interest in language and learning never diminishes in the novel, despite her dislike of finishing school. In fact, the comfort that she takes from her book seems to enhance her love of books and learning. However, her book acts as a poor substitute for being in the company of those she loves, and when she is with her family, she rarely references the book in her narrative. Further, on her travels after she runs away from finishing school, the book helps little. Instead, it is Ella's natural cunning and skills that help her through encounters with elves, ogres, and giants. Just as her mother and Mandy cannot — and will not in Mandy's case[1] — help her through all of her problems, the book has its limitations. Ella must learn to use her skills to overcome great obstacles on her own. The emphasis in this novel is on experience, not on reading, despite the importance of the book in Ella's life, and Ella must experience much of the action without adult aid — whether physical or represented by a book.

While Ella's book acts as a touchstone for home and family and represents her mother figures, other books in children's and young adult fantasy will be presented as spell books, or grimoires, or other collections of magical information. Though this type of book may seem similar to traditional uses of books in most realistic and fantasy fiction, many of these books themselves have some kind of magical property. This is the case in Garth Nix's *Abhorsen* trilogy. In the second novel of the series, *Lirael*, when Lirael is young, she asks to work in the library, one of the most dangerous jobs for the Clayr, her people, for the library contains many dangerous books (as well as mundane ones) and other artifacts of power. When she is given the position of Third Assistant Librarian, Lirael is also given three safety items, including a whistle that can be attached to her uniform so that, as another librarian tells her, "you can bend your head and blow into it, even if something's holding your arms" (82). She is also given a small mechanical, spell-activated mouse that can run and sound an alarm if she is out of hearing range for her whistle to be effective (83–4). In addition, she is given a dagger for protection. Despite its dangers — and Lirael encounters many dangerous situations while working in the library — Lirael welcomes her job and devours as many of the magical books as she can. The knowledge that she gains from these books helps her to contain a magical creature she accidentally releases and to learn to create Charter-skins, artifacts that allow her to take different animal forms.

Always feeling like an outsider among the Clayr because she has never gained the ability to See into the future that all other Clayr possess, Lirael uses her powerful Charter magic and the abilities she learns through her reading to explore depths of the library seldom entered. On her nineteenth birthday, on such an exploration, she discovers *The Book of Remembrance and Forgetting*, a book of power. Lirael knows immediately that "you could never truly finish reading such a book, for the contents changed at need, at the original maker's whim, or to suit the phases of the moon or the patterns of the weather" (*Lirael* 323). With the book, she finds two artifacts, a mirror and a set of pipes. All three items represent the artifacts of the Remembrancer, a powerful figure who has the power to see back in time and learn about events that have transpired, and Lirael's discovery of the artifacts marks her as the new Remembrancer. Her discovery also leads to her quest to help save the Old Kingdom from Orannis, a powerful figure who is trying to escape from his magical containment. When Lirael takes possession of the items, she assumes her place in the long line of Remembrances.

The other book that has great significance in the *Abhorsen* trilogy is *The Book of the Dead*, the guide for the Abhorsen, who works with the dead, returning them to the realm of death permanently. Like *The Book of Remembrance and Forgetting*, *The Book of the Dead* changes each time it is read. Both of these books represent the connection between generations of powerful and important figures in the Old Kingdom. The book is first referenced in *Sabriel*, the first novel of the series, when the title character reflects on reading and rereading it, though the book has little impact in that novel. In *Lirael*, it is revealed that characters such as Sameth, who are not meant to use these books, feel an aversion to them even if they have the ability to open and read them. The introduction to *The Book of the Dead* in *Lirael* reveals that "only someone with an innate talent for Free Magic and necromancy could open the book, and only an uncorrupted Charter Mage could close it" (267). When Sameth's mother Sabriel sends him *The Book of the Dead* to study, he becomes physically chilled at the thought of using it. Even when he sets the book aside, he "could feel the book next to him, almost as if it were a living thing. A coiled snake that was waiting to strike when he moved" (270). Sameth believes, as does the rest of his family, that he is meant to be the next Abhorsen, after his mother, yet he cannot bring himself to use the book. His reaction contrasts greatly with Lirael's. When Lirael encounters *The Book of the Dead*, she says to Sameth, "I can't explain, but I feel that I must read it" (593), and she becomes engrossed in the text, reading it all in one night even though she knows that she has retained little and that it will change its contents each time she reads it. Her innate interest in the book marks her as the true Abhorsen-in-Waiting, though this role is not revealed until later in the series. By contrast, Sameth, who prefers working with his hands, later becomes the new Wallmaker. His ability to use magic and his hands to create plays a critical role in the final battle, as does Lirael's book knowledge. The books of power act as indicators of a person's rightful role—they are the authorities that acknowledge Lirael's place in society.

Yet despite their importance for the Abhorsen and Remembrancer, these books, like all other books in the *Abhorsen* trilogy, act only as guides and cannot replace experience. Lirael observes that "knowing these secrets [of the Nine Gates in death]—even from a magical book—was not the same as having experienced them" (*Abhorsen* 389). However, as she uses the tools of her new trade, Lirael also visualizes specific pages in the books to help her perform spells (cf. 178, 353, 390). It is the blending of the book learning and practical ability that allows Lirael to succeed in her task. Only when Lirael leaves her comfort zone of the library—taking with her *The Book of Remembrance and Forgetting* and later receiving *The Book of the Dead*—does she gain self-knowledge, discovering the truth about her parentage and about the role she will play in the Old Kingdom. Books, then, are dangerous, fundamental tools in the *Abhorsen* trilogy but cannot be relied upon alone. The young characters must leave the safety and comfort of adult protection, represented by the library and the books of power, and experience the world to succeed.

In other children's and young adult fantasy books, spell books are presented differently than in Nix's *Abhorsen* trilogy. Angie Sage's novel *Magyk*, the first of the *Septimus Heap* series, references Magyk books constantly. Wizards consult them often, and when Magyk is outlawed with the assassination of the queen, Silas Heap rescues as many books as he can from being burned. Later in the novel, when Marcia Overstrand, the ExtraOrdinary Wizard, is studying Aunt Zelda's store of Magyk books, the way Magyk books are used is explained:

> The first wizard to create the spell wrote down the words and instructions on whatever he or she had at hand.... This was the **Charm**. The number of **Charms** made would depend on how many times the Wizard wrote down the spell....
>
> When a Wizard had collected enough spells together, he or she would usually bind them into a book for safekeeping; although, many **Magyk** books were collections of older books that had fallen apart and been remixed in various forms. A full **Magyk** book with all its **Charms** still in their pockets was a rare treasure. It was far more common to find a virtually empty book with only one or two of the less popular **Charms** still in place.
>
> Some Wizards only made one or two **Charms** for their more complicated spells, and these were very hard to find, although most **Charms** could be found in the Pyramid Library back at the Wizard Tower [237–8].[2]

The books, then, similar to the books in the *Abhorsen* trilogy, allow past generations of wizards to aid new generations in a tangible way, though the new wizards must implement the spells themselves.

Anyone, whether Magykal or non–Magykal, can use a Charm, though it is far easier for the Magykal to use them. The user memorizes the words of the Charm to Imprint them and can thereafter invoke the Charm by recalling the words. It takes the non–Magykal Jenna several tries to invoke her charm, whereas Boy 412, later revealed to be Septimus Heap, who has powerful Magykal abilities, learns the same spell merely by looking at the words. When he does so, "the words to the spell whizzed around his brain and filled his head with a strange buzzing sensation. Underneath his red beanie hat, the stubby hairs on the back of his head stood up. He could feel the Magyk tingling through his hand" (243). Though Magykal ability is innate in this series, reading is still a critical part of becoming a Witch or Wizard, and all Witches and Wizards must study Magyk books. The importance of reading, of studying, is emphasized at the end of the first novel when Septimus is made Marcia's apprentice. Her gift to him is an Apprentice's Diary.[3] Septimus also quickly takes to reading books that, prior to his experiences with the Heaps, were forbidden.

In addition to books used as part of apprentice study being important in the series, the Magykal Manuscriptorium and Spell Checkers Incorporated (known as the Manuscriptorium) plays a large role. At this business, scribes copy Charms and other documents for customers, and rare books and documents can be purchased. There is also a secure room — the Hermetic Chamber — where dangerous and rare books, charms, and other documents are stored. Further, the Manuscriptorium houses the Wild Book and Charm Store, which contains "two long lines of towering parallel shelves fronted with iron bars, behind which the Wild Books were crowded together. As Septimus cautiously followed Beetle [a clerk at the Manuscriptorium] along the narrow aisle he was followed by a chorus of low growls, scratching and rustlings, as the books jostled behind rusty bars" (*Flyte* 390). As with many Magykal objects in the *Septimus Heap* series, some books have powers of their own that give them near-sentience.[4] When Septimus enters the Wild Book and Charm Store, Beetle apologizes for the mess and explains that there was a "punch-up" between two sets of Charms that were mis-shelved (390–1). The importance of the Manuscriptorium is seen in the way the antagonists, from Simon Heap to Merrin Meredith, often target it, overpowering the Chief Hermetic Scribe, who runs the store, to gain access to restricted, volatile materials and the store itself. In *Darke*, the sixth book of the series, Merrin Meredith plans to make the Manuscriptorium the center of the Darke Domaine he has created to take over the Castle. In addition, Beetle, though young, has a great knowledge of materials in the Manuscriptorium and uses that knowledge to help Septimus and Princess Jenna when they are all off on various adventures.

Though books aren't given primary attention in the *Septimus Heap* series, several books do play an important role at times. Septimus keeps a copy of *The Book of Survival and Bushcraft*, a remnant of his time in the Young Army, in his emergency backpack, and it comes in handy on occasion when he is away from the Castle and must fend for himself, notably in the second novel of the series, *Flyte*. Though non–Magykal, the book does offer practical help to Septimus, and like Magykal books, it requires Septimus to apply the information it contains. Another non–Magykal book that plays a role in the sixth book in the series, *Darke*, is *The Queen's Rules*, which Jenna receives on her fourteenth birthday. This book, which Marcia Overstrand calls "that wretched book with its tiddly-squiddly type" and "the bane of every ExtraOrdinary Wizard's life" (79), lays out the rights and obligations for the Queen or Princess-In-Waiting and includes the "Right To Know" anything the Queen deems important from the ExtraOrdinary Wizard or the ExtraOrdinary Wizard's Apprentice (92–3). This rule initially thrills Jenna, though later she considers discarding the book because "she didn't care about being Queen," but she discovers "she could *never* throw it away," for "whether she liked it or not, this was who she was" (382, emphasis in original). The book's fit in her hand, and the danger affecting the Castle, make her realize "what the Day of Recognition actually meant," that she belongs in her role as Princess-In-Waiting (382). Her implementation of the Right To Know rule on Septimus later evokes quite a different response from him than from Marcia. Rather than irritating him, Jenna's demand makes him feel "less alone" than when he thought he had to keep his Darke Week task secret from Jenna: "He felt part of everything once more and he also, he realized, felt relieved. He *wanted* to tell Jenna where he was going" (499–500, emphasis in original). This non-Magykal book helps Jenna accept her role and reconnects her and Septimus after weeks of their drifting apart. It also allows her to understand and better connect to her deceased birth mother and other previous queens — similar to the way in which books of power allow Sabriel and Lirael to connect to their ancestors.

Another book that plays an important role in the series is the *I, Marcellus*. In the third book in the series, *Physik*, Septimus becomes fascinated with Alchemie and reads books on it whenever he can despite — or perhaps because of — Marcia's disapproval. Marcia calls Alchemie, now a banned subject, "a load of five-hundred-year-old drivel" and "total twaddle and a complete waste of time" (41). What most interests Septimus about Alchemie is Physik, akin to medicine, and he hopes to learn how to cure a Sickeness that has spread through the castle by studying various old Alchemie books. The *I, Marcellus*, which contains an Almanac and sections about Alchemie and Physik, was written by Marcellus Pye, the last Alchemist, five hundred years prior to the main action of the series. The importance of the book in *Physik* is less for its contents than for the letter to Marcia that Septimus hides in the book when he is taken back in time to be Marcellus's Alchemie Apprentice. Marcellus is in the process of writing the book and brewing a Tincture for eternal life. Chapter 25 of *Physik*, titled "The *I, Marcellus*," opens with entries from Marcellus's diary, which catalogs Septimus's arrival in Marcellus's time and the brewing of the Tincture, as well as the plan to Seal the *I, Marcellus*. This chapter also gives greater detail from Septimus's point of view of the *I, Marcellus* and its sections, particularly the Physik section, which Septimus has studied in great detail, recording aspects of it in his own Physik notebook. It is this information that allows Septimus to cure the Sickeness in his own time once he returns.

The *I, Marcellus* comes up again in the sixth book of the series, *Darke*, when Marcellus, who successfully used the Tincture to gain eternal life, consults the Almanac section first to find the best time for Septimus to begin his Darke Week test, in which he will enter the Darke realm to test his abilities, and later to pinpoint the entrance to the Darke Halls where Septimus is going to rescue the ghost Alther, who was accidentally banished. Like all other books in the series, the *I, Marcellus* is a tool the characters use, though it is much less accepted by everyone because of the banning of Alchemie. Marcia in particular voices her disapproval of the book and of Marcellus whenever she can, a fact that does not discourage Septimus from working with Marcellus even after his return to his own time. In fact, Septimus's reaction to Marcia's dislike of Alchemie and the books associated with it — and of Marcellus — seems to have the opposite effect on Septimus, who continues to read the books and associate with Marcellus, often in secrecy so that he does not encounter Marcia's anger about his choices. Though he is embracing books here, his actions are subversive because Marcia is a higher authority than Marcellus in society, and his choice to read those books despite the prohibition proves useful.

Perhaps the most dangerous books in the *Septimus Heap* series are *The Undoing of the Darkeness* and its companion book *The Darke Index*. While both books individually are useful — *The Undoing of the Darkeness* for countering Darke spells and *The Darke Index* for casting Darke spells — Marcia notes in *Darke* that *The Undoing of the Darkeness* is "no good for the really important stuff" without *The Darke Index* (314). The books are separated because together they are too dangerous except in extreme circumstances. Marcia loses *The Undoing of the Darkeness* in the first novel of the series, *Magyk*, but regains it with Septimus's help in the second book, *Flyte*. *The Darke Index* is first in the hands of DomDaniel, then Simon Heap, then Merrin Meredith, all of whom are antagonists at different points in the series. Merrin, who was raised by DomDaniel as Septimus Heap and resents having his identity stolen, uses *The Darke Index* in the fourth novel of the series, *Queste*, to cast a spell to Darken the Destiny of Septimus, though it proves ineffective. In the sixth book of the series, *Darke*, Merrin uses the book to create a Darke Domaine, which spreads over the entire Castle. It is only when Marcia reunites *The Undoing of the Darkeness* with *The Darke Index* (which Beetle has recovered from Merrin) and uses the Paired Codes — a two-piece amulet that when linked can be used to decode major spells in the books — to read them that she is able to remove the Darke Domaine. The books in this situation are far more critical to the survival of the Castle and its inhabitants than most books in other children's fantasy series, though, again, decoding the spell is only part of the removal; the spell must also be cast properly once it is revealed. Reading and practical application — action — unite as they do in the *Abhorsen* trilogy.

Each of the novels discussed thus far contains books playing a role, though that role is not central. Other children's and young adult fantasy novels and series revolve around a book. These books drive the plot of the novel (or series) in various ways. The books themselves may not have the power that books in the other novels discussed do, but they represent some kind of power. Eoin Colfer's novel *Artemis Fowl*, for example, opens with the anti-hero Artemis on a trip to get a copy of *The Book of the People*, the fairies' book of "instructions to our magicks and life rules" (27). The first page of *The Book of the People* explains its purpose:

> I am thy teacher of herb and spell.
> I am thy link to power arcane.
> Forget me and thy magick shall wane.
>
> Ten times ten commandments there be.
> They will answer every mystery.
> Cures, curses, alchemy.
> These secrets shall be thine, through me.
>
> But, Fairy, remember this above all.
> I am not for those in the mud that crawl.
> And forever doomed shall be the one,
> Who betrays my secrets one by one [27–8].

The Book of the People is the bible of the fairy world, the ultimate authority, complete with a warning about letting humans — "those in the mud that crawl" — gain access to it.

Once he has a copy of *The Book of the People*, Artemis must try to translate it because it is written in Gnommish. A technologically savvy child, he discovers that even advanced translation software cannot help him initially, and he is forced to determine how to read the book on his own. Only once he has printed and manually cut up and reorganized the words can he feed it through the translation program, which he has also had to configure to understand the script. After he has read the book, Artemis is able to mastermind a plan to kidnap a fairy and ransom it for gold to restore his family fortunes to the level he finds acceptable. His success comes only because he has obtained the book. He locates Holly Short, the elf he kidnaps, by reading about the fairies' need to perform the Ritual to replenish their magic in specific locations. He manipulates the fairies trying to secure Holly's release as well because he knows their rules for entering human homes, how they Mesmerize humans to get their way, and how they handle matters when negotiations fail. Though he has no practical experience with fairies until he procures the book, Artemis's confidence in his reading and reasoning skills leads to his implementation of a plan that, if unsuccessful, could kill him and all the others in his home. The book in this novel acts as a means to manipulate and control the fairies, and Artemis uses this piece of fairy authority against the people it is supposed to help.[5] He is one of the few characters in children's fantasy who embraces reading, and his skillful reading could be seen as a positive depiction of books and reading. Yet, because he uses the book's information against authority, his actions are quite subversive — something that may appeal to child readers but that may alienate adults. In *Artemis Fowl*, the message comes at the end when Artemis, having defeated the fairies, makes a deal with Holly Short to exchange part of the gold he has won for her help healing his mother, thus emphasizing the importance of family, even for a "criminal mastermind" like Artemis, over gaining more money.

Yet another novel in which a book features prominently is *Faerie Wars* by Herbie Brennan. In this novel, Brimstone, one of the antagonists, uses *The Book of Beleth* to summon the demon Beleth because Brimstone believes Beleth will make him rich and powerful. As he is using the book, Brimstone reflects, "He'd read somewhere the tome was what made all demonic invocations work, whether you had it with you or not. So long as it existed somewhere, the road to Hell was always open to a man who knew the spells" (48). Though Brimstone's own use of the book does not end well for him since he cannot keep his side of the bargain he makes with Beleth, later the book is used by the main character Henry, who is from the Analogue, or human, world, and Princess Holly Blue to call Blue's brother Pyrgus back to the Faerie Realm from Hell. Pyrgus immediately tells Henry to destroy the book. Once the book has been destroyed, Pyrgus explains, "The book was the main control portal between Hell and the Realm of Faerie. Once you destroyed it, all the other portals ceased to operate" (358). The destruction of the book ends the plan by the Faeries of the Night to overthrow the Purple Emperor because they were relying on the demons' help for success.

The actual use of *The Book of Beleth* is interesting in *Faerie Wars*. When Brimstone uses it, it glows in his hands and he feels nothing but glee at possessing it. When Henry uses the book, however, he is repulsed by it, not least because he believes it is covered in baby skin. As he is searching for something to save Pyrgus,

> Henry found himself in the peculiar position of holding a book that actually scared him. He couldn't shake the feeling it was like something out of a horror movie. In his mind's eye, he could see the innocent young hero stumble on a tome like this in some vampire's crypt. Open it, or even touch it, and the minute you turned your back it would start to glow. Shortly after that, smoke would billow out to form something with large teeth and long claws [339].

What is interesting about Henry's thought, aside from his fear of the book, is the comparison he uses. He focuses on a horror *film* rather than a book. Earlier in the novel, he does the same when he enters the kitchen of the Imperial Palace: "He had the feeling of walking into a period movie, something from Dickens or even earlier" (317). The fact that Henry associates the writer Dickens with films rather than books shows that film has had more of an impact on him than reading. Henry's choice to ignore books in his suite, despite knowing "he might learn a lot about Pyrgus's world from those books if he took the time" (317), emphasizes his interest in experience over reading—he thinks "he would probably learn a lot more if he explored the palace"

(317). Reading plays a secondary role to observation in *Faerie Wars*, despite the importance of *The Book of Beleth*, a book that serves to underscore the dangers of reading, and to discourage reading. The adult authority represented by books is not just rejected but destroyed in *Faerie Wars*.

Other children's and young adult fantasy novels contain books that play an even stronger role. Tony DiTerlizzi and Holly Black's *The Spiderwick Chronicles* revolves around the Grace children's great uncle's book, *Arthur Spiderwick's Field Guide to the Fantastical World Around You* (*Field Guide*). At the beginning of the first novel in the series, *The Field Guide*, Jared, Simon, and Mallory Grace discover their great uncle's book and learn that all sorts of mystical creatures exist. This knowledge helps them understand and fix some of the strange things that have been happening in their new home because they realize that they have angered a brownie, which has become a boggart. When the boggart returns to being a brownie named Thimbletack, he tells them, "Arthur Spiderwick's book is not for your kind. Too much about Fey for a mortal to find. All who have kept it have come to harm. Be it through violence or charm. Throw the book away, toss it in a fire. If you do not heed, you will draw their ire" (104). Thimbletack does not explain who "they" are, and the children do not heed his advice, though they all have some idea of the importance of the book. It is, Jared thinks, "an absolutely huge book, too large to even comprehend. And worst of all, they were only at the beginning" (107). This book, like the *I, Marcellus* in *Septimus Heap* and *The Book of the People* in *Artemis Fowl*, is attractive to the troubled and rebellious Jared because it represents forbidden knowledge. *The Spiderwick Chronicles* are an intrusion fantasy in Farah Mendlesohn's schema, and the book itself is the disruptive force that leads to further disruptions by the magical creatures.

In the second book of the series, *The Seeing Stone*, Simon, Jared's identical twin, is kidnapped by goblins, who believe that he has the *Field Guide*. Jared uses information from the *Field Guide* to learn how to see the Fey as well as for information about goblins and trolls, though he does not understand why the book is so important to the goblins as they cannot read it. In the third book, *Lucinda's Secret*, the Grace children argue over whether they should get rid of the *Field Guide* since it is causing so much trouble. Before they can make a decision, however, the book disappears, taken, they think, by Thimbletack. They also learn that other parties are interested in the book: the elves, who want to destroy it to protect faeries (90), and Mulgarath, an ogre. When the children question the elves about why they do not want anyone to have the *Field Guide*, the elves tell them, "That book is dangerous in anyone's hands…. There is too much knowledge therein" (92). Because the book is a general guide, it contains information about faeries that even the faeries do not know, and the elves fear that in the wrong hands, human or faerie, the information will pose a threat to all faeries. The elves' trickery in trying to obtain the book, however, angers Mallory and the other Grace children, who decide not to cooperate with the elves.

The importance of the *Field Guide* increases in the fourth book, *The Ironwood Tree*, when Mallory is kidnapped by dwarves working for Mulgarath. Because Thimbletack has taken the *Field Guide*, Jared is forced to try to remember details of the book, which he has read several times, so that he can formulate a plan to free Mallory. Ultimately, Jared and Simon save Mallory from the dwarves and Mulgarath, only to learn that Mulgarath has somehow obtained the *Field Guide* on his own. The final book of the series, *The Wrath of Mulgarath*, involves the Grace children trying to rescue their mother, who has been captured by Mulgarath, as well as retrieving the *Field Guide*. After their success, they decide to take the *Field Guide* to the elves, who "return it to you for safekeeping" because "you have proven that humans may use the knowledge it contains for good" (127–8). Like many of the children's and young adult fantasy novels and series in which books play such a significant role, it is the information in the books that makes the books dangerous rather than any magical properties the book may contain — and the *Field Guide* does not contain any magical properties. The danger in which the Grace children find themselves can be directly attributed to the *Field Guide*. Further, it is the non-reader Jared who becomes most obsessed with the *Field Guide*, and it is he who plans to supplement it with additional information that he has gathered from his experiences with the creatures, though he never becomes an active reader. Instead, his singular experience with the *Field Guide* makes him more aware of the world around him and makes him appreciate the practicality of recording what he discovers to help others. However, the *Field Guide* does not aid the Grace children when they are in trouble; they must rely on their wits and each other to succeed. The book causes the trouble; it does not fix it.

What is perhaps more interesting about this series is the way the fictional books are created. Each of the novels in *The Spiderwick Chronicles* opens with a letter to the reader from Holly Black, one of the authors, detailing how the authors "met" the Grace children and obtained the story that they present in *The Spiderwick Chronicles*. Printed beside Black's letter is a letter from Mallory, Simon, and Jared to Black and Tony DiTerlizzi, asking them to publish the *Field Guide*. Further, in each of the novels, a picture of a "real" document is presented, whether it is a handwritten note by Arthur Spiderwick (*The Field Guide*) or an expulsion letter for Jared (*The Ironwood Tree*). The result is that the fiction of the series is placed into question, something that is extended by the later publication of *Arthur Spiderwick's Field Guide to the Fantastical World Around You, Care and Feeding of Sprites*, and DiTerlizzi and Black's next series, *Beyond the Spiderwick Chronicles*, in which the *Field Guide*, the Grace children, and even DiTerlizzi and Black make appearances.

Rather than focusing on the dangers of *The Field Guide*, *Beyond the Spiderwick Chronicles* revolves around the danger of over-relying on books and emphasizes the need to find a balance between reading and experience. In this series, the main character, Nick, and his new stepsister, Laurie, clash. Nick is a studious, practical character who has great respect for adult authority, while Laurie spends much of her time reading about and imagining faeries and other mythological creatures. Laurie shares her interest in faeries with the disinterested Nick, showing him her copy of the *Field Guide* in the first novel of the series, *The Nixie's Song*. They then launch into a debate about whether the *Field Guide* is fictional. Nick points out, "It says 'fiction' inside. Explain that," to which Laurie responds, "They had to put that in there.... So they don't get in trouble or sued" (8). Nick's initial reaction to the book and to Laurie is negative because he sees the text as fanciful and not realistic. Soon Laurie is proved right in her belief in faeries when they encounter a nixie, and she becomes entranced with the creature, refusing to listen to Nick's warning that the nixie is dangerous, something Laurie would realize, Nick says, "if you actually read that book you keep carrying around" (60). Here Nick's studiousness — and grounding in reality, however unusual or shifting — clashes with Laurie's idealizing of the faeries, a common clash for the characters.[6]

As events escalate out of control in the story, Laurie reveals that she didn't really believe faeries existed. Instead, they were part of the fantasies that she continually weaves to make her life more interesting. She has read the *Field Guide* and "knew there were monsters. I just didn't think we'd find any. I thought we'd see sprites or something pretty.... I guess I didn't think we'd see anything at all" (91). This admission is followed by her comment that the reality of having a brother similar in age is also nothing like she had dreamed; she ends with "I hate you [Nick], and I really hate faeries" (92). It is this admission that makes Nick sympathize with her, at least to some extent, rather than just resent her, and they begin to work together to get help solving the faerie problem — the arrival of giants.

Their plan, to seek out the authors of the *Field Guide* at a book signing, leads to a chapter titled "IN WHICH We Nearly Break the Fourth Wall." At this book signing, Nick asks the authors — who are never named, though labeled pictures of them appear on pages 104–105 of *The Nixie's Song*— how to stop the giants, but the authors' advice is mostly platitudes and recommendations to read fairy tales. The female author ends the recommendations with "I don't have any more specific suggestions than that, but since you're the hero of your own story, I know you'll come up with a good ending" (106). Disgusted, Nick and Laurie leave, Nick declaring, "They're nothing but fakes" (107). Black and DiTerlizzi have simultaneously tied the series more completely to reality by placing themselves in the story and placed the reliability of the *Field Guide* into question by acting as if the work is fictional. The question of what is real becomes even more complicated moments later when Nick and Laurie encounter the Grace children from the original *Spiderwick Chronicles* series and convince them to help deal with the giants. Nick and Laurie learn that Grace is not Jared, Simon, and Mallory's real last name because, Jared tells them, "Mom made them [the authors] change our last name" (145). They are given the new last name of Fennelly, but a footnote indicates it is "still not his [Jared's] real name" (145). The continued play between reality and fiction underscores the theme of balancing imagination and action. Neither Nick nor Laurie is balanced, and their experiences dealing with the nixies, the giants, and finally the wyrm king all help them to achieve a better balance. Nick learns to be self-reliant, to act physically, rather than to play video games or watch films. He is forced to be the hero even though he views Jared as "the real hero" at the start of the final novel of the series, *The Wyrm King* (5). Laurie, on the other hand, learns to live in the real—albeit fantastic—world rather than in her imagination. She also discovers that her avid reading of various books about the fantastic has served her well, for she realizes that the creature Sandspur is a spriggan and not mentioned in the *Field Guide*, something Jared does not know because he is not a reader of any book besides the *Field Guide* and "comics" (158), a trait of his carried over from the original series. The *Field Guide*, then, is not definitive as it is in the first series, and Laurie reveals that she can negotiate multiple texts to learn what she need to know once she realizes the creatures are real.

Though *Beyond the Spiderwick Chronicles* does not revolve around a book in the same way that *The Spiderwick Chronicles* does, the *Field Guide* remains an important element and dangerous in its own way, for overreliance on it for information and treating it as the definitive guide, does not work well. The characters must complete additional research, including field research, to succeed. As Nick thinks in the first novel, "Books don't always tell the whole story" (115). Though he is referring to Jared's place in books, the comment applies as well to the *Field Guide*, for though useful to them at times, it does not solve all their problems. Books aren't the threat as in the first *Spiderwick Chronicles* series, but characters are not encouraged to be readers; instead, action is stressed, as it is in most children's fantasy in which books play a prominent role. The end of the series also encourages the reader to be the writer: a poem following the authors' biographies declares the end of the Spiderwick tales, offers a lesson — "friends and family form a bond / which cuts through any knot" — and indicates that there are more tales to share. The final two stanzas of the poem tell the reader that the job of creating and being the hero of new stories may "fall to you" and urges, "Please keep a pen with you to write, / a pad, a brush, and ink" because the readers' tale may "start / SOONER / THAN YOU THINK!" Once again Black and DiTerlizzi have blended fiction and reality with their final words.

Like the *Spiderwick Chronicles*, Michael Scott's *The Secrets of the Immortal Nicholas Flamel* young adult series revolves initially around the theft of the Codex or *The Book of Abraham*, which Nicholas Flamel and his wife Perenelle have been guarding for centuries. This book, "a book of ancient magic" as Nicholas Flamel describes it in *The Alchemyst*, contains the recipe for the elixir that has given Nicholas and Perenelle immortality for centuries, as well as stories about the world and spells for various rituals, including ones that create gold and jewels. The final pages of the Codex contain the means of allowing the Dark Elders to return to the human world and take over. At the start of the first novel, *The Alchemyst*, the primary antagonist John Dee steals all but the final two pages of the Codex, and much of the action in the first four novels in the series involves Dee's pursuit of Nicholas Flamel and the main characters, twins Josh and Sophie Newman. The Codex, then, is similar to the *Field Guide* in *The Spiderwick Chronicles*, containing information dangerous in the wrong hands.

Though small amounts of information are revealed about the Codex in the first four books and Nicholas Flamel emphasizes its importance to Sophie and Josh, the background of the book is not revealed until the fifth novel of the series, *The Warlock*. At the start of this novel, Josh has just defected to Dee's side, taking with him the final two pages of the Codex, though he does not inform Dee that he has the pages. Several characters who lived during the time in which the book was created, including Josh and Sophie's Aunt Agnes, who turns out to be Tsagaglalal, the wife of Abraham the Mage, talk about the book's creation and its contents. In addition, Perenelle Flamel, who with Nicholas has been guarding the book for five hundred years, tells Sophie,

> I was a child when Marethyu [a long-lived character, often called Death, who passes the book to Nicholas] told me that my husband and I would become the guardians of a metal-bound book. We would be the last in a long line of humans to protect this precious object. He said the book contained the entire knowledge of the world ... but when I first saw it, I knew that could not be the truth. There were so few pages in it. How could the entire knowledge of the world be con-

tained in twenty-one pages? It was much later before Nicholas and I began to discover the secrets of the Codex and its ever-changing text [*Warlock* 150–1].

Like *The Book of Remembrance and Forgetting* and *The Book of the Dead* in the *Abhorsen* trilogy, the Codex has magical properties that cause the text to change, something Sophie and Josh witness when they look at the two pages Josh tears from the book when Dee is stealing it in *The Alchemyst*. They observe that "the letters shifted on the page like tiny beetles, shaping and reshaping themselves, becoming briefly almost legible in recognizable languages like Latin or Old English, but then immediately dissolving and reforming into ancient-looking symbols not unlike Egyptian hieroglyphs or Celtic Ogham" (27). Further, the recipe for the elixir that Nicholas and Perenelle must take every month to prolong their life changes each month and cannot be copied down or duplicated (*Magician* 70). As a result, Perenelle and Nicholas age significantly as the series progresses because they have lost the Codex and cannot brew the elixir without it.

Also in the Codex is the prophecy about a pair of twins: "The two that are one must become the one that is all. One to save the world, one to destroy it" (*Warlock* 274). Though Sophie and Josh hear about this prophecy from the Flamels once they are on the run from John Dee, Sophie does not see it in writing until the fifth novel in the series, when she receives a green marble tablet written by Abraham the Mage ten thousand years before her birth—and a thousand years after he first recorded the prophecy. This prophecy has driven the Flamels for five hundred years to search for the twins who fit the prophecy, and they believe that Josh and Sophie are those twins, though which role each will play is uncertain until the very end of the series. As with most prophecies, this one is vague and ominous-sounding, and though the natural inclination is to believe that the "one to destroy" the world will be a "bad" twin, this inclination falls apart when it is revealed that one twin—Josh—must destroy the Elders' world Danu Talis[7] so that Earth, his world, may come into being. Sophie is the twin who must save the Earth, though in reality, Josh's destruction of Danu Talis leads to the saving of the earth as well. They are able to fulfill the prophecy with the aid of the Codex and Abraham the Mage's messages to them.

Though the theft of the Codex does set the events of *The Secrets of the Immortal Nicholas Flamel* series into motion, the Codex itself is not a focal point in much of the series, especially in books two (*The Magician*), three (*The Sorceress*), and four (*The Necromancer*). Dee continues to chase Nicholas, Josh, and Sophie around Europe to get the last two pages of the book, but his plans for the book, initially to bring the Dark Elders to Earth, change when he has a rift with them. Instead, he decides to use the Codex, if he gets the final two pages, "to destroy the Elders" (*Warlock* 65) so that he can take over all of the different Shadowrealms that exist. Much of the series itself revolves around Awakening the twins' magic and teaching them different types of magic — Air, Earth, Fire, Water. The teachings, however, do not involve book learning but interaction with a master of that magical ability. In addition, the shifting point of view in the series, similar to that employed by Angie Sage in the *Septimus Heap* series, spreads the focus among an increasingly large number of characters, most of whom are not focused on the Codex. As a result, though the Codex remains an important aspect of the series, it does not have quite the same impact as the *Field Guide* does in *The Spiderwick Chronicles*.

In the final novel of the series, *The Enchantress*, Josh, given the Codex by Abraham's wife Tsagaglalal, returns the two pages he has held for most of the series to the Codex, and it magically repairs itself. Before he sees to the destruction of Danu Talis, he looks at a section of the Codex — "the history of the world after the Fall" (496) — but stops his reading quickly: "He didn't want to read any more. Not yet. He was going to have to keep this book safe for over nine and a half thousand years, until he sold it to a penniless French bookseller [Nicholas Flamel]" (498). Josh's destruction of Danu Talis leads to his becoming Marethyu, "Death, the destroyer of worlds" (500), and not Josh Newman. He sets in motion the events chronicled in the series. The Codex, which seemed so important in the start of the series, is only a tool ultimately, something Abraham and Marethyu use to spur Nicholas and Perenelle into finding, protecting, and training the twins of the prophecy.

In contrast to the main characters of *The Spiderwick Chronicles*, however, Josh and Sophie are both strong and engaged readers, encouraged by their parents, who are archaeologists. In fact, Josh first meets the Flamels when he applies for a job in their bookshop in San Francisco. Both Josh and Sophie also have a strong knowledge of myths and legends, thanks to their parents, and this knowledge helps them as they learn more and more about Immortals, humans given immortality by an Elder or through other means, and Elders, usually thought of as gods from different ancient religions.[8] Their active reading also allows them to questions the authority of the adults around them, though the results are not always positive, as when Josh decides that he cannot trust the Flamels and abandons them and Sophie to join John Dee. Even then, however, he does not trust Dee enough to give him the final two pages of *The Codex*. The most important questioning of authority comes in *The Enchantress*, when Josh and Sophie refuse to do their parents' bidding because they do not wish to be pawns any longer.

Further, Josh and Sophie, especially Josh, are technologically savvy, and technology plays a big role in the first few books in the series. Josh uses the internet to research John Dee and Nicholas Flamel right after Dee destroys the Flamels' bookstore and steals the Codex. He continues to use his laptop and other technology for research through the first few novels, as do other characters, especially the Immortal Machiavelli, who uses the titles of his books as passwords to his files.[9] However, as the events unfold and become more magic-oriented, technology is used less and less. The Codex itself, when Dee opens it in the car he, Josh, and Virginia Dare are in, causes "Sparks [to dance] across every metal surface in the car.... Every indicator on the dashboard lit up with red warning lights. The heavy car jerked and stalled" (*Warlock* 56). Only after Dee closes the Codex can Josh restart the car. The ancient technology of the magical book defeats the modern, and the power of the Codex frightens Josh, especially since he can feel the pages he is carrying warm against his skin when Dee opens the book. Though early novels in the series show a heavy utilization of technology, by the fifth book, *The Warlock*, the role of modern technology is diminished. Action dominates over reading and using technology. As with most children's and young adult fantasy, it is the physical practice that becomes focal, not book learning or other types of reading.

Like *The Spiderwick Chronicles* and *The Secrets of the Immortal Nicholas Flamel* series, the first six books of Rachel Caine's young adult series *The Morganville Vampires* focus on a single book. The main character of the series, sixteen-year-old Claire Danvers, is in her first year of college at Texas Prairie University in Morganville, Texas, despite her preference to attend any of the other universities to which she has been accepted — MIT, Caltech, and Yale. Her parents' insistence that she is too young to travel far from home, however, has forced her to attend an in-state university more known for partying than academics. Claire finds most of her entry-level classes far too easy and has difficulty fitting into the college where her academic abilities greatly surpass her classmates' abilities. Early in the first book of the series, *Glass Houses*, Claire's attitude to book learning is revealed: "The problem was that Claire really *loved* school. Loved books, and reading, and learning things — okay, not calculus, but pretty much everything else. Physics. What normal girl loved *physics*? Abnormal ones. Ones who were not ever going to be hot" (4, emphasis in original). Immediately, Claire places herself into an "other" category, an "abnormal" one, because of her love of books and learning, and this view of her intelligence never really changes in the first six books of the series. More than any other character discussed in this chapter, Claire clings to the adult authority represented by her books. Her own view of her intelligence is echoed by her dorm mates, some of whom beat Claire so badly, and threaten to kill her, after she has shown them up, that she looks for a place to live off campus. Once Claire moves into Glass House with Michael, Eve, and Shane, her obsession with books and studying is slowly tempered by the others, especially Shane, who draws her out, encouraging her to do more than just study and go to class. Claire never loses her love of learning, but she becomes a more balanced person. Once she leaves the dorms, Claire also learns Morganville's big secret: the town is run by vampires, and residents make deals with different vampires to protect themselves and their family. Those unprotected are fair game for all vampires.

Though Claire's intelligence and quest for knowledge play a large role in the series, a particular book comes to take precedence. This untitled book is something for which the vampires have been searching for years, and when Shane, who is unprotected, runs into problems with a specific vampire for helping Claire, she learns about the book and determines to find it and exchange it with a higher ranking vampire for protection for Shane. Eve explains the little she knows of the book to Claire: "They [the vampires] just put out a notice about ten years ago that they were looking for it. I heard they have people all over town going through libraries, bookstores, anyplace it could be hidden. But the weird thing is that the vamps can't actually read it" (*Glass Houses* 121).[10] The book has a "brown leather cover. Some kind of symbol on the front" (121), which the vampires have tattooed on all residents of Morganville as a reminder of what to look for. As Claire begins her own search, knowing she is unlikely to find the book, but hoping to learn how to create a fake one, she goes through the college library with some trepidation and thinks, "Dammit, she resented being scared in a library! Books weren't supposed to be scary. They were supposed to ... help" (156). Her love of learning and her trust in adult authority are being challenged by the school she attends and the new knowledge she has gained about the world around her, and Claire is not happy with the changes, though she does not give up her quest. When she manages to find the actual book, which a professor had hidden inside a bible in his home, she must fight with one vampire faction to retain it with the help of Shane, who swaps book covers with a collection of Shakespearean sonnets to disguise the book. Amelie, the head vampire, offers to protect the household if Shane guards the book for her. The book, she reveals, contains the directions for creating another vampire, knowledge held only by Amelie in Morganville because the vampires "removed the knowledge of how to create more vampires, simply by refusing to teach it" (232) so that vampires would not outnumber humans. Similar to *The Book of the People* in *Artemis Fowl*, this book represents a guide for the supernatural creatures who seek it.

As the series progresses, focus on the book wanes to some extent, but Amelie capitalizes on Claire's book smarts in the third novel of the series, *Midnight Alley*, and sets her to work with Myrnin, an old, nearly insane vampire trying to discover the cure to the insanity that has begun to plague all of the local vampires. Claire's continued fascination with books and learning, particularly science — balanced to some extent by her burgeoning relationship with Shane — makes her interested in this task since it challenges her as much as the new college classes in which Amelie enrolls her, and in fact her study with Myrnin earns her college credit. The fifth novel of the series, *Lord of Misrule*, brings the book back to the forefront when Amelie's father, Bishop, arrives in town and demands to be given the book. Once he manages to procure it at the end of that novel, he uses it to control Claire:

> Bishop broke the lock on the book that Myrnin had given him, and opened it to flip the pages, as if looking for something in particular. He ripped out a page and pressed the two ends together to make a circle of paper, thickly filled with minute, dark writing. "Put this on your arm," he said, and tossed it to Claire. She hesitated, and he sighed. "Put it on, or one of the many hostages to your behavior will suffer..."
>
> Claire slipped the paper sleeve over her arm, feeling stupid, but she didn't see any alternatives.
>
> The paper felt odd against her skin, and then it sucked in and clung to her like something alive. She panicked and tried to pull it off, but she couldn't get a grip on it, so closely was it sticking to her arm.
>
> After a moment of searing pain, it loosened and slipped off on its own.
>
> As it fluttered to the floor, she saw that the page was blank. Nothing on it at all. The dense writing that had been on it stayed on her arm — no, *under the skin*, as if she'd been tattooed with it.
>
> And the symbols were *moving*. It made her ill to watch. She had no idea what it meant, but she could feel something happening inside, something...
>
> Her fear faded away. So did her anger [229–30, emphasis in original].

The book's words are embedded in Claire's arm, making her susceptible to Bishop's orders. The book has been her downfall, or so it appears at the end of *Lord of Misrule*. Claire has been subsumed by those in authority through the page of this book. The book and its possessor Bishop control her.

However, in the sixth book of the series, *Carpe Corpus*, Claire thinks that the tattoo "had gotten a little lighter since the day that Bishop had forced it on her, but maybe that was just wishful thinking" (4), and she hopes that "*if it fades out, maybe it'll stop working*" (4, emphasis in original). Though she is doubtful about her observation and hope, both prove true, and by the end of the sixth novel, she, along with the others, are able to reclaim the book from Bishop and destroy it by ripping out its pages and burning them (the cover will not burn). The overthrowing of the book's hold on her represents her moving beyond vampire (and adult to some extent) authority and into control of her own life. At the same time, the research she and Myrnin have been doing to find a cure bears fruit when they discover that Bishop's blood is the key to the cure.

The book's dangerous content, like the content of books in *The Spiderwick Chronicles* and *The Secrets of the Immortal Nicholas Flamel* once again reveal books to be a threat as well as a benefit — in this case, the threat is such that the book must be destroyed. Further, Claire's love of books is what puts her in danger from the start of the series. It gets her mocked and attacked by classmates; it brings her to the attention of the head vampires, who then conscript her into labor; and it forces her to become a permanent resident of Morganville — she will not be able to transfer to a different university now that she is Myrnin's apprentice. Though she thinks herself happy, "at least for tonight" (*Carpe Corpus* 241), her happiness will be transitory, for she is trapped in this town thanks to her "abnormal" interest in books and learning. As with other children's and young adult fantasy series, *The Morganville Vampires* presents books and book learning as dangerous. Further, though Claire's interest in education remains important, it is the practical application of science — the original work that she does with Myrnin — that saves the vampires, not book learning alone. Claire is learning to balance books and reading with the practical, both in educational settings and outside of them.

A final young adult fantasy novel that focuses on a single book is Pearl North's *Libyrinth*. The novel opens, "The wind howled and the flames roared, but the books, as they died, merely fell silent" (11), setting up the primary conflict in the novel. One faction, known as Eradicants by the Libyrarians, another faction, and Singers to themselves, is performing a sacrifice, burning a certain number of books from the Libyrinth, a community focused on literacy and protecting and studying its massive collection of books. The main character of the novel, fifteen-year-old Haly (short for Halcyon), has the unique ability to hear written text without reading or looking at it, and it is her thoughts that open the novel, for only she notices the silencing of the books being burned.[11] Early in the novel, the focal text, *The Book of the Night*, is mentioned: "No book was more sought after — by Libyrarian, Thesian, Ilysian, or Eradicant — than *The Book of the Night*. The tome held the secrets of the Ancients, all of their machines and miracles, and most importantly, the method for making the Eggs that powered them" (21). A single Egg "could light and heat the Libyrinth for generations.... Whoever possessed a Maker of Eggs would rule over the others" (21). *The Book of the Night*, then, represents knowledge desperately needed by most of the people in this fantasy realm. When Haly, her friend Clauda, her superior at the Libyrinth Selene, and the imp Nod discover *The Book of the Night* quickly on their quest, they find that it is written in no known alphabet, though Haly can understand it perfectly, something Selene does not realize since Haly has learned to hide her ability. The quick recovery of the book goes wrong when Eradicants capture and torture Haly, though Selene and Clauda manage to escape with the book.

Once Haly has been taken to the Eradicants' lands, she learns the importance of the book and of herself to them. The Singers, as they call themselves, are so named because all of their knowledge is learned through Song. They are illiterate, and all books are banned; residents caught with books are imprisoned and tortured. Singers believe that writing represents the death of words, and at their sacrifices, they chant, "*When a word is spoken, it is born, when it is written, it dies*" and they believe that burning the books releases the words from death (11, emphasis in original). The Singers have been searching for *The Book of the Night* because of a prophecy by their founder Yammon: "one day *The Book of the Night* would be found and a Redeemer would come, a child of Iscarion [whom the Singers believe founded the Libyrinth] for whom text is song. This Redeemer would revive the murdered Word and restore to the Singers what had been stolen from them" (114). The prophecy is part of a longer tale that Siblea tells Haly about the origins of the Singers, who were once joined with Libyrarians but split apart when Iscarion refused to teach the illiterate Yammon to read after Yammon helped him defeat the Ancients. Haly, once recognized as the Redeemer, is treated well and taught about Singer society, a male-dominated society as opposed to the gender-balanced society of the Libyrarians and the female-dominated society of the Ilysians. Haly begins to respect Singer society greatly for their technology that the Libyrinth lacks, and questions some of her beliefs. At the same time, she tries to convince some of her captors, particularly Gyneth, a student assigned to attend her, that reading and books are not evil as they have been taught.[12] Haly wants to unite the Singers and Libyrarians into a productive society that shares its knowledge, something she tries to put in motion when the Singers bring her back to the Libyrinth for the Redemption by reading from *The Book of the Night*. However, problems arise when the book is not at the Libyrinth because Selene's mother, the queen of Ilysies, steals it from Selene, and a battle ensues. The true redemption comes when Clauda returns from Ilysies in the stolen Wing of Tarsus, a flying craft controlled with the pilot's energy. She diffuses the battle by spreading Song over all the combatants, tempering the power by recalling her favorite book, *The Cricket in Times Square*. This Song unites all who experience it, and they try to label Clauda the true Redeemer, though she rejects the label. The reading of *The Book of the Night*, which Clauda took from the queen and gives to Haly, is almost an afterthought for the people united by the Song, which is fortunate, for the information that everyone yearns for is absent. Iscarion writes in *The Book of the Night*, "I have failed. The secret of making Eggs remains a mystery" (318). The news devastates all at the Redemption until Haly unites them again, encouraging the formation of a new city in which the inhabitants share knowledge — the creation of a utopian society. As with other children's and young adult fantasy, practical knowledge and action overshadow the books at the end. Books have power and lead to great problems, but only actions can defeat a book's importance. For *Libyrinth*, it is the union of Song and book, represented by Haly's unique talent, that foreshadows the need for the balance the characters plan to strive for with the creation of their new society.[13]

Though attitudes towards books and reading vary from character to character in the novels discussed in this chapter, one thing remains clear: books, no matter how comforting, dangerous, or powerful, cannot replace experience and action. The young protagonists may use books as tools, but ultimately they must act using their own wits, including applying knowledge they may have gleaned from books, to succeed. Since books can be seen as representative of adult and other types of authority, the characters' actions represent moving beyond the circle of protection cast by adults. These young characters are creating their own knowledge set that combines the past — books — with the present — experience and action.

3

Interacting with Books

As discussed in Chapter 1, children's literature — even children's literature with a subversive element — usually contains a didactic element. Regardless of genre, the need for adult authors to embed didacticism into their books exists. Claudia Nelson, in her article "Writing the Reader: The Literary Child in and beyond the Book," argues that "one of the standard messages of children's metafiction is 'Read!'" (228), even while she also argues that children's metafiction is subversive. For Nelson, as for many other critics, subversion is accompanied by a message, in her case a message that reading is positive. Joe Sutliff Sanders, who dismisses Nelson's argument of subversion (along with other critics who also claim children's metafiction is subversive) without acknowledging her tempered message, also emphasizes the positive relationship between books and readers in children's metafiction, as discussed in Chapter 1. Though Sanders does temper his negative response to Nelson's argument as his article develops, he does not acknowledge her reference to "one of the standard messages of children's metafiction," a problematic choice given the ultimate similarity of their arguments.

One type of children's fantasy in particular would seem to be the place to emphasize the importance of reading: fantasy in which the child reader interacts physically with a book's characters, whether by being pulled into the book or from characters exiting the book. David Lewis, in his article "The Constructedness of Text: Picture Books and the Metafictive," in his discussion of the rules of realistic fiction, notes that "in its most extreme forms, where we become 'lost' in a book, the medium itself — language — becomes invisible as we read or listen" (135). In the type of fantasy being discussed in this chapter, the medium is not just invisible: it is absent, allowing characters or readers to move between text and reality. Books such as *The Pagemaster* by David Kirschner and Ernie Contreras, *Beware of Storybook Wolves* and *Who's Afraid of the Big Bad Book?* by Lauren Child, *The Neverending Story* by Michael Ende, the *Cracked Classics* series by Tony Abbott, *Attack of the Mutant* by R.L. Stine, and *Malice* and *Havoc* by Chris Wooding all contain child characters who interact physically with fictional texts whether by entering those texts or through characters emerging from the texts. Though this type of fantasy would seem to be a way to encourage reading in its audience given the close connection between characters and readers, in fact the messages about reading are quite mixed even as other messages are more obvious.

David Kirschner and Ernie Contreras's *The Pagemaster* (perhaps better known for its animated film version) best fits the mold of didactic expectations for children's fantasy with an interactive quality. In this chapter book, ten-year-old Richard fears nearly everything and can quote statistics about the dangers of different activities, from how many household accidents are associated with ladders (8) to the correlation of shin splints to blood clots in the legs (6). After overhearing his parents' worried discussion about him one night, Richard resolves to try harder to fit his father's idea of a "normal" son, which leads to his biking to a hardware store for some nails his father needs to work on the tree house that he is building for Richard. On his way there, Richard is caught in a violent thunderstorm and seeks shelter in a building he discovers is the public library. Mr. Dewey, the librarian, tries to interest Richard in a book, but Richard's focus is on calling his parents to collect him. Despite Richard's encyclopedic knowledge of statistics involving dangers and his vivid imagination that leads to dreams of "being struck by lightning, getting sucked into tornadoes, or falling into the Grand Canyon" (5), Richard is not much of a reader, at least of fiction, and does not possess a library card until Mr. Dewey gives him one on his arrival at the library.

The main action of *The Pagemaster* occurs when Richard, heading toward the telephone, slips and hits his head. Upon waking, Richard discovers that the mural on the rotunda, which features different characters from classic literature, is empty and that the central figure, "an old man with a long white beard ... wearing an amazing cloak made out of book pages" (19), is standing near him. Introducing himself as the Pagemaster, the old man directs Richard toward the exit through "Fiction A to Z! Where all is possible!" telling him, "When in doubt look to the booooooks" (20). From this point, Richard must navigate through the fiction section with the help of three new characters, books representing the genres Adventure, Fantasy, and Horror, each of which agrees to help Richard if he promises to check them out once they reach the exit. As they navigate the fiction section, they must make their way through portions of several classic stories, including *The Strange Case of Dr. Jekyll and Mr. Hyde*, *Moby Dick*, and *Treasure Island*, and they encounter elements of *Gulliver's Travels*, *Arabian Nights*, and "Jack and the Beanstalk," among other stories. Each time they enter a different genre section, the books in that section create obstacles they must face, as when they encounter Dr. Jekyll/Mr. Hyde in horror and Captain Ahab in adventure.

Despite the dominance of books with exciting stories in this chapter book, *The Pagemaster's* focus is less on the importance and value of reading than on Richard's learning to face and overcome his fears. He begins the journey afraid of everything to the point that his fear paralyzes him, leaving him unable to help Horror, whose fears are greater than Richard's, when he is in trouble (14). By the end of the adventure in the library, however, Richard has become brave enough to risk his life to save his friends by facing a dragon even though he would be able to escape the danger without them (87). Though his final defeat of the dragon, who has swallowed him whole, comes when he remembers the Pagemaster's reminder to "look to the books"—which he uses to grow a beanstalk in the dragon's stomach to escape—the medium of success is less important than that he stays calm enough to face his fears. When Richard and the books encounter the Pagemaster following their adventure, the Pagemaster attributes Richard's new-found confidence to the stories, but it is not reading that has made the difference; in fact, the books are the direct danger. Yet Richard becomes attached to the books and, as promised, checks them out of the library when he wakes—his adventure having occurred while he was unconscious after falling in the library. The dream has had a strong impact on him, however, for not only does he borrow the fictional books, but he also has the courage to enter the tree house he had never wanted his father to build. His parents find him there asleep with "three books nestled in his arms" (93). Kirschner and Contreras have tied adventure and courage with reading, and though they never show Richard reading the books, the implication is that he has become a reader of fiction and in fact that reading is life-changing for him. The message is not subtle, though it seems at odds with the actual events of the chapter book. In fact, the message seems to be more akin to the focus of Chapter 2: action is more important than reading, which is a dangerous occupation.

By contrast with *The Pagemaster*, Lauren Child's picturebooks *Beware of Storybook Wolves* and *Who's Afraid of the Big Bad Book?*, the sequel to *Beware of Storybook Wolves*, focus on an avid book consumer, Herb. *Beware of Storybook Wolves*, the first of the books, discusses the nightly ritual of Herb's mother reading him a story, something he enjoys immensely, though he insists she take his favorite book of fairy tales out with her because "there's a wolf in it." His mother humors him despite believing "storybook wolves are not at all dangerous." When one night she accidentally leaves the book behind in Herb's room, Herb discovers that his fears of storybook wolves are real, for the two wolves from his fairy tales book emerge from the book and Herb must devise a way to stop them from eating him. His clever first attempt to foil the wolves' attack is stopped by the wicked fairy from "Sleeping Beauty," who "hated little boys only slightly less than she hated little girls," so he turns to the book for help, finding "the page with the Fairy Godmother, and [shaking] it until she tumbled out of the book and onto the floor." Though she is irritated by Herb's actions, she eventually helps him defeat the wolves.

Beware of Storybook Wolves focuses more on the humorous situation in which Herb finds himself than it does on reading, though the fairy tales book is certainly a focal point of the picturebook. Books represent danger if left open and unguarded, and once the problems begun with the escape of the wolves are resolved, Herb piles them under his bed so that the characters cannot escape to harm him again. Further, the changes made by the fairy godmother, who turns one wolf into a caterpillar, are permanent, as the end of the picturebook demonstrates when the story shows Little Red Riding Hood encountering a caterpillar in the woods on the way to her grandmother's house. Though books are dangerous, they also offer adventure for the consumer, and in this respect, *Beware of Storybook Wolves* could be seen to promote reading. Certainly Herb has no desire to discard his books; he merely takes precautionary measures to protect himself from the villains while he sleeps.

The second book, *Who's Afraid of the Big Bad Book?*, presents a slightly older Herb as an avid reader and focuses on the treatment — or mistreatment — of books. The first sentence of the picturebook, "Herb loved storybooks," establishes Herb's relationship with books immediately. He enjoys his books so much that he "read his books everywhere. This was why many of the pages were stickily stuck together, soggy around the edges, and usually had bits of banana, cookie, and the odd pea squashed between the pages." Herb's love of books does not stop him from mistreating them, though this mistreatment is primarily attributed to "last year, when he was much younger." In addition to the food stains, he has defaced the books in numerous ways, including by drawing mustaches on characters, removing furniture and even characters from the story, and adding telephones and stickers to the illustrations, a fact the reader discovers once Herb is transported into one of his books — "a book of fairy tales." Like Richard in *The Pagemaster*, Herb's entrance into the book comes with unconsciousness: he falls "asleep with his head on the page" and wakes in a different bed when Goldilocks wakes him by shrieking, "WHAT ARE YOU DOING HERE? HOW DARE YOU BE ON THIS PAGE? I AM THE STAR AND I SAY YOU ARE NOT ALLOWED IN THIS STORY!" Goldilocks and the other characters in the book are aware that they are characters in a book, and none appreciates Herb's appearance, particularly when they realize that he is the owner of the book, and, especially in the case of the characters of "Cinderella," responsible for the vandalism of their story.

Sylvia Pantaleo, in her essay "Postmodernism, Metafiction, and *Who's Afraid of the Big Bad Book?*," explores the different postmodern and metafictional elements in *Who's Afraid of the Big Bad Book?* (she presents twelve elements). Part of the metafictional in *Who's Afraid of the Big Bad Book?*, she argues, is "the constructedness of the text" (36). In addition,

> as a reader of his fairy tale book, Herb became involved and took on a co-author role as he physically changed the text and illustrations in the book. Herb became intimately involved with the text when he fell into the book. Again he participated in constructing the story as he traversed the land of fairy tales. However, his involvement in the diegetic, in the fictional world in which the events and situations that are narrated occur, taught him lessons about the importance of critical detachment [36].

While Herb's romp through his fairy tale book is amusing for the reader, it is showing the need for a balance between engagement — active involvement — and detachment.[1] Certainly the detachment is paramount for Herb at the end of the text, for as soon as Herb escapes thanks to a combination of climbing the text and Goldilocks' voice shaking the book hard enough to dislodge it from Herb's bed and send him tumbling to the floor in his room, he and his friend Ezzie, who has slept through the adventure, spend the night repairing most of the damage with one exception: they alter Goldilocks' story by padlocking the door to the bears' house and putting a "mousy brown" wig on her. If there is anything didactic in the picturebook, it is that while reading is enjoyable, books are not meant to be defaced, even to make a card for one's mother — as Herb does when he removes Prince Charming from the book. Unlike *The Pagemaster*, which is heavily didactic, *Who's Afraid of the Big Bad Book?*, like *Beware of Storybook Wolves*, focuses more on fun than lessons and even seems to undermine its message with the final two pages, which focus on Goldilocks' transformation.

Like Herb in *Who's Afraid of the Big Bad Book?*, Bastian in Michael Ende's *The Neverending Story* reshapes the story he enters. Also like Herb, Bastian loves books and his first contact with *The Neverending Story* leaves him so entranced that he steals the book from the shopkeeper who was reading it. He is fascinated by the book because "here was just what he had dreamed of, what he had longed for ever since the passion for books had taken hold of him: A story that never ended! The book of books!" (11). A combination of fear of being caught with the stolen book and a desire to read it immediately lead Bastian to skip classes and hide in the school's attic, where he spends the day reading *The Neverending Story*. Bastian as a character closely resembles

Richard from *The Pagemaster*: both boys are isolated, lonely, and picked-upon. Though Bastian does not possess Richard's level of fear, he too uses his experiences in *The Neverending Story* to grow and develop.

When he first starts reading *The Neverending Story*, Bastian becomes captivated by the story of Atreyu's quest to find the savoir of Fantastica, the magical world of *The Neverending Story*. Bastian remains separate from the story with his point of view inserted through italics while the text of *The Neverending Story* is in standard font. As the story progresses and Bastian becomes more and more engaged in it, he realizes that at times characters can hear, and even see, him, though he also thinks this connection to the characters is unlikely. For example, when he cries out upon reading of Ygramul and that cry is recorded in *The Neverending Story*, he thinks, "*Could she have heard my cry? ... But that's not possible*" (77). He starts to wonder if he could be the savior for whom Atreyu searches. Yet his self-esteem is so poor — he is described as "fat and bowlegged" (21), is neglected by his distant, grieving father, and picked upon by schoolmates — that he dismisses the possibility of entering *The Neverending Story* to give the Childlike Empress her new name and save Fantastica from the encroaching Nothingness destroying it. His fear of disappointing the Childlike Empress and Atreyu inhibits him from entering the story, leading the Childlike Empress to force his hand by traveling to the Old Man of the Wandering Mountain, who is recording *The Neverending Story*, and asking him to repeat *The Neverending Story* over and over until Bastian realizes he must break the storytelling cycle and save the Childlike Empress and Fantastica: "*and so it would go on for ever and ever, for any change in the sequence of events was unthinkable. Only he, Bastian, could do anything about it. And he would have to do something, or else he too would be included in this circle*" (198). When he calls out to the Childlike Empress with her new name — "Moon Child" — that he is coming, the boundaries between his world and Fantastica disappear and he becomes lost in the book literally. As Fanfan Chen notes in his article "From Hypotyposis to Metalepsis: Narrative Devices in Contemporary Fantastic Fiction," "The diegetic hero becomes a hypodiegetic hero and interacts with the hypodiegetic characters within the embedded story" (399). Bastian becomes not just the hero of the external story but the hero of the one he enters. His entry into the book, unlike in *The Pagemaster* and *Who's Afraid of the Big Bad Book?*, is not an unconscious event; it is urgent and active, though he is surprised to discover that he enters into darkness. Only his ideas, his stories, can recreate Fantastica, and that is what he does, starting with Perilin, the Night Forest.

While the focus of *The Pagemaster* is Richard's overcoming his fears, *The Neverending Story* presents Bastian pushing his fears away under a new identity.

As the savior of Fantastica, Bastian has the power to make his wishes and stories come true. As the Childlike Empress tells him, "Fantastica will be born again from your wishes.... Through me they will becomes reality" (204). These wishes include the creation of lands and origin stories for different creatures of Fantastica, and part of his early wishes are to change himself in appearance and skills. The Childlike Empress sees him as a hero, and the reflection he sees of himself in her eyes is what he longs to be, and once he sees this reflection, "he was transported, carried out of himself, and when he returned, he found he had become the handsome boy whose image he had seen" (209). Even then, he is not satisfied and adds strength and other skills to his handsome appearance. He becomes the perfect storybook hero in many ways and decides he would rather stay in Fantastica than return to his life in the Other World — what little he remembers of it, memories that disappear with each wish he makes. As this power goes to his head, he becomes more and more arrogant and isolated from his true friends Atreyu and Falkor and is manipulated by Xayide into distrusting them. Only when he has completely cut himself off from Atreyu and Falkor, by wounding Atreyu in battle, does Bastian realize he must return home to save Fantastica and himself. To do so, Bastian must lose everything, including his own name, and pass through the Waters of Life and strip himself of all Fantastica elements. In other words, he must embrace his own identity again, accept himself and all of his faults.

As with *The Pagemaster*, the travels in *The Neverending Story* change Bastian when he returns to his world. He re-forges a relationship with his father and returns to the bookstore to confess his theft of *The Neverending Story* (which has disappeared from the attic where Bastian left it) to the shopkeeper. Though the book and Bastian's travels are what lead him to change, books are not the focal point at the end. In fact, they seem to have diminished in importance, for the focus at the end is on Bastian sharing his story, not in a book, but orally. Mr. Coreander demands that Bastian "tell me the whole story" (443) and informs Bastian after that "it's not just books. There are other ways of getting to Fantastica and back" (445). Storytelling, sharing stories, becomes more important than reading, a communal activity in contrast to the isolation of Bastian's experience as a reader hidden away in the attic of the schoolhouse. Though didactic in nature, *The Neverending Story* does not promote reading in the way it might be expected to do.

By contrast with the texts discussed thus far, with characters either interested in books or in gaining some kind of knowledge, Tony Abbott's *Cracked Classics* series presents the main characters Devin, the narrator, and Frankie, his "best-pal-even-though-she's-a-girl" (*Trapped* 1), who are not just reluctant readers but hostile ones, actively avoiding reading of any kind. They particularly hate the "chubby book[s]" (6) assigned to them by their English teacher, Mr. Wexler, and even when assigned to do a report for class as in *Trapped in Transylvania*, the first novel in the series, they manage to avoid doing so. In this first book, their punishment for not reading is to be sent to the library where, Mr. Wexler tells them, "the librarian will make you learn to love every single one of [the books]" (11). From the start of the series, these reluctant readers are given book work as punishment for not reading, a tactic that seems counterintuitive, and in fact throughout the series, they never become voluntary readers.

The opening of each book—Devin and Frankie ending up in the library—leads to their entrance into the focal book via the broken old security "zappers" kept in the workroom of the library. Often the book has been assigned for class, though in a couple of cases (*A Christmas Carol, Around the World in Eighty Days*), the book they enter into has not been assigned specifically but is on display or otherwise important to the story. After the first book, in which they must come to terms with the transportation, they know immediately what has happened and what it will take for them to return to their world: they must go through the events of the story. However, unlike Herb, Bastian, and even Richard to a lesser extent, Devin and Frankie cannot change the events of the original text despite their interaction with the characters; instead, they become participants in the classic stories. Whenever they try to explain events to a character that he or she should not know, the characters cannot understand their language (*Trapped* 43). Further, if they try to read ahead in the book, which they have with them throughout the story, the words start to blur. On occasions when they flip past scenes, at least once per novel, there is a ripping sound and the story world becomes unstable, throwing Devin and Frankie forward in the narrative (59).

Though Devin and Frankie remain reluctant readers even in the stories, they find themselves becoming attached to the characters, even thinking of them as people rather than characters by the end of the story. At the end of *Trapped in Transylvania*, Devin thinks, "It's the people in the stories that make people read them over and over" (111). Their attachment to characters becomes particularly harrowing at the end of *Crushing on a Capulet*, when they enter into *Romeo and Juliet*, for despite all their attempts to avert disaster, Romeo and Juliet die. The experience also leads to their discussing the purpose of tragedy: "We can ... make sure the bad things don't happen again" (136). It is a facile message, but it underscores that they are taking something from the experience. By the end of each classic text they have entered, Devin and Frankie have gained an appreciation of that book, though they still have no desire to read (or reread), as evidenced from the continuing frame for the narratives. There is an argument to be made that the message of the series is, as Claudia Nelson indicates in her article, "Read!," for presumably the readers of *Cracked Classics* are expected to want to read the classic books Devin and Frankie have experienced in an attempt to make the same connection with the characters and story as Devin and Frankie. Yet that message, like the message in *Who's Afraid of the Big Bad Book?*, seems to be undermined by Devin and Frankie's continued attitude toward books and reading. Even the subversive element of the series — Devin and Frankie's secret undermining of Mr. Wexler by knowing well books that they had seemingly not known just minutes before — is undermined by the hint that the librarian Mrs. Figglehopper is fully aware of what the zappers do. On their return from *Dracula*, after Devin tells Mrs. Figglehopper that *Dracula* "wasn't as boring as we thought," he observes Mrs. Figglehopper's reaction: "Now I won't say her eyes exactly twinkled when she said that ["Oh, I know" in response to Devin's comment about *Dracula*], but they were very bright" (127). Further, at the end of each book in the series, there is a note "From the Desk of Irene M. Figglehopper" to the reader that gives background on the classic book's author and the story. The note also comments about the security gates' instability, though Mrs. Figglehopper never confirms knowledge of what they do, even having a repairman try to fix the gates in *What a Trip! (Around the World in Eighty Days)*. If adults like Mrs. Figglehopper and Mr. Wexler ultimately control the children — and the fact that Mrs. Figglehopper gets the last word in each book points toward adult control of the narrative — Devin and Frankie's subversiveness rings hollow. Certainly, the series presents itself as didactic, but its success is questionable for all that it comes closest of the children's fantasy texts discussed to promoting reading among its audience. The one text in the series that is most didactic, *Humbug Holiday*, in which Devin and Frankie enter *A Christmas Carol*, parallels the didacticism of the original text, for Devin, like Scrooge, must learn the true meaning of Christmas and the importance of giving to the less fortunate, in this case sharing the cookies his mother has made for the school's Community Christmas Banquet.

In contrast to the books discussed thus far, in which the main characters interact with either classics of literature or otherwise artistic works (in the case of *The Neverending Story*), in both R.L. Stine's *Attack of the Mutant* and Chris Wooding's *Malice* series, the focal books are comic books, a medium often viewed negatively, seen as not worth reading, especially compared to literary works. This perspective is clear in *Attack of the Mutant*, a Goosebumps book — a series also often viewed in a negative light. In this novel, the main character Skipper is obsessed with comic books. He collects them and seems more concerned with their value as collector's items than in reading them, for he tells his friend Wilson, "If you read them, they lose their value" (2) and later informs Libby that she is "not a real collector" because she has no interest in selling her comics in the future, just wanting to read them (20). However, Skipper particularly enjoys the comic *The Masked Mutant*, which he reads obsessively and against his parents' wishes. His father blames Skipper's low grades on his obsession with comic books, which he reads rather than doing homework and studying. Both of his parents disapprove of his comic books, his father calling them "trash" (11) and his mother calling them "dumb comics" and wondering, "When is the last time you read a good book?" (37). Neither parent is successful at diverting Skipper's attention away from his comic books, even when his father confiscates them and threatens to throw them out, for Skipper knows that it is an empty threat (11–12). If anything, his parents' disapproval of comics has the opposite effect on Skipper, encouraging rather than discouraging his covert reading. As Darigan, Tunnell, and Jacobs note in *Children's Literature: Engaging Teachers and Children in Good Books*, "Direct attacks on positive reading responses to poor quality books ... almost always guarantee that a rift will develop between teacher and student" (23). The effect is similar between child and parent or really any authority figure, as was also evident in *Septimus Heap*.

Most of *Attack of the Mutant* revolves around Skipper's discovery that the villain and title character of *The Masked Mutant* may actually be real, for one day, he sees what he believes is the character's secret lair. An exploration of the lair reveals that it houses the printing press for *The Masked Mutant*, that Skipper has become a character in the comic book, and that the Galloping Gazelle, one of the good characters in the comic book, is waiting for Skipper to rescue him. Both the Masked Mutant and the Galloping Gazelle believe that Skipper has superpowers like them, and eventually, in an attempt to defeat the Masked Mutant, Skipper takes on the mantle of "The Colossal Elastic Boy" (112). After he battles the Masked Mutant and seems to have succeeded in killing him, Skipper decides that he doesn't need comic books any longer until he cuts himself and discovers that he now bleeds ink. The Masked Mutant's comment that he "changed you [Skipper] into a comic book character" (111) has come true, making Skipper realize "my comic book career wasn't over" (117). *Attack of the Mutant* does not focus on reading, though Skipper's obsession with comic books does not seem healthy, but instead focuses more on adventure and the surprise ending, a feature of the Goosebumps series. Like the Masked Mutant and the Galloping Gazelle, Skipper is now made of ink rather than flesh and blood. Though there is never any explanation of how the Masked Mutant and the Galloping Gazelle come to be in the real world, Skipper's transformation is explained by the Masked

Mutant: "Remember when you walked through the glass door and a beam of light passed over you? ... Well, that was a scanner.... When you stepped through it, it scanned your body. It turned you into tiny dots of ink" (111). Skipper can still interact with his family at the end of the novel, but his life has been utterly changed with his transformation. Like most of the Goosebumps books, the ending of *Attack of the Mutant* is open, concluding with Skipper's realization that his role in comics is just beginning.

Yet despite the prominent role of comic books in this novel, the focus of the story is not "Read!" Instead, it points to the dangers of reading comic books. As with *The Pagemaster*, books pose a threat rather than offer safety in escape. Yet the apparent warning about the dangers of becoming obsessed with comic books may in fact encourage further reading because of the possibility of excitement, even transformation. Even Skipper, who appears ready to give up comic books after living an adventure, must return to them at the end of the novel.

By contrast with the focal comic book in *Attack of the Mutant*, which is well-known and widely distributed, the focal comic books in Chris Wooding's two-book *Malice* series, also called *Malice*, is an underground comic book that few characters have seen or even believe exists. The comic book itself is printed using ink that, when exposed to the air, eventually fades, so it is difficult to share the comic, and it cannot be copied. Rumors swirl about the comic book and its villain, Tall Jake, and kids will often perform a ritual to call Tall Jake to "take me away" (*Malice* 8), not really believing it will work but titillated by the possibility. The series revolves around main characters Seth and Kady trying to find out what has happened to their friend Luke, who performs the ritual at the beginning of *Malice* then disappears. Tracking down his actions prior to his disappearance, they discover a comic book shop in London that has copies of *Malice*, though the store proprietor denies having it. When they look at the copy that Seth has stolen, they find a section containing Luke. This section is presented in comic book form in the novel, which contains several other comic book sections at points of critical action in Malice, the name of the land in the comic book. Not wanting to believe that Luke is really dead as the comic depicts, Seth plans to do the ritual and follow his friend, to attempt a rescue. The possibility of entering a world full of real, life-and-death adventure excites Seth, who longs for real adventure rather than the "fake" danger of the modern world:

> His dreams were full of new frontiers, of explorers like David Livingstone, the first European to cross the African continent, or Neil Armstrong, the first human being ever to set foot on the moon. Kady had fascinated him with tales of Lewis and Clark, the men who trekked across North American long before anyone had

mapped it, and of Columbus and Magellan, the great sea voyagers. These were men who cast themselves into the unknown, far from help, facing terrible and extraordinary danger. These were his heroes.

Today's explorers were sponsored by soft-drink corporations, all their challenges pointless because there was nothing left to explore.... [27–8].

Seth's desire for real adventure, with genuine risks, comes up again and again in the series. His interest in Malice is more for its real dangers than anything else; he wants to help Luke and later others, but it is the danger that drives him. Malice the place suits Seth, and he has no desire to return to his life in small-town England.

Reading in this series is not paramount. Though the character most knowledgeable about Malice, Justin, read the comic book for a year before performing the ritual to call Tall Jake, most characters have done little, if any, reading of the comic — which is difficult to get — and learn the pitfalls of Malice as they occur, or die in the process like Luke. Seth reads a single comic before entering Malice the first time. Kady does little reading as well before she too returns to Malice after learning she had been there the previous year but had escaped with no memory of being in Malice. She later learns that all who escape from Malice lose their memory of being there. Rather than books and reading playing a major role in the series, it is rumor, speculation and fear that are focal. In the first book, the tie between Malice the place and *Malice* the comic book is not entirely clear. In this book, Malice the place could be a parallel world that the comic's creator, Grendel, can see into and draw, but not literally be a comic book. However, in the second book, *Havoc*, the origins of Malice are explained: Grendel, a deformed, mentally-impaired man sequestered in a mental institution, imagined the world and drew it. The Lack, one of the Six, the original rulers of Malice, explains the origins of Malice to Seth and other members of the opposition group Havoc:

> Our world began with Grendel. Him, and only him. I do not know where he came from. I do not know exactly what he is. I do not know if you would call him a god or a fool. But he possesses the most extraordinary mind. A mind that would build a world, and craft every inch of it in exquisite detail. He painted and sketched and drew, tuning and testing. Eventually, he had imagined it, so perfectly, he believed it so much, that the world inside his head became real. It took on a life of its own and passed beyond his control [287].[2]

Thus Grendel's obsession with the images in his mind led to his drawings, which led to the creation of Malice. In Wooding's series, unlike the other series discussed, the books are not the danger: belief is the danger. Tall Jake was able to overthrow the other members of the Six by becoming the character most believed in. He uses the rumors, fear, and belief to help create bridges between Malice and the real world, emerging from a large portrait of himself that Grendel drew, and his ultimate plans are to merge the two worlds and rule both. With the help of Icarus Scratch, who owns the former mental institution in which Grendel lives and draws and who publishes the comic books, Tall Jake has gained great power. The Lack explains why Tall Jake kidnaps children as part of the plan:

> Because if he didn't, nobody would be interested. If Malice was just a comic, nobody would care. But it's a dangerous comic. It's a dark secret. Forbidden. Scratch knew kids would read it if they believed those were real kids fighting for survival. If not for that, it would be only one comic among many, and it would disappear without trace [289–90].

The rumors about the comic are so strong that, though it is only published in small runs in England, kids around the globe, communicating in chat rooms and elsewhere on the internet, have heard of it and believe, performing the ritual and giving Tall Jake more power. In Malice, Seth and Kady encounter other children from the United States, Russia, and Sweden. The reading matters less than the belief; however, the comic book's production helps fuel the belief. Thus once Tall Jake is defeated in Malice, Seth, Kady, and Justin return to the real world and plan to take Grendel, thereby stopping the comic book production. Plans go awry, naturally, and it is Grendel, Tall Jake's creator, who ultimately weakens him — with the very tools that created him. Grendel blinds and burns Tall Jake by painting over the eyes of his portrait with black ink, allowing Seth to stab Tall Jake with Grendel's pen: "From where the pen stuck out of his collar, Tall Jake began to smolder. The same smoldering that Grendel's paintbrush had caused, like he was a ball of paper burning up in the heart of a fire" (381). The tools of the creator have destroyed the creation.

The end of the series underscores the lack of focus on books and reading, for Seth, Kady, and Justin have the chance to return home and live normal lives, but only Kady embraces the chance.[3] Seth and Justin, however, feel out of place in their world and plan a return to Malice, Seth because it still represents real adventure and danger rather than the simulated adventures of the real world. To this extent, the message of the *Malice* series is mixed. Seth and Justin reject their lives and their families and all that is familiar for the chance to live in a fictional world, albeit one that they have made moderately more stable. Their conversation at the end of *Havoc* presents this decision:

> "Are you sure about this? I mean, going back for good? What about your folks? What about Kady?" [Justin asks.]
> Seth felt some of the good humor drain out of him. "I don't want to leave her," he said. "I don't want to leave *them*. You think I haven't thought about

that? I mean, how can I explain to Mom and Dad where I've gone? How I can't even send them a postcard or make a phone call now and then?"

"That's rough," Justin said. "It's easy for me; I mean, I don't have nothin' worth crying about that I'm leaving behind. But you..."

Seth sighed. "Kady's gonna be happy here. My parents are happy here ... or as happy as they get, I suppose. But this place isn't for me. I know where I'm supposed to be" [390, emphasis in original].

They have rejected reality so that they can continue enjoying the excitement of Malice — a selfish choice, particularly on Seth's part because, unlike Justin who was raised in an abusive environment, Seth comes from a stable, caring family. Kady's refusal to go with them shows her greater maturity and willingness to work for her happiness in reality. Perry Nodelman, in *The Hidden Adult: Defining Children's Literature*, notes that one of the common patterns of children's literature is home/away/home: the child character leaves home, has adventures and conflicts that change him/her, and returns home a changed person (61). In the *Malice* series, this pattern is broken, and though Seth and Justin discuss the negative impact staying away will have on Seth's family, he nevertheless chooses to stay away. Given that this series is aimed at young adults, it is arguable that the choice Seth makes is one that shows maturity since people his age — late teens — are forging out on their own by leaving home for college or to start a new job. However, his choice is suspect given its disconnection from reality — Seth and Justin are remaining lost in a fictional world rather than coping with the real world. It is not a healthy choice.

This focus on adventure, on experience, carries through most of the books containing interactive elements, from *The Pagemaster* and *The Neverending Story*, in which Richard and Bastian gain confidence through their adventures, to the more humorous adventures of Lauren Child and Tony Abbott, in which reading is also secondary to experience, to Stine and Wooding, in which characters become the adventure. There is no denying that the stories contain messages. But both Sanders's and Nelson's belief that books and reading are central and positive does not fit with the books discussed in this chapter. Perhaps the true message behind this particular type of metafiction is not "Read!" but "Experience!" By experiencing, the characters create their own stories rather than relying solely on stories supplied by adults.

4

The Writer-Character in Children's Fantasy

The majority of children's fantasy books discussed thus far contain characters interacting with books that are either powerful artifacts and/or allow characters to enter and exit the books and become part of a different story. However, another type of interaction exists, one in which the characters of the books are also writers or storytellers. Often these writer-characters are children, though they may also be adults writing about children. Not surprisingly, these books are heavily metafictional, often focusing as much on the process of storytelling as on the story itself. Maria Nikolajeva, in the chapter "Metafiction in Children's Literature" of her book *Children's Literature Comes of Age: Toward a New Aesthetic*, focuses on "texts that in some way or other consciously discuss the art of writing and their own existence" (191), one aspect of metafiction. Though most of the texts she examines have a heavy realistic component, most also have supernatural elements, and Nikolajeva notes that "it is these [supernatural] elements that evoke the characters' (and the readers') doubts as to the credibility of the stories, draw our attention to whatever seems incoherent, and, consequently, also stimulates reflections on metafiction" (201). Nikolajeva further argues that "the essence of metafiction ... is to erase the illusion of a boundary between fantasy and reality, and in so doing it also questions the reality of 'reality'" (202). In other words, without the supernatural elements in these texts—which include Robert Cormier's *Fade*, Geraldine McCaughrean's *A Pack of Lies*, and Mary Rodgers' *Freaky Friday*—the metafictional elements would stand out less because these supernatural elements underscore the fictional nature of the story in a way that enhances the role of metafiction to question "the reality of 'reality.'" As discussed in Chapter 1, there can be a close connection between fantasy and metafiction because both resist and break the bounds of realistic fiction.

Pseudonymous Bosch's novel *The Name of This Book Is Secret*, the first in the *Secret* series, demonstates Nikolajeva's claims well. This novel does contain a story: Cass and Max-Ernest's developing friendship as they investigate the death of a magician whose diary they have found and decoded, and their rescue of a classmate who has been kidnapped by the same people they suspect of killing the magician. However, this story is frequently subsumed by the implied writer, who talks of the dangers of the story he is telling, crosses out the first chapter of the story and then explains why it is crossed out, and eventually tells the readers to imagine their own character names and setting for the story if they don't like those that he is creating to protect the reader from the dangers of real knowledge of these characters. Though it might be easy to forget the framework of the novel and the implied author's discussion of writing the story once the story itself begins, the implied author frequently inserts metafictional comments into the story through footnotes and parentheticals among other techniques, reminding readers of his role in shaping the story. Chapter 17, "I've Changed My Mind," is perhaps the most intrusive insertion of the implied author into the story. He writes,

> Rather than continuing to narrate the adventures of Cass and Max-Ernest, I'm going to end this book here — while they're still safe.
> More importantly, while you're still safe.
> I know, you're angry with me. You've read this far — you feel you've earned the right to know how the story ends [170].

From this point the implied author goes into a discussion about how good it is the reader cannot find him and bribe him into telling the rest of the story — before he manages to bribe himself with some chocolate into finishing the story. This humorous episode underscores the control the implied author has over Cass and Max-Ernest's story, a control he relinquishes briefly at the end of the novel. In the first Chapter 32, "Do-It-Yourself Ending," the implied author explains that "Only bad books have good endings" and that, moreover, "endings are hard to write" (314). Rather than write a narrative ending, then, he goes one by one through the characters in the story and explains how he would "imagine" their story would end (315), language that tempers his role as absolute authority over the story. This list, he informs the reader, can then be shaped into a narrative ending by the reader, and he offers a place in the book to write the ending, in the second Chapter 32, "Your Version," which is comprised of two lined pages for the reader to complete and the instructions, "PLEASE WRITE IN BLACK OR BLUE INK ONLY. ATTACH EXTRA PAGES AS NEEDED" (326). Despite this apparent relinquishing of the ending, however, the implied author takes over the story again for Chapter 0, "The Denouement," explaining first what a denouement is and then writing one that acts more as a precursor to the next book in the series than as an actual denouement. As the implied author indicates, based on the definition he has given, denouement "is exactly the wrong word to describe this chapter. This chapter will make nothing clear; it will raise many questions; and it may even contain a surprise or two. But I say we call it the denouement anyway because the word sounds so sophisticated and French" (333–4). The implied author's conscious control over the narrative has spanned the entire novel.

As with the examples of metafiction that Nikolajeva discusses in her chapter about metafiction, *The Name of This Book Is Secret* contains very few supernatural or fantasy elements; even the magician's tricks are explained realistically. The main supernatural element of the story, Ms. Mauvais's lack of aging except in her hands, serves to help underscore the fictional nature of the story, much as the intrusion of the implied author does. Though he talks frequently about there being a real story that is the basis for the one he is telling, his conscious disguising of elements from the names of characters and the setting to the ending serves to emphasize the fictional nature of the story.

Nikolajeva does not, however, analyze metafictional texts that are classified as pure fantasy (though her texts come close in some cases). Texts such as Rick Riordan's *Percy Jackson & the Olympians* and *The Kane Chronicles* series fit securely in the fantasy genre and have a metafictional element to them, yet this metafictional element serves less to "evoke ... doubts as to the credibility of the stories" than to offer up the possibility that these fantasies are real. They attempt to "erase the illusion of a boundary between fantasy and reality" by offering the possibility that the fantastic events are real and not fictional through the metafictional techniques employed by Riordan.

The Lightning Thief, the first novel in Rick Riordan's *Percy Jackson & the Olympians* series, opens with the narrator Percy addressing his audience:

Look, I didn't want to be a half-blood.
If you're reading this because you think you might be one, my advice is: close this book right now. Believe whatever lie your mom or dad told you about your birth, and try to lead a normal life.
Being a half-blood is dangerous. It's scary. Most of the time, it gets you killed in painful, nasty ways.
If you're a normal kid, reading this because you think it's fiction, great. Read on. I envy you being able to believe that none of this ever happened.
But if you recognize yourself in these pages — if you feel something stirring inside — stop reading immediately. You might be one of us. And once you know that, it's only a matter of time before *they* sense it too, and they'll come for you.
Don't say I didn't warn you [1, emphasis in original].

Percy's warning, loaded with urgency and directly addressed to two reading audiences, immediately demands that these implied readers take him seriously and question what they believe is reality. His initial address to potential half-bloods (or demigods) like him stresses the danger of his, and other half-bloods', life, and the use of the word *lie* in "Believe whatever lie your mom or dad told you about your birth" places into question the reality of life as half-bloods know it. If their mundane, realistic life is a lie, then the book, the story that Percy is narrating, may be real. The subsequent statement that Percy makes to "normal kid[s]" directly addresses the idea that the text is supposed to be fiction, but his tone and his comment about envying these readers who are "able to believe that none of this ever happened" again call into question the fictional nature of the text. Percy is willing to let his readers believe he is telling a fictional story, but there is no doubt that for him the story is not fictional. His return to addressing potential half-bloods — and his order to "stop reading immediately" — serve once more to stress the reality of the situation being narrated. Yet his warning against reading the story seems contradictory: Why tell this story when it could possibly resonate with other half-bloods and put them in danger? Certainly the implied readers of the opening paragraphs are more likely to be titillated by the cryptic warning than to stop reading, despite (or perhaps because of) his parting salvo of "Don't say I didn't warn you," just as the actual reader of the novel is. The story could be seen as a backhand manner of recruiting more demi-gods, as opposed to the overt recruitment used by Carter and Sadie Kane in *The Kane Chronicles* (see below). *The Name of This Book Is Secret* uses similar techniques to attract readers — warning them away in the opening as a means to pique their interest in the story. Percy's reading prohibition is just as tempting as the prohibitions in *Septimus Heap* and *Malice*.

This opening warning in *The Lightning Thief* is the main metafictional element of the *Percy Jackson & the Olympians* series. This novel and the remaining four books in the series do not contain additional overt addresses like this to the reader; however, Percy's narrative style continues to be quite conversational. In fact, the narrative seems to be much more like verbal storytelling than a written narrative despite his reference to a book in the opening warning, a technique that Monika Fludernik calls "pseudo-orality" ("Conversational" 65). In her article "Conversational Narration/Oral Narration," Fludernik discusses "narratives that give prominence to a pseudo-oral narrative voice, a teller figure whose style suggests that the discourse has been uttered rather than written down" (65). These narrators, she indicates,

> are often garrulous, repetitive, contradictory and illogical; they keep interrupting themselves and tend to address a fictive listener or audience familiarly; they seem to have an intimate rapport with the fictional world, to which they apparently belong, and also do not shy away from expressing their feelings and views

emphatically, thus setting themselves off from the typical narrators or literary texts — aloof, bland, reliable, neutral [65].

This style, evident to a small extent in Bosch's *The Name of This Book Is Secret*, is distinct in *Percy Jackson* and in *The Kane Chronicles* discussed below. Fludernik adds that

> it must be noted that the evocation of orality in literary texts is just that: an evocation or stylization produced by highlighting the most striking features of oral language. What counts for narrative purposes is not a faithful copy of the "original" utterance in all its linguistic detail, but the effect of deviation from the norm through quaintness, informality, intimacy, lack of education, cultural difference, class ascription. The simplifications and exaggerations of the linguistic features of orality and/or register therefore serve the purpose of facilitating identification, stereotyping, "local color," or *effet de reel* [66].

The style also blurs the distance between fantasy and reality. Percy's style is so close to the contemporary child's vernacular that the fantastic component of his narrative seems more believable than of it were presented in third person or in an elevated style. Percy's warning to the reader is clearly pseudo-oral: conversational and highly informal in nature with its direct address to the readers.

Following his warning, Percy introduces himself and reveals, "I'm twelve years old" (1). This detail establishes a near-consonant self-narration for this first novel, to use Dorrit Cohn's term describing a first person narrative told with little or no time between the events being narrated and the narrator (153). In Percy's case, he is twelve at the time of the telling, as revealed through the use of present tense, as well as during the events that transpire during the novel.[1] The lack of time between narrator and events in the story helps cement the urgency and reality of Percy's story as well. If he were narrating from several years past the end of the events, his warning about the dangers of being a half-blood would ring false. And though there are no more lengthy addresses to the implied readers, Percy frequently uses narrative cues to acknowledge his readers or otherwise indicate that he is aware of his audience. In *The Lightning Thief*, he often uses a tag such as "I dare you" ("I dare you to try not listening if you hear your best friend talking about you to an adult" [19]). He uses similar tags in the other books in the series, particularly "I mean" ("I mean, I've met plenty of embarrassing parents..." [*Sea* 254]; "I mean, I knew the legends about Apollo..." [*Titan's* 45]; "I mean, I wasn't exactly a gardening type..." [*Battle* 213]; "I mean, sure, she'd always been cute..." [*Last* 70]); "I know" or "you know" (cf. *Sea* 98; *Titan's* 238; *Battle* 7; *Last* 34); and "I'll admit" (cf. *Lightning* 347; *Sea* 210; *Titan's* 52, 167; *Last* 46, 345). All of these rhetorical devices point more toward an oral storytelling than a written one, as do many other devices Percy uses in the story.² There are a few more indications that Percy's story is being written. The reference to writing is most noticeable in the fourth book of the series, *The Battle of the Labyrinth*, in which the Greek letter delta, the mark indicating entrances to the labyrinth, is usually represented with the actual symbol and not the word (Δ), though Percy does explain that the symbol is "the Ancient Greek Delta" the first time it appears (60). Later the symbol is just shown without explanation (cf. 121, 240, 276, 334). In addition, Percy makes a comment that points toward a written narrative in *The Battle of the Labyrinth*: "I would never say this out loud or she'd [Aphrodite] blast me to ashes..." (212). While the focus of the series is not on storytelling itself, while the series does not often "consciously discuss the art of writing and [its] own existence" (Nikolajeva 19), there is never any doubt that Percy the narrator is conscious of his implied readers throughout the storytelling in all five novels in the series. And the constant addresses to the readers keep the story feeling realistic despite its fantastic elements.

Further, the oral nature of his narrative style underscores Percy's attitudes towards books and reading in the series. As he introduces himself in the first chapter of *The Lightning Thief*, Percy indicates that he is "a boarding student at Yancy Academy, a private school for troubled kids in upstate New York" (1) when the story begins. He also details some of the problems he has encountered in traditional educational settings, not least because he has "dyslexia and attention deficit disorder" (7). The dyslexia makes reading very difficult for him, and though he later learns from Annabeth, another half-blood, that all demigods have dyslexia because their "mind is hardwired for ancient Greek" (88), he never becomes comfortable reading and books never play a prominent role in the series aside from the ones he narrates.³ Even Annabeth, a daughter of Athena and one of the smartest of the half-bloods, rarely spends time reading because she too struggles with non–Greek books.⁴ Once again, the fact that Percy is consciously narrating a written text is seemingly contradictory for the half-blood audience, for they too would have problems reading the very book he warns them to close in his introductory comments.

Whereas the *Percy Jackson* series contains only a small metafictional element and focuses on the written texts that Percy refers to in *The Lightning Thief*, Riordan's *The Kane Chronicles* trilogy contains a much larger metafictional component that also blurs the line between fantasy and reality in a similar fashion. The layers of narration in *Percy Jackson* consist only of Percy the narrator relaying Percy the character's story to his implied readers. However, *The Kane Chronicles* has an additional layer of narrative. All three volumes in the trilogy open with a Warning to the implied reader from the implied author. This Warning, like the first few paragraphs in *Percy Jackson*, serves to blur the line between fantasy and reality by referencing how the implied author came to write the story. The Warning in *The Red Pyramid*, the first novel in the trilogy, reads,

> *The following is a transcript of a digital recording. In certain places, the audio quality was poor, so some words and phrases represent the author's best guesses. Where possible, illustrations of important symbols mentioned in the recording have been added. Background noises such as scuffling, hitting, and cursing by the two speakers have not been transcribed. The author makes no claims for the authenticity of the recording. It seems impossible that the two young narrators are telling the truth, but you, the reader, must decide for yourself.*

Like the opening of *Percy Jackson*, this Warning calls into question the truthfulness of the events in the story about to be told. However, this time the implied author blurs the line rather than the narrators, siblings Sadie and Carter Kane, who tell the story without there being a question about its validity.[5] As with the *Percy Jackson* series, readers of *The Kane Chronicles* know the text is fantasy, and this Warning blurs the separation of fantasy and reality, and even challenges the implied reader to decide on the story's truthfulness, though interestingly, the author never questions whether Sadie and Carter themselves are real or constructs. In addition, the Warning demonstrates the power that the implied author has over the text. He has made "best guesses" about sections of the recording, inserted illustrations (hieroglyphs), and removed certain sounds. Further, because he controls the shape of the final "transcription," he is responsible for the physical make-up of the text, which presents two chapters by Carter alternated with two chapters from Sadie until the final chapter of the novel, which is a stand-alone by Carter, Sadie having narrated the previous two chapters. There is no explanation as to why the author has chosen to work in two-chapter increments for each narrator, nor is there an explanation about why the final narrative by Carter is in a single chapter instead of two like all of the other Carter segments of narrative. Each chapter is also named by the author, though he employs first person in many chapter titles, including "Imprisoned with My Cat" (Chapter 3, Sadie) and "I Face the Killer Turkey" (Chapter 13, Carter), giving the author another layer of control of the final text. Though the content of the narrative is attributed to Carter and Sadie, the implied author controls the final format and content of the written text. The manipulation can be seen as a way of pointing to the fantastic elements of the story; however, it can also be seen as the Author's desire to keep readers' attention through the shaping of the story, to underscore its truth.

This control is emphasized at the end of the book, for following Carter's final chapter is an Author's Note, which again questions the reality of Carter and Sadie's story: "*Much of this story is based on fact, which makes me think that either the two narrators, Sadie and Carter, did a great deal of research ... or they are telling the truth*" (515). He details several elements of Egyptian culture that are real as a means of demonstrating their accuracy and ends by saying, "*Should further recordings fall into my hands, I will relay the information. Until then, we can only hope that Carter and Sadie are wrong in their predictions about the rise of chaos...*" (516). The end of *The Red Pyramid* keeps fantasy and reality blurred, and the author's final sentence seems to lean toward a belief that the story is real because he hopes the predictions are wrong — not lies or fiction, which are impossible, but *wrong*, which is possible, if improbable.

The Warning in the second book in the trilogy, *The Throne of Fire*, continues the implied author's movement toward believing Carter and Sadie:

> This is a transcript of an audio recording. Carter and Sadie Kane first made themselves known in a recording I received last year, which I transcribed as The Red Pyramid. This second audio file arrived at my residence shortly after that book was published, so I can only assume the Kanes trust me enough to continue relaying their story. If this second recording is a truthful account, the turn of events can only be described as alarming. For the sake of the Kanes and for the world, I hope what follows is fiction. Otherwise we are all in very serious trouble.

Though the author doesn't know if the story is "a truthful account," the tone of this warning seems to point toward his belief in the Kane siblings because rather than the story "seem[ing] impossible" as in the first book, now he hopes it is a fiction, a statement that implies belief that the story is real, that Sadie and Carter are telling the truth. The statement also parallels his Author's Note in *The Red Pyramid* with the use of the word *hope*. Like *Percy Jackson*, the implied author of *The Kane Chronicles* points toward the events being real via his discussion of the content of the text. This metafictional element blurs the fantasy/reality line, allowing the implied reader to take the story at face value. And once again, the text of *The Throne of Fire* concludes with an Author's Note that shows why the implied author is starting to believe Sadie and Carter are telling the truth: "Before publishing such an alarming transcript, I felt compelled to do some fact-checking on Sadie and Carter's story. I wish I could tell you they had made all this up. Unfortunately, it appears that much of what they have reported is based on fact" (447). Once again, the blurring of fantasy and reality — in favor of reality — comes up, and though the implied author does not guarantee the truth of the narrative, he does end the Author's Note with an even stronger statement of belief in the story as truth than in the first novel: "In short, I believe they might be telling the truth. Their call for help is genuine. Should further audio recordings fall into my hands, I will relay the information; but if Apophis [the god of Chaos] truly is rising, there may be no opportunity. For the sake of the entire world, I hope I'm wrong" (447). The use of *hope* in this passage has shifted from Sadie and Carter's story to the implied author's understanding of what they have revealed. Though he is still hedging on stating what he believes — "I believe they might be telling the truth"— his belief is strong enough that there is no hope that Sadie and Carter are wrong; instead, it is a hope that he is wrong in his assessment of the speed with which Apophis will rise. His skepticism is nearly gone now, and in the final book in the trilogy, *The Serpent's Shadow*, no doubt remains.

The Warning for *The Serpent's Shadow* reads,

> *This is a transcript of an audio recording. Twice before, Carter and Sadie Kane have sent me such recordings, which I transcribed as* The Red Pyramid *and* The Throne of Fire. *While I'm honored by the Kanes' continued trust, I must advise you that this third account is their most troubling yet. The tape arrived at my home in a charred box perforated with claw and teeth marks that my local zoologist could not identify. Had it not been for the protective hieroglyphs on the exterior, I doubt the box would have survived its journey. Read on, and you will understand why.*

Unlike the Warning in the first two books in the trilogy, this warning casts no doubt on the veracity of the story. Instead, the implied author describes the state of the box containing the tapes he received for transcription. The charred state and the unidentifiable "claw and teeth marks" add credence to the story, which sounds unbelievable on the surface. Further, the "protective hieroglyphs" reference indicates that the implied author now believes in the magic that has been presented in the previous stories by Carter and Sadie. No doubt exists about the reality of this story now, and the implied author's final comments merely encourage reading to understand the state of the box he received, not to decide if the story is real as the previous Warnings do. For the implied author, the story is now real. Also unlike the first two books in the trilogy, *The Serpent's Shadow* does not end with an author's note. Instead, Sadie (who starts and ends the narrative in this novel) has the final comments. Following the story are two non-fiction sections, a Glossary of commands with accompanying hieroglyphs and Egyptian terms, and a list of Egyptian gods and goddesses mentioned in *The Serpent's Shadow*. The implied author has no need to write a note questioning the reality of events or promising publication of the next installment because the story is over, at least for now.[6] There is no question of the reality of the story now; for the implied author, the story is real.

Carter and Sadie's narratives, the main part of the trilogy, are presented much like the transcripts the Warning tells the reader they are. As with *Percy*

Jackson, there is a sense of urgency from the narrative in the first two novels in the trilogy. *The Red Pyramid* opens with Carter saying,

> We only have a few hours, so listen carefully.
> If you're hearing this story, you're already in danger. Sadie and I might be your only chance.
> Go to the school. Find the locker. I won't tell you which school or which locker, because if you're the right person, you'll find it. The combination is 12/32/33. By the time you finish listening, you'll know what those numbers mean. Just remember the story we're about to tell you isn't complete yet. How it ends will depend on you [1].

Like the opening of *The Lightning Thief*, *The Red Pyramid*'s narrative start focuses on a specific type of audience — descendants of pharaohs like Sadie and Carter, though that information isn't made clear until later in the story. The urgency of the narrative continues in other parts of the novel, as when Carter starts the second section of his narrative: "It's Carter again. Sorry. We had to turn off the tape for a while because we were being followed by — well, we'll get to that later" (49). Also like *The Lightning Thief*, the audience is being warned; however, rather than trying to drive away the audience like Percy does, Carter and Sadie are trying to recruit help for the upcoming battle between the forces favoring Ma'at, or order and harmony, and the forces of Chaos. Those who hear the recording and can find the locker are the primary target of the recording, though at the end of the story, Carter also indicates a wider audience: "We're going to send out this tape to a few carefully chosen people and see if it gets published. Sadie believes in fate. If the story falls into your hands, there's probably a reason..." (514). The author who writes the Warning and Author's Note is clearly *not* one of the people able to open the locker; if he were, he would presumably not have doubts about the truthfulness of the story. The address to the reader, to "you," by Carter also adds to the reality of the story because it makes the audience a part of the story.[7]

The Throne of Fire, the second book in *The Kane Chronicles*, opens with a similar urgency:

> Carter here.
> Look, we don't have much time for long introductions. I need to tell this story quickly, or we're all going to die.
> If you didn't listen to our first recording, well ... pleased to meet you: the Egyptian gods are running around loose in the modern world; a bunch of magicians from the House of Life is trying to stop them; everyone hates Sadie and me; and a big snake is about to swallow the sun and destroy the world.
> [Ow! What was that for?]
> Sadie just punched me. She says I'm going to scare you too much. I should back up, calm down, and start at the beginning.
> Fine. But personally, I think you *should* be scared [1, emphasis in original].

Carter's direct address to the readers serves both to engage them and to impress upon them the urgency of what he is saying. These stories are told for a specific purpose — to recruit help — and at the end of *The Throne of Fire*, Sadie, like Carter in *The Red Pyramid*, articulates that purpose. This time, the recording they're making is encouraged by Walt, one of the new recruits, who tells Sadie, "Tell people what happened.... Don't let ... the others spread lies about your family. I came to Brooklyn because I got your first message — the recording about the Red Pyramid.... You asked for help, and we answered. It's time to ask for help again" (443). Encouraged by Walt, Sadie and Carter make the second recording, concluding with

> We're sending out this tape to set the record straight....
> The point is, wherever you are, whatever type of magic you practice, we need your help. Unless we unite and learn the path of the gods quickly, we don't stand a chance.
> I hope Walt is right and you'll find me hard to ignore, because the clock is ticking. We'll keep a room ready for you at Brooklyn House [445–6].

The purpose behind Sadie and Carter's narrative is quite clear for both the reader that the implied author addresses and the listeners Sadie and Carter address.

The final novel in the trilogy opens with less urgency as the crisis is over once Carter and Sadie sit down to tell the story, though Sadie still manages to titillate the reader:

> Sadie Kane here.
> If you're listening to this, congratulations! You survived Doomsday.
> I'd like to apologize straightaway for any inconvenience the end of the world may have caused you. The earthquakes, rebellions, riots, tornadoes, floods, tsunamis, and of course the giant snake who swallowed the sun — I'm afraid most of that was our fault. Carter and I decided we should at least explain how it happened.
> This will probably be our last recording. By the time you've heard our story, the reason for that will be obvious [1].

Rather than focusing on recruiting new initiates (though they still welcome them), the focus of this story is on explaining the events surrounding Doomsday. Again, the direct address to the audience — "Congratulations! You survived Doomsday" — draws readers/listeners into the story, making them part of it and emphasizing the reality of events. There is no imminent danger to the Kanes as in the first two novels, but the opening still grabs the reader's attention. The end of the story contains similar references to the audience, including a reference to the implied author when Sadie says, "We'll put this tape in a secure box and send it along to the chap who's been transcribing our adventures" (401). She also encourages listeners to join them: "As for you lot out there, listening to our recording — we're never too busy for new initiates. If you have the blood of the pharaohs, what are you waiting for? Don't let your magic go to waste. Brooklyn House is open for business" (401). Though the adventures are over for the moment, magic and new initiates aren't disappearing.

Like *Percy Jackson & the Olympians*, *The Kane Chronicles* employ near-consonant self-narration, evident from information about how and when the stories are recorded. In *The Red Pyramid*, Carter tells the reader at the end of the novel, "Just when things were settling down to a nice safe routine, Sadie and I embarked on our new mission. Our destination was a school that Sadie had seen in a dream. I won't tell you which school, but Bast drove us a long way to get there. We recorded this tape along the way. Several times the forces of chaos tried to stop us..." (513). Once the narrators drop off the tape, the narrative shifts to the present tense and the sending out of the tape, an indication that the version sent to the author was at least slightly different since the version dropped off in the locker would not contain a past tense narrative of the delivery of the tapes. The true indication of consonance lies, like *Percy Jackson*, in reference to ages — Carter is fourteen, Sadie twelve at the time of the story and of the recording. A further indication comes in the second novel in the trilogy, which occurs within six months of the end of the first novel but which makes reference to the tapes of the first and the fact that those tapes have resulted in the arrival of new recruits. The recording of the second story occurs within days of the final battle of the story. The effect of this consonance is more important in *The Kane Chronicles* than in *Percy Jackson* because the story is being utilized as a recruitment tool in the first two novels and *must* occur in near-consonance for effective recruitment. The third novel is less clearly consonant since it is recorded following Doomsday and Carter and Sadie now have leisure time. The style, however, is still consistent with the first two novels, and the use of present tense in the final section of the last chapter indicates that the changes to Brooklyn House being described are current and ongoing, and not long after the main story ends.

Stylistically, like *Percy Jackson*, *The Kane Chronicles* appear very much like the transcriptions of oral recordings that they are supposed to be. In addition, Riordan attempts to present dialect difference between Sadie, who has been raised in England by her maternal grandparents and has a British accent, and Carter, who has been raised by his American father and speaks with an American accent. There are a few dialect issues with Sadie in terms of her vocabulary (her use of *disoriented* instead of *disorientated*, for example), and her dialect is fairly stereotypical, though most readers of the series will likely not notice the discrepancies. The references to recording and to listening are unambiguous indications of oral storytelling. However, the manner in which the stories are told also has an oral feel. There are frequent exchanges between Sadie and Carter, usually presented in brackets, as when Carter says, "[Ow! What was that for?]" at the start of *The Throne of Fire* (1) or early in *The Red Pyramid* when he says, "[Shut up, Sadie. Yes — I'm get-ting to that part]" (5) or toward the end of *The Serpent's Shadow* when Sadie says, "[Yes, I said that. Don't get a big head, brother dear. You're still a huge dork]" (350).[8] In addition, as in *Percy Jackson*, there are frequent tags that point toward their audience, including "I have to admit" ("I have to admit: it felt amazing" [*Red* 226]) and "I know" ("I know. It surprised me too" [*Red* 364]). There are also references to storytelling itself, particularly in *The Throne of Fire* and *The Serpent's Shadow*. Often references will focus on the difficulty of describing or explaining things, as when Carter in *The Red Pyramid* says,

> But the weirdest things were the *displays*.
> I don't know what else to call them [158–9, emphasis in original].

and when Sadie says in *The Throne of Fire*, "Should I describe Waterloo Station as it was before or after we destroyed it?" (119). The references to storytelling in *The Throne of Fire* and *The Serpent's Shadow* also reflect Carter and Sadie's separation at times during the story and their developing awareness of plotting. Early in the novel, Sadie travels to London to meet friends for her birthday, and her segment of the narrative ends with a cliffhanger — an inhuman voice welcoming her home. The next chapter begins with Carter saying,

> Thanks a lot, Sadie.
> Hand me the mic right when you get to a good part [68].

Then when Sadie gets the microphone back, she tells Carter,

> Well, you *talked* long enough, brother dear.
> As you've been babbling on, everyone's been imagining me frozen in the doorway of Gran and Gramps's flat, screaming, "AAHHHHH!" [99].

Similar exchanges between Sadie and Carter occur when they present the narratives of the times they are separated in *The Serpent's Shadow*. The narrators are aware of shaping the story they're telling much more so than in the first novel of the trilogy. This conscious manipulation of story is strongly metafictional, much more so than the *Percy Jackson* series, and continues blurring the line between fantasy and reality begun by the implied author. These aspects would seem to counter the author's emerging belief in the truth of the story because they are contrivances of fiction, not indicative of the rushed narrative this "transcription" purports to be. However, *The Throne of Fire*, unlike *The*

Red Pyramid, is narrated in Sadie's bedroom, at least initially, not in a car, and the narrative is not interrupted by the dangers described in the first recording, allowing for a more leisurely, if still urgent, recording. For *The Serpent's Shadow*, there is no urgency in the relaying of the story, allowing for even more reflection on storytelling itself. In addition, Carter and Sadie, having already narrated one story, will have gained more comfort and awareness of storytelling, which will allow greater self-consciousness in their story.

Both *Percy Jackson & the Olympians* and *The Kane Chronicles'* metafictional elements work to counter the fictional nature of the fantasy for the implied readers. The urgency of the narratives, the addresses to the audiences, the focus on stories either as artifacts to warn readers to "close this book" or as a recruiting tool make them feel more realistic. This effect is quite different from Nikolajeva's argument that small supernatural elements in metafictional texts help to "evoke the characters' (and the readers') doubts as to the credibility of the stories" (201). In Riordan's pure fantasy metafictional novels, the metafiction makes the fantasy less fantastic and more realistic.

By contrast with Riordan's two metafictional series, Dav Pilkey's *Captain Underpants* series presents a different type of metafiction, one that has nothing to do with making a story seem realistic but that is more focused on poking fun at society, including "obnoxious children's books" (*Nostril Nuggets* 160). Like *The Name of This Book Is Secret* and *The Kane Chronicles*, *Captain Underpants* contains an implied author, though his appearance in the series is more limited — his primary appearances come in the first chapter of each novel in the series, when he introduces main characters Harold and George. Each first chapter also ends with the refrain "But before I can tell you that story, I have to tell you *this* story." The implied author establishes his control of the story with that sentence, reminding the reader that he decides how the story will be told. As the series develops, he makes more frequent appearances: naming chapters to remind readers that the story is a construct (e.g. Chapter 31 in the eighth book, *Captain Underpants and the Preposterous Plight of the Purple Potty People*, "The Chapter Where Nothing Bad Happens") and reminding readers of elements mentioned previously in the book (e.g. in the fourth book, *Captain Underpants and the Perilous Plot of Professor Poopypants*, when the implied author says, "Remember that Poopypants guy I was telling you about in Chapter 2?" [49]).

Unlike the books discussed thus far, however, the *Captain Underpants* series also presents its main characters recognizing that they are part of the fiction created by the implied author, who, like the implied author of *The Name of This Book Is Secret*, presents Harold and George's story in third person. In part, Harold and George's awareness comes in their own writing. These characters are notorious for rearranging the words on signs — as when they change a flower shop sign in *The Adventures of Captain Underpants*, the first book of the series, from "Pick your own roses!" (1) to "Pick our noses!" (2) — and for the comic books that they create and distribute in their school. One such book is *The Adventures of Captain Underpants*, the entirety of which is presented as Chapter 3 of the first book in the series (which bears the same name), and it is their creation of Captain Underpants that drives the story, for their fictional creation comes to life when they hypnotize their principal Mr. Krupp into thinking he is Captain Underpants, and they are unable to reverse the hypnosis permanently. In fact, some elements of the comic books they write for each novel in the series come true in different ways.

Beyond the creation of comic books in the novels, which don't reveal their self-consciousness, Harold and George reveal their awareness that they are in a fictional story in two main ways. First, they, not the implied author, give instructions for the Flip-O-Rama sections of the novels. George indicates in their first introduction, "We proudly bring you the latest in cheesy animation technology" (80), showing that he is talking not to other characters in his story but to the implied reader of his story. Harold and George offer similar introductions to Flip-O-Rama in each of the subsequent books, and because the illustrations are by Pilkey, not Harold (whose style is depicted differently from Pilkey's), they are removed from their story to introduce part of that same story. They are clearly aware of their role as fictional characters.

The other way in which Harold and George show awareness of their story is at the beginning of each novel starting with *Captain Underpants and the Attack of the Talking Toilets*, the second novel in the series. As they do with Flip-O-Rama, Harold and George directly address the implied readers to present a comic book that they have written to summarize the events in the rest of the series. The second book starts with George saying, "Um ... hello. Before you read this book, there's some things you should know," and Harold warns readers, "Please don't let this comic fall into the wrong hands" (8). Not only are they aware of their place in the series, then, but they are also making sure readers know what has happened before they enter the implied author's narrative. As the series has progressed, more and more comments about the story, particularly toward the end of the novels, occurs. In *Attack of the Talking Toilets*, for example, George and Harold are trying to defeat the Talking Toilet 2000, and George declares, "We need to invent a character who can defeat a giant robot toilet" (106) — which has come into being as a result of Harold and George copying their comic book about a talking toilet on a classmate's science project that can convert pictures into real beings. George's declaration isn't metafictional, nor is Harold's suggestion —"How about a robot urinal?

... We can call it *The Urinator!*" (106) — but George's response shows his consciousness of his story: "No way! ... They'll never let us get away with that in a children's book. We're skating on *thin ice* as it is!" (106, emphasis in original). This comment addresses the issue of appropriate content for children's texts and seems to mock the lines that are drawn — talking toilets are acceptable but not urinals. The series, then, in its self-consciousness of standards in children's literature, parodies that same literature. It is, in fact, one of the most subversive series discussed in this book.

This parody becomes stronger further in the series when references to the story having a moral in *Captain Underpants and the Perilous Plot of Professor Poopypants*, the fourth book, occur. At the end of the novel, George and Harold discuss the resolution of the story:

"I learned that it's not nice to make fun of people," said George.
"Wow," said Harold. "I think this is the first time one of our stories ever had a *moral!*" [149, emphasis in original].

While this self-mocking could have been the end of the conversation, leaving the book with a positive message, George and Harold's next exchange:

"Probably the last time, too," said George.
"Let's hope so," said Harold [149].

continues to poke at the expectations of children's books by adults — compared to what children may actually want to see in their books. Even the implied author enters the moral discussion, commenting, "But George and Harold had forgotten all about the *other* moral they had learned along the way which was: 'Don't ever, ever, *EVER* hypnotize your principal'" (150). This moral exists only because of the grief that Principal Krupp/Captain Underpants causes George and Harold throughout the series and it is clearly tongue-in-cheek.

Captain Underpants and the Wrath of the Wicked Wedgie Woman, the fifth book in the series, continues with the mocking self-references. This time George and Harold are tussling with Wedgie Woman in their tree house and something spills in her hair, alarming George and Harold, who have the following conversation:

"This is the juice we got from that spaceship back in our third book!"
"You mean the one with the annoyingly long title?" asked George.
"Yeah!" said Harold. "This is the EXTRA-STRENGTH SUPER POWER JUICE! And a whole bunch of it got in her hair!"
"Don't worry," said George. "None of it got in her mouth. What's the worst that could happen? Her *hairstyle* would have superpowers?"
"Well," said Harold, "I guess you're right. That *is* pretty stupid ... even for one of *our* stories" [91, emphasis in original].

Here they mock their own story's plot, as well as foreshadow what happens to Wedgie Woman, whose hair does indeed gain superpowers. Similar references to specific passages in the books exist throughout the series.

In other places, they mock genre fiction, as when the boys are tied up and have an axe swinging toward them. Harold says,

> "Maybe the blade will fall and slice through the ropes and not harm us at all."
> "I doubt it," said George. "That kind of thing only happens in really lame adventure stories."
> Suddenly the blade fell and sliced through the ropes, not harming George or Harold at all. The two boys looked at each other and decided it was best not to comment on the situation [112–3].

The boys' dismissive comment about adventure stories comes true, self-consciously emphasizing that their adventure story is a parody of the genre. Similar comments about "obnoxious children's books" (*Nostril Nuggets* 160), "lame children's books" (*Robo-Boogers* 172), and "poorly written children's stories whose authors have clearly been running out of ideas" (*Preposterous Plight* 43) are made by other characters.

The effect of these self-mocking novels is to shine a light not just on the creation of text, though they certainly do "consciously discuss the art of writing and their own existence" (Nikolajeva 191), but to poke fun at the conventions they are part of. As Waugh indicates, the parodic structure acts as a frame-break and "the frame-break, while appearing to bridge the gap between fiction and reality, in fact lays it bare" (33). Unlike the *Percy Jackson & the Olympians* and *The Kane Chronicles* series, which do bridge the gap between fiction and reality, *Captain Underpants* makes no attempt to do so and actually emphasizes its fictional nature, much as *The Name of This Book Is Secret* does. The writer-character can thus do one of two things: emphasize the fictional nature of a novel — underscore its constructedness — or bridge the fantasy/reality split. The first person narratives of Rick Riordan, with their pseudo-oral style, encourage belief in the fantastic stories. The parodic third person narrative of *Captain Underpants* and the less parodic but heavily metafictional (and only slightly fantastic) nature of *The Name of This Book Is Secret*, on the other hand, emphasize the fictional nature of the stories much as Nikolajeva discusses. In Pilkey's case, the characters themselves recognize their place in a fictional story. More than any type of children's fantasy book discussed thus far, these series focus on action rather than books and reading, with the exception of the books being created by the characters.

5

Books and Storytelling in Film

Paralleling the three previous chapters, films and television programs aimed at children and young adult audiences, whether adapted or original, will use books in similar manners to their written counterparts. Some films and programs place great importance on books either as artifacts of power or, more often, as tools containing dangerous information. Other films and programs present books as interactive, with characters entering or departing fictional texts. Still other films and programs focus on characters as writers or storytellers. Like many children's fantasy books, films and television series will contain a message; however, given the wider target audience of films, the messages may be less overt than those in books. Family films, those rated G or PG, contain the strongest messages while films rated PG-13 or television series rated TV-14 have far more mature messages. As is the case with children's fantasy in which books are prominent, the books are not usually central to the message and the focus is on action rather than on reading.

Books as Artifacts

Like the books discussed in Chapter 2, many fantasy films for a child or young adult audience may include books as artifacts of power or resources containing dangerous information. Though many of these films have been adapted from children's or young adult novels, even the original films utilize books in a similar manner. *Ella Enchanted* is a feature film based on Gail Carson Levine's novel.[1] However, whereas the book Mandy gives Ella in the novel is used as a comfort and represents Ella's mother figures, the film version alters the book's purpose and origins. The film version of the book acts as a humor device. Much younger than her counterpart in the novel, Mandy (Minnie Driver), as a household fairy, cannot perform magic very well. As a result, she has turned her boyfriend Benny (Jimi Mistry) into a book during a haircut spell gone awry. Because Benny "knows everything," he acts as a near-encyclopedia for Ella (Anne Hathaway) on her travels. However, his power is limited to showing Ella what she asks through images rather than text, though when Ella initially flips through the pages, they are full of text. Ella must deduce from the images the location of Lucinda (Vivica A. Fox), the fairy who has cursed her with obedience. Though Benny as a character is humorous, his role as a book is purely informational, a marked contrast from the enchanted book in the novel, which offers Ella folktales to read and enjoy as well as information. The film as a whole downplays the seriousness of Ella's curse and many other situations to focus on the humor. As in the novel, Ella is smart and well-read, but those qualities are undermined, mostly notably in a debate she and Hattie (Lucy Punch), her new stepsister, have in a class at community college — as opposed to the boarding school of the novel, where no debating occurs. In this scene, though Ella is clearly the better informed and more articulate debater, Hattie defeats Ella by ordering her to "just admit you're stupid and don't know what you're talking about." Similarly, Ella's encounter with the ogres, in which she uses her linguistic skills to defeat them in the novel, is replaced by Prince Char (Hugh Dancy) rescuing her and the elf Slannen (Aidan McArdle). The only other books used in the film appear when Ella checks the Census records at the castle in an attempt to find Lucinda, but these books are merely informational. Unlike the novel, in which books are a comfort to Ella during times of loneliness and despair — enchanted or not — in the film they play a negligible role. Even the enchanted book, Benny, acts merely for humorous effect rather than anything else. Books' role, relatively small in the novel, has been diminished further in the film. Given the greater focus on humor in the film, it is no surprise that the message that Ella (and by extension children) must forge her own path and break the curse by herself is downplayed.

By contrast, *The Spiderwick Chronicles*, based on the series by Tony DiTerlizzi and Holly Black discussed in Chapter 2, maintains the dangerous nature of the focal book, *Arthur Spiderwick's Field Guide to the Fantastical World around You* (*Field Guide*). Though many details of the series are altered in this adaptation, from the role of the elves being removed to the greater prominence of Mulgarath, the danger the book poses does not change. The film opens with Arthur Spiderwick (David Strathairn) completing his *Field Guide*. The moment the book is complete, a supernatural ripple of sound echoes through his study and the wind howls outside the house, underscoring the dangers the book poses and making it seem as if the book itself is magical, though this does not prove to be the case. Then the scene shifts to eighty years after the completion of the book and the arrival of the twins Jared and

Simon Grace (Freddie Highmore), their sister Mallory (Sarah Bolger), and their mother, Helen (Mary-Louise Parker), at the Spiderwick house. Jared finds the *Field Guide* not long after their arrival and, ignoring the warning message against reading the book, opens it. The same sound that accompanied the completion of the book occurs as soon as he opens it, along with a visual of a magical ripple extending outside the house and into the woods surrounding it, scaring him into retreating to a trunk to read it, but not deterring his reading.

As he begins reading the book, a voiceover of Arthur addressing the reader comes to the film audience. He introduces the book and the fantastical creatures "hidden through mimicry and magic," and mentions how the book contains "tools and techniques" to find the creatures. Arthur also warns the reader about the ogre Mulgarath, saying, "I implore you, dear reader, to use this information wisely, for the ogre Mulgarath seeks this knowledge with relentless persistence." Mulgarath, then, is introduced earlier in the film than in the written series. As in the series, Jared is not much of a reader, and his sister Mallory mocks his reading of the *Field Guide*. Because Jared has caused trouble quite often in the past, his mother and siblings also believe that he is responsible for some of the destructive events that occur shortly after their arrival at the house. Simon and Mallory refuse to believe the information in the *Field Guide* until after Jared, using Arthur's Seeing Stone, shows them the creatures attacking them and the house. It is Thimbletack the brownie, who worked closely with Arthur, who gives them background information about the *Field Guide*, including the argument he and Arthur had on whether to destroy the book or protect it. Because the book has not been destroyed, Thimbletack tells Jared, it must be protected by being kept within the protective circles surrounding the house. The fear most creatures have is that if the book falls into the wrong hands, it will be used to destroy the creatures.

After Simon is injured by goblins who mistake him for Jared and kidnap him to get the *Field Guide*, the children try to destroy the book but discover that it has protective charms on it. The rest of the film revolves around the Grace children's attempts to protect the *Field Guide* from the ogre Mulgarath (Nick Nolte), and they discover firsthand how dangerous the book's information can be when Mulgarath gets several pages from it and learns how to break the protection circles around the house. In addition, Hogsqueal the Hobgoblin (Seth Rogen) tells how Mulgarath killed his family with the information he had gleaned from the single page he had previously acquired. The Grace children track down Arthur Spiderwick, who was kidnapped by sylphs angry at the creation of the book, and try to convince him to destroy the *Field Guide*, but he refuses, telling Jared, who has read the entire book, "You are the book now," emphasizing the internalization of knowledge from reading. The successful battle to protect the book at the end of the film leads to Thimbletack telling Lucy (Joan Plowright), Arthur's daughter, who has been in a mental asylum for years, that the book is safe again at the end of the film. Mulgarath, the primary threat to the book, has been killed, swallowed by Hogsqueal, allowing for a happy ending and no need to destroy the book — even if that were possible.

Like the written series, the film version of *The Spiderwick Chronicles* presents a book that, though it doesn't possess any magical properties itself, represents a danger to those referenced in its pages and those who possess the book. The knowledge contained in the *Field Guide* is dangerous, and Arthur Spiderwick is punished in the film for creating the book, though the creatures themselves gave him the knowledge to create the book. All of the events in the film, the dangers to the Grace children, are a direct result of the *Field Guide*. Despite its divergence from the DiTerlizzi and Black novels, the film's message about the *Field Guide* remains the same: it is a threat to all who possess it, whether they've read its contents or not. Reading, and the knowledge gained from reading, is dangerous.

Another adaptation of a written series containing focal books is the short-lived television series *The Secret Circle*, based on L.J. Smith's trilogy. Though the novels are for a young adult audience, the television series, like many with teenage main characters, targets both young adults and adults (though a fairly young demographic of adults). *The Secret Circle* aired on the CW network during the 2011–2012 season, a network known for targeting a youthful demographic. Even more than the previous two adaptations discussed, *The Secret Circle* diverges from the original texts on which it is based. It has a completely different setting — Chance Harbor, Washington as opposed to New Salem, Massachusetts — and a reduction of characters forming the circle — six instead of twelve. Particularly early in the twenty-two episodes, *The Secret Circle*, which follows the lives of six teenage witches, focuses in part on the young witches' desire to find the Book of Shadows for each family. These books contain the records of different spells and other information pertinent to performing magic, and in fact it was Diana's (Shelley Hennig) discovery of her late mother's Book of Shadows that revealed to her and the other four witches who grew up in Chance Harbor with her — Adam (Thomas Dekker), Nick (Louis Hunter), Melissa (Jessica Parker Kennedy), and Faye (Phoebe Tonkin) — that they are witches. Since the discovery of this Book of Shadows, the group has been practicing magic in secret, learning from the spells and other information contained in the book. The arrival of Cassie Blake (Britt Robertson) in Chance Harbor means the opportunity for the six witches to bind a circle that will give them more power collectively than they have individually. The side effect, however, is the loss of individual power for most of them, the initial exception being Cassie thanks to the dark magic she possesses from her father's side of the family. Later in the series, Diana will also gain individual power because she and Cassie share a birth father (Diana believes for most of the series that the man raising her is her birth father). At the conclusion of the pilot episode, Cassie discovers her mother's Book of Shadows along with a note from her mother in which she indicates her regret that Cassie has been drawn into the life of magic from which her mother tried to protect her.

Early in the series, the Books of Shadows play a fairly important role. They offer spells the teens can try and reveal information about those spells—their purpose and the dangers they may pose. However, the books can also be dangerous, as Cassie and Faye discover in the episode "Heather." The character Heather (Camille Sullivan) has been rendered catatonic by a spell Cassie's mother placed on her, and Cassie believes the spell was cast to cause harm and to keep Heather from revealing what happened in the boat fire that killed half of the circle members' parents. When Cassie finds the spell that rendered Heather catatonic in her mother's Book of Shadows, she wants to undo it, but Diana, the leader of the circle, refuses, arguing that they need more information about the spell before they remove it. Convinced she is right, Cassie enlists Faye, who is impulsive and self-serving, to help by promising to let her read Cassie's Book of Shadows since Faye has been unable to locate her family's. They perform the spell and Heather wakes, a violent, unstable woman possessed by a demon. Shortly after, Diana, in her own Book of Shadows, discovers that the sigil that kept Heather catatonic was a suppression spell to keep the demon in check. Cassie's instinct to help Heather has actually unleashed the demon, who, after Heather's death, passes into Melissa and then Nick, who in the next episode, "Slither," is killed so that the demon can be killed.[2] Cassie learns the hard way that the Book of Shadows is limited in its information and that it is important to do additional research on spells before trying them just because they're in the book. She learns the importance of critical reading. As with the *Field Guide* in *The Spiderwick Chronicles*, the Books of Shadows in *The Secret Circle* are themselves benign, but the information they contain may be used for good or evil.

Though Cassie learns her lesson well with Heather, the more impulsive Faye must experience the lesson again in the episode "Fire/Ice." Frustrated by her lack of individual power, Faye steals a page from Cassie's Book of Shadows that contains a spell to regain her powers by siphoning Cassie's dark magic. Cassie discovers the page is missing when she is searching for information about her father's medallion, which she found in the burnt-out ship where the parents died. Faye promises to return the page to Cassie at the Fire and Ice Dance at the school so that Cassie will be close enough for the spell to work. Faye completes the spell with the help of Lee (Grey Damon), a voodoo practitioner. However, as with the spell Cassie used to release Heather from her catatonia, Faye does not have enough information about the spell to understand its effects. When she gains independent power, she soon discovers that, though she was supposed to gain Cassie's dark magic, in fact she is gaining the power from the other members of the circle, not Cassie, and that she is harming them. She soon reverses the spell. Once again, the lack of full information about a spell leads to harm being done, and though it is not as damaging as Cassie's mistake, it sends a message about the importance of understanding a spell before performing it.[3] Certainly the circle does not again use the Books of Shadows without knowing as much about the spell as they can gather.

Instead, they start to turn their trust to the adults surrounding them, which poses its own problem. As discussed in earlier chapters, books can be seen as representative of adults and adult authority, and young characters often learn that the information contained in books is limited, forcing them to experience life beyond the books — beyond the protection and knowledge of adults — to get a better sense of the world. These same texts in which adult authority in the form of books is either rejected or supplemented with practical experiences often feature absent or uninvolved adults, a fact that allows for the young character to be self-sufficient. However, in *The Secret Circle* television series, there are numerous adult figures who remain involved in the action, and the focus gradually shifts from books as adult authority — and the knowledge that the information in books is limited — to actual adult authority and who can and cannot be trusted.[4] With the return of Cassie's father, John Blackwell (Joe Lando), who everyone thought was dead, the circle must negotiate the slippery world of adults, most of whom have been keeping secrets. The circle members do not know whom to trust, for these adults are all parents or grandparents, who, as such, are thought of as trustworthy, but who all have different agendas involving the circle. The final episode of the series, "Family," explores the role that family plays, as the circle members realize that John Blackwell — Cassie and Diana's biological father — has been manipulating them all along in an attempt to dissolve the circle and to destroy all witches who are not of his line. They also discover that Charles (Gale Harold), Diana's father, and Dawn (Natasha Henstridge), Faye's mother, both of whom have committed criminal acts in an attempt to regain the powers that were stripped from them following the boat fire, are in fact as caring parents willing to risk themselves to help their children. As they did with the Books of Shadows, representatives of past generations of family, the circle members negotiate the minefield of adults and learn how to read and understand them so that they may become self-sufficient.

Another television series featuring young adult characters, *Buffy the Vampire Slayer* presents book in a different manner.[5] From the first episode "Welcome to the Hellmouth," Buffy Summers (Sarah Michelle Gellar) is clearly an active character not interested in books or reading. She has relocated to Sunnydale, California, with her mother following her expulsion from her previous school in Los Angeles, and her first visit to the library to get books for her new classes leads to an encounter with Rupert Giles (Anthony Stewart Head), the school's new librarian and, she discovers a short time later, her Watcher. At this encounter, Giles tells Buffy that he knows what she is looking for before she can ask and places an enormous tome labeled *Vampyr* on the check-out counter. Though Buffy is reacting negatively to the title rather than the book, the fact that she flees from Giles and the knowledge he represents, however briefly, is characteristic of her attitude toward slaying: she does research only as needed and relies upon her physical skills and quick thinking more than research. While this trait may seem natural for someone whose job is to slay vampires and other creatures, in fact Buffy is not a traditional Slayer. During the episode "What's My Line" in the second season, a second Slayer, Kendra, appears in Sunnydale to help because her Watcher has told her "signs indicate that a very dark power's about to rise in Sunnydale."[6] Unlike Buffy, Kendra has known she was a potential Slayer all of her life and has been training both physically and in the history of Slayers, Watchers, and supernatural creatures. Kendra is a veritable encyclopedia of information pertinent to her role as Slayer. Though it is likely that Kendra is no more typical a Slayer than Buffy, she does demonstrate that Slayers are expected to do more than glean knowledge as needed during crises. Yet given Kendra's short-lived stint as a Slayer — she dies at the end of season two — it becomes clear that an overabundance of book learning, even supplemented with physical training, is ineffective.

Though Buffy does not enjoy the research aspect of being a Slayer, she appears positively bookish when Faith (Eliza Dushku), who becomes an active Slayer upon the death of Kendra, appears. Faith embodies the opposite traits of Kendra: she is an uninhibited, emotional Slayer reliant only on her physical skills to get through crises. This reliance fails her nearly as much as Kendra's reliance on book knowledge failed her, and Faith ends up susceptible to the Mayor's invitation to join his side after the Watcher's Council tried to take her in for killing a civilian by mistake. Buffy comes to represent a balance between Kendra and Faith: she favors action but knows the importance of research to help plan her battles. This knowledge comes the hard way in the first episode of season two, "When She Was Bad," when Buffy believes an initial translation of a spell to bring back the Master (Mark Metcalf), the villain of season one, means that she, as the "closest" person to the Master upon his death, "someone connected to the vampire," as Giles indicates, is part of the spell. As Buffy takes the bait, believing a message sent to her with Cordelia's bracelet attached will allow her to face the vampires, further research on the translation reveals that "closest" actually means "nearest physically," and Giles, Willow, Cordelia (Charisma Carpenter) and Jenny Calendar (Robia LaMorte), who were in the same room as the Master when he died, are kidnapped. Had Buffy waited for Giles to complete his research, she would have been there to help protect Giles and Willow, though not Jenny and Cordelia, who were kidnapped the previous day; instead, she is forced to rescue them all. The lesson she learns about the importance of thorough research is similar to the lessons Cassie and Faye learn in *The Secret Circle*, and Buffy generally balances research and action quite well after this incident, though she remains impatient with the research process. Times of heightened emotions also lead to a dismissal of research, as in the season three episodes "Bad Girls" and "Consequences" in which she goes out of control with Faith shortly following the Watcher's Council's eighteenth birthday test for her that stripped her temporarily of her powers and endangered her mother.

A second character in *Buffy the Vampire Slayer* who must learn to balance book learning and action is Willow Rosenberg (Alyson Hannigan). For the first couple of seasons of the series, Willow is the antithesis of Buffy: she is one of the smartest students at Sunnydale High School, introverted, shy, and eager to study, though she also longs for a social life, particularly a romantic one. It is Willow's computer skills in "Welcome to the Hellmouth" and "Harvest," the first two episodes, that give Buffy and Giles information about the town's electrical tunnel system as well as additional information about local events possibly related to the Master. Throughout the series, Willow's computer skills often offer supplemental help to Giles's books, though it can also lead to problems, most notably in the episode "I, Robot ... You, Jane" in which Willow, during a computer class project to digitize old library texts, scans in *The Book of Moloch*, a text that held the demon Moloch trapped in its pages. The scanning releases Moloch into the internet, and he uses his persuasive skills to establish a connection to two of the other students from the class so that they will help construct a body for him. Moloch also establishes a relationship with Willow through a chat room, and she is drawn to him, rejecting Buffy's concerns for her until Moloch reveals information about

Buffy that he shouldn't know. Knowing he has lost her trust, Moloch arranges for Willow to be kidnapped. At this point in the series, though Willow is smart, she is one of the frequent victims of the supernatural creatures and must be rescued, in this episode by Buffy and Xander (Nicholas Brendon) while Giles and Jenny Calendar perform the spell to remove Moloch from the internet. This removal does not, however, return him to his book; rather, it traps him in the robot body that was created for him. Willow, Buffy, and Xander must defeat this physical form, and though Willow is not the one to defeat him — that falls naturally to Buffy — she does take shots at him with a fire extinguisher, showing an early willingness to get involved physically despite her preference for the research side of the battle.

As the series progresses and Willow starts to explore witchcraft, she becomes more and more involved physically, often leaving the library to be in the field with Buffy, as when she performs a spell to help Buffy retrieve a box from the Mayor's office in the season three episode "Choices" and ends up imprisoned by the Mayor (Harry Groener). Though once again she is rescued by Buffy, this time in a trade for the box Buffy and Angel (David Boreanaz) have stolen from the Mayor, Willow is a much stronger character than in the first and second season, and holds her own. She kills a vampire guarding her and, trusting that Buffy will rescue her, remains in the Mayor's office to examine the Books of Ascension that contain the information about the Mayor's plans for graduation day rather than taking the chance to escape. This decision allows her to steal pages from the books that may help defeat the Mayor and to give them to Giles and new Watcher Wesley Wyndam-Pryce (Alexis Denisof). At this point in the series, Willow has a solid balance between books and action, much like Buffy, and this balance continues in season four when they enter college. Because of her academic interests and strengths, Willow excels more in college than Buffy, who has difficulty adapting to the new venue.

It is in season six that the balance starts to shift for Willow, who becomes addicted to witchcraft and starts to reject the mundane. In the first episode of the sixth season, "Bargaining," Willow, convinced that she must bring Buffy back from the hell to which her death has sent her, convinces Xander, Tara (Amber Benson), and Anya (Emma Caulfield) to help her perform a spell to return Buffy to life. Much like Cassie's misguided desire to help Heather in *The Secret Circle*, Willow has convinced herself that she is helping Buffy, though she lacks the information she needs to know for certain. In fact, as Buffy reveals first to Spike (James Marsters) in "After Life" and later to the rest of her friends in "Once More with Feeling," she was in heaven, not hell: she was "finished" and happy. This devastating news is compounded for Willow when Tara discovers in the same episode that Willow has used magic to alter her memory, to make her forget a fight, and confronts Willow. In a last-ditch effort to make everything better, in the episode "Tabula Rasa," Willow casts a spell to make Buffy and Tara forget and accidentally erases everyone in the group's memory, including her own. This spell is the final straw for Tara, who ends her relationship with Willow, and Willow becomes out of control with her magic until her actions nearly kill Dawn (Michelle Trachtenberg). Realizing that magic is her addiction, Willow struggles to gain control of herself and succeeds for a while. However, when Tara is killed shortly after they reconcile, Willow loses all control. While previously she used spell books to find specific spells to perform, in "Villains," she goes to the Magic Box, the shop that now houses all of the books they use for research, and, using magic to gather all the "black arts books," she places her hands in them and physically absorbs the books: the words crawl up her arms and torso and over her face and absorb into her, turning her hair as black as the ink from the now-blank books. Willow has become the magic, rejecting the patience associated with using books or technology for research, and uses her new knowledge to kill Warren (Adam Busch), who shot Tara, and to try to get Jonathan (Danny Strong) and Andrew (Tom Lenk), who were part of the trio making Buffy's life hell for most of the season. Only Xander in "Grave," the final episode of the season, can stop her from her path of destruction. The final season of *Buffy the Vampire Slayer* sees Willow regaining her balance slowly. She still performs magic, but she has control of herself and has returned to using magic only as a necessity rather than as a convenience. In addition, her computer and research skills become utilized again. Willow has learned though a more difficult path than Buffy the importance of a balanced life.

Books themselves in *Buffy the Vampire Slayer* play an interesting role. For the first three seasons of the series, the school library becomes a focal location for the characters. It is Giles's primary location, most research is completed there, and Buffy even trains physically in the library. Given the function of a library — a place for quiet, undisturbed study — it would seem logical to expect the library to be a haven for the characters. However, though Buffy, Willow, Xander, and Giles can often meet there in peace to complete the research they need to do, quite often this sanctuary is disturbed by the very creatures being studied. In "I, Robot ... You, Jane," as discussed above, the library is the site both of the release of Moloch and of the spell to contain him. In "Prophecy Girl," the final episode of the first season, the characters discover that the Hellmouth opens in the library, and the final battle of the season takes place in part in the library. In this same episode when Buffy overhears Giles telling Angel of the prophecy he has found in *The Codex* that she will die, she rejects her role as Slayer and Giles, telling him, "You're so useful sitting here with all your books!" Though her reaction is a natural offshoot of learning she is fated to die, the language she uses — railing against the information in the books Giles relies upon — is telling. Though the information Giles has is useful, sometimes it is overwhelming for her. Further, at the end of the episode, after the Hellmouth has been closed and the Master dies in the library, Giles himself briefly rejects the library, saying, "I don't like the library much anymore." Though all of the characters return frequently to, and rely upon, the library in later episodes, it is never quite the haven they feel it should be. The Hellmouth, which opens again in "The Zeppo" episode from season three, opening in the library could be read as a metaphor for the dangers of knowledge. While knowledge is the key to destroying the creatures who attack, it also endangers those who possess the knowledge, much as it does in *The Spiderwick Chronicles*, and, as will be discussed below, *The Vampire Diaries*.

In the second season opener, "When She Was Bad," Giles and Willow are taken from the library to be part of the sacrifice to bring the Master back. The final episode of season two, "Becoming," finds the other Slayer Kendra being killed in the library. The library is the place Oz (Seth Green) goes to lock himself each month when he becomes a werewolf. In the third season episode "Gingerbread," many of Giles' most useful books are confiscated by parents who have been brainwashed by the villain of the episode, a creature that poses as Hansel and Gretel type children, and used as the kindling for fires to burn Willow, Buffy and another witch. And in the final episode of the third season, "Graduation Day," the library is the place to which Buffy lures the transformed Mayor so that they can kill him with the massive amount of explosives with which they have replaced the books. Once again, if books — and the library as the house of books — represents adult authority, by destroying the library, the students are showing that they have moved beyond adult authority and graduated, as the episode title indicates, to being self-sufficient. They haven't rejected books — Giles and others have removed the most valuable and useful ones — but they play a different role following the destruction of the library.

The fourth season finds Buffy and the others at a loose end when it comes to research. Since Buffy has quit working with the Watcher's Council and Giles is no longer part of the Council, their resources become limited, and with the introduction of the Initiative, a secret government agency fighting creatures, a new kind of information comes to the fore: high-tech and government-funded. This information is incomplete, as Buffy discovers when Initiative member Riley Finn (Marc Blucas) does not what a Slayer is. In fact, the high-tech world of the Initiative is short-lived; books cannot be replaced, and in season five, a new venue for research is established when Giles purchases the Magic Box, a magical supplies store. The dangerous, sensitive, and otherwise valuable books are stored above the sales floor, and, as they did in the library, the characters frequently gather in the Magic Box to complete research. Also, like the library, this place of research comes under frequent attack, culminating in its destruction at Willow's hands at the end of season six. The seventh season moves the primary site of research to the Summers' house, but in this season the representatives of knowledge in the series' universe, the Watcher's Council, are destroyed in a bomb blast in "Never Leave Me" by the First Evil. Prior to the explosion, servants of the First Evil had been killing Watchers and potential Slayers across the globe as well as taking files and records belonging to the Council. The creatures attacking Buffy throughout the series know the importance of knowledge and, culminating with season seven, attempt to strip her of her resources. Though the creatures are never fully successful, their attacks underscore the danger of knowledge and the books that house the knowledge in the series.

Many of the films and television series that contain books as focal objects, like the written series, show the potential dangers of the books and of the need for young characters to establish a balance between knowledge and action. The didacticism of the films and series, when focused on knowledge, emphasizes the importance of looking critically at authority, whether textual or actual adult authority figures.

Interactive Stories

Like films and television programs containing books as artifacts of power, films with interaction between main characters in books — similar to books discussed in Chapter 3 — can be both adaptations and original, or a combination. *The Pagemaster* bears a close resemblance to its written counterpart, likely because the original authors of the book, David Kirschner and Ernie Contreras, were also two of the screen writers, along with David Casci.[7] As with the written version, main character Richard (Macaulay Culkin) fears almost everything, and the focus of the film concerns Richard's overcoming his fears with the help of imaginative fiction. A smart boy, Richard focuses his reading initially on non-fiction, which feeds his fears; he has even brought a medical journal to his baseball team's practice to show the correlation between shin splints and blood clots. The main action of the film revolves around Richard's adventures at the library at which he seeks shelter from a wicked storm. While searching out the phone to call his parents, Richard falls

5. Books and Storytelling in Film 93

in the rotunda of the library and hits his head. When he wakes, the mural of scenes from different books that is on the rotunda begins to drip all over the library, including onto Richard, turning him from a live-action character to an animated one. Upon noticing the transformation, Richard exclaims, "I'm a cartoon!" only to be corrected by the Pagemaster (Christopher Lloyd), who tells him, "You're an illustration." That Richard associated himself with the television medium of a cartoon rather than the textual medium of an illustration demonstrates that film has had a greater influence on him than books, a common trait in the contemporary world, and something depicted commonly in books and especially film, where characters turn toward and reference visual technology more than written resources. This is especially true of film in which it is easy to see the modern world — video screens, internet sites, text messages. Though *The Pagemaster* was released in 1994, before the proliferation of cell phones and computers, visual media still heavily influence Richard's life.

The Pagemaster sends Richard through the fiction section of the library on his way to the phone and exit, telling Richard that he will "face three tests: horror, adventure, and fantasy," and reminding him to turn to the books when in doubt. As Richard sets off, the books begin whispering to him passages from their pages. Much of this film parallels the written version; however, there are a couple of notable alterations. The three books representing Adventure (Patrick Stewart), Fantasy (Whoopi Goldberg), and Horror (Frank Welker) are all quite conscious of their role as books and make frequent references to books and storytelling. For example, after Richard, having been offered help by Fantasy to get home, asks, "Do I have to click my heels or something?" Fantasy says, "Honey, you in the wrong story." In addition, when Horror and Fantasy discuss their story types, Horror declares, "Horror always has sad endings," while Fantasy declares her home the "land of happy endings." And Adventure grumbles as he is saving Horror from Liliputians, "You're lucky I was published with a thick hide." Further, though the Pagemaster's role is minimal in both the books and film, he intrudes more in the film than in the book, telling Richard at several junctures to "seize the courage," thus underscoring the nature of Richard's adventure through the library — to overcome his fears. As with the book version of *The Pagemaster*, the true test of Richard's developing courage comes at the end when he has a chance to escape without Adventure, Horror and Fantasy and chooses to try rescuing them, succeeding only when, having been swallowed by the dragon, he turns to the books. Upon finding "Jack and the Beanstalk" in the dragon's stomach, he opens the book and releases the beanstalk, riding it out of the dragon. The courage Richard shows in what turns out to be a dream he has while unconscious extends into his real life. When he wakes — and the film returns to live action — Richard checks out the books and races home on his bike, then climbs into the previously-unwanted tree house, where he falls asleep with his arms on the books. As with the written version, the film version of *The Pagemaster* is strongly didactic, emphasizing the importance of reading fiction to help cope with and overcome fears even though reading itself has had nothing to do with Richard's change of attitude since he is never shown reading any books. Richard's entry into the world of books, even if only in a dream, has transformed him.

By contrast with *The Pagemaster*, which differs little from its original form, the adaptations of Michael's Ende's *The Neverending Story* bear little resemblance to the novel. According to Dieter Petzold in "A Neverending Success Story? Michael Ende's Return Trip to Fantastica," "The final version of the script exasperated Ende so much that he tried (in vain) to take legal action against it" (230). The first adaptation, released in 1984, a film that "popularized *The Neverending Story* on the international stage" (229) in fact adapts only the first half of the novel — from Bastian's theft of *The Neverending Story* to his naming of the Childlike Empress and rebuilding of Fantasia[8] from the single grain of sand that remains of the land. The second film, *The Neverending Story II: The Next Chapter* (1990), contains some of the elements of the second half of the novel, notably Xayide's manipulation of Bastian and his loss of memory. The third film, *The Neverending Story III: Escape from Fantasia* (1994), is an original film that utilizes many of the popular characters from previous films — the Rock Biters, Falkor the Luckdragon, the Childlike Empress — and introduces the Old Man of the Wandering Mountain, the keeper of *The Neverending Story*, though the part he plays in both the novel and the film is quite small. In each film, Bastian is the focal character, the only one who can save Fantasia, and like Richard in *The Pagemaster*, Bastian must overcome his fears to succeed.

In the first film, much like the original novel, Bastian (Barret Oliver) discovers *The Neverending Story* in a book shop where he seeks shelter from bullies. In his discussion with Mr. Koreander (Thomas Hill), Bastian reveals himself a reader with "186 books at home," many classics of literature (*Treasure Island, The Last of the Mohicans, Lord of the Rings*, etc.), and explains that he likes to pretend to be Tarzan or Nemo or other characters. Mr. Koreander dismisses Bastian's enjoyment of "safe" books and, at Bastian's curiosity about the book Mr. Koreander is currently reading, tells Bastian, "This book is not for you," a comment that works to get Bastian to steal the book when Mr. Koreander turns to answer the phone. This theft appears to have been manufactured by Mr. Koreander given the shot of him smiling and nodding as

Bastian runs away with the book. The reverse psychology — the prohibition of reading the book — makes Bastian want to read it, much as prohibitions have worked in previous children's texts discussed. Because the majority of the film from this juncture focuses on Bastian reading *The Neverending Story*, the film employs frequent voiceovers of Bastian reading the book while the action — primarily Atreyu's quest to find the savior of Fantasia — happens. The film cuts between Atreyu (Noah Hathaway) and Bastian's reactions to events affecting Atreyu, but the characters remain separate for much of the film. The first time Bastian interacts with the story comes when, reading that the "mountain" Atreyu is climbing is actually Morla the Northern Oracle, he yells out and is heard in Fantasia, though even as he realizes the characters have heard him, he says aloud to himself, "But that's impossible. They couldn't have heard me." Only when Atreyu has reached the second gate in his search for the Southern Oracle and, looking in the magic mirror, sees Bastian reflected back at him does Bastian articulate what is happening, though still with disbelief: "What if they really do know about me?"

As in the novel, where Bastian slowly comes to see himself in *The Neverending Story*, in the film, he also begins to recognize himself. However, he has little self-confidence and thus resists his instincts to offer help by giving the Childlike Empress (Tami Stronach) a new name.[9] Atreyu's despair over Bastian's lack of help leads to the Childlike Empress indicating that the savior is "listening to every word we say," but Bastian continues to resist helping, saying, "It's only a story. It's not real!" Only the Childlike Empress directly addressing him and demanding, "Call my name!" gets Bastian to give her the name Moon Child, his late mother's name. Once he does name her, Fantasia and the real world connect, allowing Bastian and the Childlike Empress to interact physically. Taking the single grain of sand that remains of Fantasia, Bastian recreates the land, bringing back many of the characters who had been lost to the Nothingness. The worlds cross again when Bastian is shown riding the Luckdragon Falkor through the streets of his town, chasing the bullies who had chased him at the start of the film. The film ends with a narrator indicating, "Bastian made many other wishes and had many other amazing adventures before he finally returned to the ordinary world. But that is another story." This final line parallels part of the refrain common in Ende's novel, though it is only used in this place in the film version. For Bastian, this adventure is about gaining self-confidence, being able to see himself as worthwhile and facing the bullies who have tormented him. It is also a resolution to his father's comment at the start of the film that Bastian needs to "stop daydreaming. Start facing problems." Daydreaming, in the form of being wrapped up in a book, is not Bastian's problem; in fact, his day spent reading *The Neverending Story* has led to a transformation: he becomes able to face down the bullies, albeit on Falkor's back.

Bastian's confidence does not last, however, and in *The Neverending Story II: The Next Chapter*, he faces a new fear: diving off the high platform at school when he is trying out for the school's swim team. The film opens with Bastian (Jonathan Brandis) reading aloud in the kitchen and playacting some of the adventures of the book, only to create a steadily worsening mess. Bastian has remained an active, imaginative reader, though it still causes him some problems. Not long after his failure to dive from the platform, Bastian returns to Mr. Koreander's book shop to look for self-help books about courage. There he hears *The Neverending Story* calling to him, "Help us," and "Please come back, Bastian." Mr. Koreander (Thomas Hill) tells Bastian that "books change each time you read them" but denies Bastian's request for *The Neverending Story*, so Bastian steals it once again — and again Mr. Koreander seems to expect the theft based on his knowing smile when Bastian leaves.[10] As Bastian examines the book back in his room at home, the ouroboros on the cover comes alive, hissing before becoming dormant again, and Bastian removes it — it is the medallion the Auryn — and opens the book, only to discover the words on the pages are fading. Bastian enters Fantasia through the picture of the Childlike Empress (Alexandra Johnes) along with the viewing audience. The actual means of transportation into Fantasia is not clearly shown. Bastian looks at the picture of the Childlike Empress and the shot moves into the picture and then fades to a different part of Fantasia. Presumably, Bastian's claiming of the Auryn allows him to enter Fantasia. Then the character Xayide (Clarissa Burt) is introduced. Like her counterpart in the novel, Xayide desires to take over Fantasia, but her power is greater in the film than in the novel, for she has a machine that removes Bastian's memories one by one with the wishes he makes using the Auryn. This element of the film contrasts with the novel, in which it is the Auryn itself that causes memory loss in humans using it to wish. In the novel, Bastian's ego also initially spurs on the wishing. In other words, Bastian is his own worst enemy in the novel, where in the film Xayide is the antagonist who is responsible both for feeding Bastian's insecurities — something she also does in the novel — and for robbing him of his memory.

While Bastian is trying to help Fantasia through its current problem with the Emptiness encroaching, the result of humans' lack of interest in stories, his father Barney (John Wesley Shipp) discovers him missing and, finding *The Neverending Story* in Bastian's room with information about Mr. Koreander's bookstore in it, approaches Mr. Koreander about Bastian. Mr. Koreander suggests that Bastian's father read the book for an explanation of

Bastian's absence, and when he glances through the book, he sees references to Bastian and goes to the police thinking that Mr. Koreander is involved in Bastian's disappearance. However, the store is empty when they return to it, and the police officer will not believe him. Incensed, Barney tells them, "I'm not the type of person to make things up. Look, I'm an engineer, all right? What I see is what I see." As in the first film, Bastian's father is facts-oriented, uninterested in anything imaginative, and this trait makes it hard for him to relate to his son who, influenced by his mother, enjoys reading and making up stories. In fact one of the memories he loses early in the film shows him and his mother talking about *The Neverending Story* shortly before her death. With no help from the police, Bastian's father returns home and to the book and, as Bastian did in the first film, becomes more and more involved with events. Also like Bastian in the first film, a voiceover of Barney occurs as he reads *The Neverending Story*. By the end of the film, Barney is voicing his encouragement to Bastian aloud. Also similar to the first film is the thinning of the separation between Fantasia and the real world. At the end of the film, having used his last wish and memory to give Xayide a heart, thus saving Fantasia by replacing the Emptiness with Love, Bastian must jump from a waterfall to demonstrate his courage and, as the Childlike Empress says, "heal both of our worlds." His father shouts his encouragement of Bastian at this point, and Bastian can hear him, much as Atreyu could hear Bastian despite their physical separation in the first film. With his father's voice in his ears, Bastian is able to make the jump and return home to "tell my dad I love him." As with the first film, *The Neverending Story II* emphasizes the importance of the imagination and, to a lesser extent, reading. However, only one book, *The Neverending Story*, offers true danger and a means of gaining self-confidence (in the first film) or courage (in the second film). All other books pale in comparison to *The Neverending Story*, a fact articulated by Mr. Koreander in the first film when he calls other books "safe." The relationship between *The Neverending Story* and Bastian is reciprocal as well: his involvement with the story helps him, but he also saves the story, first by defeating the Nothingness and then the Emptiness.

    The third film, *The Neverending Story III: Escape from Fantasia*, introduces a new threat both to Bastian (Jason James Richter) and to Fantasia: the Nasties, "an evil force that first takes hold in young humans when they turn away from books and reading." The only one who can save Fantasia is "a voracious reader of great imagination and extraordinary courage"—Bastian. Though the plot of this film does not spring from the novel, the way story is presented relates to the novel's explanation of story. *The Neverending Story III* opens with the Old Man of the Wandering Mountain (Freddie Jones), the character who records *The Neverending Story*, and the film shows the book being written as events happen. Similarly, when Bastian receives *The Neverending Story* after the Nasties are introduced, this time in his new school's library where Mr. Koreander (Freddie Jones) is librarian,[11] he reads the events that have led him to the book and to his present situation, looping the chase scene visually to show the connection between the book and Bastian's life. At his new school, the Nasties are a gang of unpleasant seniors who have repeated their final year of school several times. In an attempt to escape the Nasties, Bastian demands to be transported back to Fantasia and gets his wish; however, the Nasties discover the book and Bastian's place in it and decide to make Bastian's life miserable while he's in Fantasia, which negatively affects Fantasia itself. To save Fantasia, Bastian must return to his world and face the Nasties to recover *The Neverending Story*. The Childlike Empress (Julie Cox) gives him the Auryn so he can wish his way home and then wish *The Neverending Story* to its keeper. However, the wish to return goes awry and several Fantasia characters also transport to the real world, forcing Bastian to rework his plans. For the characters to return home, Bastian must gather them all and wish them back to Fantasia before he can wish the book back to its keeper.

But because the Nasties can read Bastian's actions and plans, they make their own plans to steal the Auryn and thus retain control of *The Neverending Story* (and get whatever they wish) forever. The successful resolution of the story comes after the Nasties wreak havoc in both Fantasia and the real world, but eventually Bastian, with the help of his new step-sister Nicole (Melody Kay), returns the book to Mr. Koreander, who tells him, "The story's not over yet." With this film, *The Neverending Story* has become Bastian's story as much as the story of Fantasia and of fantasy. Bastian in fact owns the story late in the film, declaring, "This is my story, and I'm not gonna let it [the destruction of Fantasia] happen." Once again it is Bastian's imagination that plays a role in the film, at least on the surface. Certainly his belief in and experience with Fantasia make the events possible, yet it is also his use of the book to escape from the Nasties that causes the problems: they would not have discovered *The Neverending Story* had Bastian not escaped into the book and left it open for them to find. This last film demonstrates the importance of facing problems rather than running from them, and the book is a tool to force that lesson.

Like *The Neverending Story* and *The Pagemaster*, the original Disney film *Enchanted* shows the power and importance of imagination, but it also reveals the importance of a balance between imagination and reality. Unlike both *The Pagemaster* and *The Neverending Story*, however, *Enchanted* moves from the fictional, a book, to the real world. An intertextual mix of different Disney fairy tales, the film commences with a pop-up book of *Enchanted* opening and a narrator (Julie Andrews) beginning the story, quite common in many fairy tale oriented films.[12] This animated fairy tale, the story of Giselle (Amy Adams) and Edward (James Marsden), seems to be heading toward a typical fairy tale ending: love at first sight leads to a marriage the next day. Instead, Edward's stepmother, the Evil Queen Narcissa (Susan Sarandon), steps in before the happy ending and, in the guise of an old woman much like Snow White's evil stepmother, convinces Giselle to make a wish at a well. When Giselle leans over the well, she is pushed into it and falls a great distance to the world outside the book, in this case contemporary New York City. At this point in the film, the majority of it is presented in live action, and the absurdity of fairy tale expectations becomes clear, for Giselle and later Nathaniel (Timothy Spall), Edward, the chipmunk Pip, and the queen all have difficulty adjusting not just to the modern world, but also to the more cynical nature of modern society. Giselle in particular is perennially optimistic and cheerful, never doubting that Prince Edward will come for her or that they have found true love.

By contrast with Giselle is Robert (Patrick Dempsey), a divorce attorney and single father to young Morgan (Rachel Covey), who loves fairy tales and fairy tale princesses. Robert plans to remarry for rational reasons and to soften Morgan up for the news, he presents her with a gift, the book *Important Women of Our Time*. He tells her he knows it is "not that fairy tale book you wanted, but this is better" because the women are all great role models for her. Immediately Robert is set up as the rational, cynical character who rejects fairy tales and the idea of true love while Giselle is his polar opposite. Their paths meet when he and Morgan, returning home, see her calling for help on a billboard for the Palace Casino. He catches her when she falls from the billboard—her enormous hoop-skirted wedding dress making mobility difficult in the real world where it did not affect her in animation. As Giselle explains her problems, Robert becomes convinced that she is mentally unstable, but he ends up helping her, giving her a place to spend the night. The next morning, after Giselle has cleaned up the apartment with the help of New York City's version of animal helpers—pigeons, rats, and cockroaches—and has used Robert's curtains to fashion a new dress, he tells her, "It's like you escaped from a Hallmark card or something." He is unable—and initially unwilling—to fathom her innate optimism and cheerfulness, just as she has difficulty with his cynicism.

However, as they spend time together and discuss their different views, they start to understand each other and both begin to bend—Robert becoming more romantic with his fiancée Nancy (Idina Menzel) and Giselle demanding that she and Edward go on a date to become better acquainted before they marry. Not surprisingly, Giselle and Robert fall in love, though both feel committed to their fiancés and don't wish to hurt them. It is at the ball that matters come to a head. After Giselle bites the poisoned apple, Edward is unable to wake her with "true love's kiss," and both Edward and Nancy, who have observed Giselle and Robert's interactions, encourage Robert to kiss her, which naturally works. Others at the ball witnessing these events think they are a performance and one comments that it is "much better than last year's show," emphasizing the contemporary view that fairy tales and magic are impossible. In response, Queen Narcissa, intent on winning, declares, "If I'm going to remain queen, I'm going to need some kind of story when I go back [to Andalasia]." At this point in the film, the metafictional element becomes quite heavy, as the queen creates her story, though traditional fairy tale roles become subverted, particularly when the queen, after transforming into a dragon, takes Robert. She taunts Giselle, saying, "Come along, Giselle. I wouldn't want you to miss this ending." Sword in hand and having removed her impractical shoes, Giselle chases the queen, who observes, "This is a twist on our story. It's the brave little princess coming to the rescue. I guess that makes you the damsel in distress, huh, handsome?" With the queen's defeat and return to the book from which she has come, Giselle and Robert help each other from falling to their deaths from the building roof on which they are perched. The end of the film comprises several epilogue scenes presented as pages in the book opened at the start of the film, starting with Nancy finding Giselle's shoe and Edward putting it on her foot, much like Cinderella. They run away together, Edward taking her to Andalasia, the land of the book, and, now animated, they marry. Another page shows Giselle with a new business — clothing designer for Andalasia Fashions, which makes dresses for little girls. The narrator returns, declaring, "And so they all lived happily ever after" as the book closes.

While *Enchanted* does show some of the absurdity of fairy tales and self-consciously discusses the creation of story, ultimately it returns to the idea that a fairy tale ending is possible for everyone. Though Giselle has learned the importance of getting to know whom she is marrying and of fighting for her love, she has changed little at the end of the film, for her dress factory is staffed in part by the creatures that helped her earlier and she has gotten her happily ever after. It is the cynical Robert who has undergone the greatest change in the film, becoming someone who believes in true love, magic, and happily ever after. It is imagination that wins, just as in *The Pagemaster* and *The Neverending Story*, and it happens through action, not through reading.

Writing and Storytelling in Film

Like films with books as artifacts of power or interactive books, which often stress some kind of balance in life— between study and play or between imagination and reality—films and television programs that feature writing or storytelling also often stress finding a balance in life (or trying to do so). In these films and television series, which are intrusion fantasies, the characters struggle to cope with what they know is real amid the fantastic events happening around them. Unlike their written counterparts discussed in Chapter 4, these films and television series do not attempt to bridge the gap between the real and the fantastic (or vice versa).

The CW's television series *The Vampire Diaries*, based loosely on L. J. Smith's young adult series of novels,[13] features two primary journal[14] writers among the main character: Elena Gilbert (Nina Dobrev) and Stefan Salvatore (Paul Wesley). The pilot episode opens with Stefan saying, "For over a century I have lived in secret, hiding in the shadows, alone in the world until now. I am a vampire and this is my story." It is interesting that this series, which is more about Elena than Stefan, opens with him claiming the story being told. His narrative voiceover continues, though he is not shown writing yet, before the scene shifts to Elena, whose voiceover occurs as she writes in her own journal about seeing the day, the first day of her junior year of high school, as a fresh start. The first half of the first season of *The Vampire Diaries* features Elena and Stefan as writers quite frequently. In fact, the end of the pilot episode and the beginning of the second episode, "The Night of the Comet," has Elena and Stefan writing in journals while their narratives intertwine. Much of their writing focuses on the changes going on in their lives. For Elena, it is adjusting to life after her parents' death four months prior to the start of the new school year. For Stefan, who has been a vampire for 145 years, the adjustment is to returning to Mystic Falls, Virginia, and coming to terms with his interest in Elena, who makes him feel alive again after years of just getting by. Journals for both Stefan and Elena are places to express their feelings of difference, of isolation, of loneliness, and of confusion. When Elena suspects that Stefan is a vampire at the end of the episode "You're Undead to Me" and again at the beginning of the following episode, "Lost Girls,"[15] she pours her confusion out in her journal:

> Dear Diary, I'm not a believer. People are born, they grow old, and then they die. That's the world we live in. There's no magic, no mysticism, no immortality. There is nothing that defies rational thought.... People are supposed to be who they say they are and not lie or hide their true selves. It's not possible. I'm not a believer. I can't be. But how can I deny what's right in front of me? Some-

one who never grows old. Never gets hurt. Someone who changes in ways that can't be explained. Girls bitten. Bodies drain of blood.

Then, setting her journal aside, she goes to confront Stefan. After this point in the series, the act of writing in journals becomes infrequent for both Stefan and Elena; instead, the drama of living in Mystic Falls, Virginia, a hot spot for vampires, witches, and, after the first season, werewolves, overshadows the writing.[16] While both Elena and Stefan remain journal writers, most of the shots of them with their journals following this turning point show them unable to write in their journal, as in "Lost Girls" when Elena is staring at a blank page in her journal, or in "History Repeating" when Stefan is doing the same.

However, journals remain an important part of the series. Elena's ancestor Jonathan Gilbert, a contemporary of Stefan and his bother Damon (Ian Somerhalder) when they were human in the 1860s, kept a detailed journal with illustrations that becomes critical for gathering research about both vampires and the town's Founders' Council and its plans to destroy the vampire population. Jonathan Gilbert's journal is first referenced in the episode "History Repeating," in which Elena's brother Jeremy (Steven R. McQueen) discovers one journal in a box of his father's materials as he tries to find resources to help him with an extra credit history paper for the new history teacher Alaric Saltzman (Matt Davis).[17] In the next episode, "The Turning Point," a voiceover accompanies Jeremy's initial reading of the journal: "I live in fear. It consumes me. In the early evening, when I see the sun begin to fade, the fear comes. Because I know that the night brings death." Later he learns from Aunt Jenna (Sara Canning) that Jonathan Gilbert was known for his fictional works. She and Jeremy initially attribute the journals as part of his fiction.[18] Jonathan Gilbert's journal becomes a point of contention in the first season when vampires hoping to open a tomb that sealed twenty-seven vampires under Fell's Church believe the journal contains the location of the witch Emily Bennett's grimoire. This grimoire is thought to contain the spell that will unseal the tomb. Unlike Stefan and Elena's earlier journal writing, used to introduce their characters, establish their personalities, and explore their angst about each other, Jonathan Gilbert's journal is a dangerous resource in the first season as it contains information about vampires, spells, and other things that the average person would find unbelievable but that, in the wrong hands, endangers those possessing the journal or its information. In this sense, Jonathan Gilbert's journal resembles *The Field Guide* in *The Spiderwick Chronicles* (or many of the books discussed in Chapter 2). Once the vampires locate the grimoire—with the help of the journal—the journal becomes less important. However, Elena's journal returns to prominence again when Jeremy, knowing that Elena is hiding something about the death of his girlfriend Vicki (Kayla Ewell), steals it from her room and reads it in the episode "Under Control." Because at this point he already believes in vampires thanks to a budding relationship with the vampire Anna (Malese Jow) and his readings of Jonathan Gilbert's journals, Jeremy knows that Elena's writing is truthful when he reads that Vicki, a new vampire, attacked Elena and was staked by Stefan. He also learns that Elena asked Damon to remove Jeremy's memory of the events using vampire compulsion. As with the information in Jonathan Gilbert's journal, the information in Elena's journal is a danger in the wrong hands — though to a lesser degree with Jeremy, whose anger makes him lash out against Elena without revealing his new knowledge to others.

The second season of *The Vampire Diaries* focuses even less on journals and shifts instead, especially early in the season, to academic resources Elena's birth mother Isobel (Mia Kirschner) collected before becoming a vampire herself.[19] This anthropological research includes information about Katherine, the vampire who turned Damon and Stefan and of whom Elena is a doppelganger. There is also information about vampires in general and, more important in this season, on werewolves. In particular, the resources contain a legend about an Aztec "curse of the sun and the moon" that explains the origins of vampires being limited to darkness and to werewolves shifting on the full moon. They also learn that vampires were the prey of choice of werewolves, and that, according to legend, a werewolf bite is fatal to a vampire, though they are not sure how much of the folklore to believe. This curse — and various factions' desire to break the curse — drives much of the second season, though Elijah (Daniel Gillies), one of the Original vampires, eventually reveals in the episode "Klaus," that the legend — and indeed many other legends across different cultures — is a hoax perpetrated by his brother Klaus (Joseph Morgan) to keep both vampires and werewolves searching for the ingredients Klaus needs to break the real curse. The real curse was placed on Klaus alone to stop him from being a hybrid vampire and werewolf.[20]

The other textual focus of season two is on grimoires, defined in the series as a "witch's cookbook." Bonnie Bennett (Kat Graham), a descendent of Emily Bennett, whose grimoire is so critical in season one, retains that grimoire and has become more adept at magic by studying the grimoire. When new witches come to town, Bonnie discovers in "By the Light of the Moon" that Dr. Jonas Martin (Randy J. Goodwin) collects grimoires, because, so his son Luka (Bryton James) tells her, "my dad is obsessed with finding them and making sure that our family heritage stays intact.... The way he sees it, all witches are family. We're all bonded together by a code of loyalty to help each other." These grimoires contain powerful spells of all types, and Bonnie consults them frequently in her various attempts to help Elena. Just like any text, however, the grimoires can be used to mislead people: in the first season, Bonnie pretends to deactivate a device to harm vampires, and in the second season, Luka chooses a spell to do with Bonnie that will not work to destroy the moonstone, a key ingredient in the curse-breaking spell. What is most interesting about the grimoires in the series, however, is that, though characters are often shown looking through the grimoires for specific spells, when it comes time to cast the spell, the grimoire, while it will be in the shot, is not read — and is in fact rarely held by the witch. Presumably the witch must memorize the spell before he[21] or she casts it; however, this aspect of witchcraft is never discussed. Books are predominately a resource in the second season of *The Vampire Diaries*, often a misleading one, as in the case of the curse of the sun and the moon and later with the spell Bonnie and Luka perform. The season seems to be about questioning sources, trying to find out what is truth.

Season three shows a further diminished role of books, though Stefan's journals become a reference at times for Elena and Damon as they try to locate Stefan after he leaves Mystic Falls with Klaus after making a deal with the now-hybrid to save Damon from a werewolf bite, which indeed proves to be fatal to a vampire. Having located Stefan in Chicago, Damon, in the episode "The End of the Affair," gives Elena Stefan's journal from the previous time he was in Chicago — the 1920s — telling her, "Read this. Paints a pretty little picture of Stefan's first experience in Chicago," and, after her initial refusal to read Stefan's private thoughts, adding, "You need to be prepared for what you're about to see." At this point in the series, Stefan has reverted to being a "Ripper," almost out of control, and when Elena still refuses to read it, Damon begins reading it aloud to her. The journal is informational as it was at the start of the series, though now it serves as information for Elena as well as the viewers of the series. Stefan's journals are referenced again in "Ghost World": Elena, having read them, asks her brother, who has gained the ability to talk to ghosts following his death and revival at the end of the second season, to contact Lexi (Arielle Kebbel), the now-dead vampire who repeatedly helped Stefan reclaim his humanity. When ghosts start materializing suddenly all over Mystic Falls, Lexi is among them and she tells Elena, "Looks like today was a good day to be thinking about me." Later in the season, in "All My Children," Stefan is shown writing in his journal again.

Another journal writer of importance in the third season is Samantha Gilbert, Jonathan Gilbert's granddaughter. Hoping to find an explanation for a rash of murders of Council members, Damon, Stefan, and Elena begin looking up information on a similar group of murders from 1912. When Elena finds Samantha's journal in the episode "1912," she initially thinks that Samantha Gilbert "went just as crazy as Jonathan Gilbert." However, as she reads the journal, and with the discovery of Stefan's reflections about the 1912 incident in one of his old journals, she comes to believe, like Samantha Gilbert did, that a ring passed through the Gilbert family that reverses death caused by supernatural events causes the wearer to become insane after it is activated several times. In 1912 it was Samantha Gilbert responsible for the deaths; in present-day Mystic Falls, it is Alaric, who has worn the ring — and been killed while wearing it several times — responsible for the deaths. He has no memory of the events as the ring triggers a type of dissociative personality disorder: Alaric kills Council members as one personality, but his primary personality is unaware of what he is doing. Once again, the journals act as a type of reference for the unusual events occurring in Mystic Falls.

A further type of family record in the third season is the cave carvings/paintings that Alaric finds in tunnels on the old Lockwood property at the end of "Ghost World." In the next episode, "Ordinary People," Alaric begins to decipher what Damon labels the "Lockwood[22] diaries — Pictionary-style" and realizes that the carvings well pre-date the official founding of Mystic Falls. In addition to the pictographs are Runic inscriptions of names — the names of the Original vampires. Alaric examines photographs of the images, marking them with notes as he tries to decipher them, to discover the story the images tell. As with the paper journals, this pictographic and Runic writing allows Elena, Damon, and Alaric to piece together necessary information about the Originals as they try to find a way to kill Klaus. Though Elena goes to Rebekah (Claire Holt) to get the story first-hand, she discovers with further analysis of the pictographs that Rebekah does not know the true story of her mother's death — that she was killed by Klaus. Later in the season, in the episode "All My Children," the pictographs again become important, this time for Rebekah and Klaus, when Rebekah discovers by looking at a section of them that the white oak tree that is the source of the only wood capable of killing an Original was not destroyed as she and her siblings thought. This knowledge leads her on a search for the location of the tree so that she can destroy it properly.

Another type of writing that plays a role in *The Vampire Diaries*, much as it did in *Buffy the Vampire Slayer*, is internet research. The more advanced technology of *The Vampire Diaries* offers the characters greater opportunity for quick research, though none of the characters is a computer whiz like Willow in *Buffy the Vampire Slayer*. Technology is ubiquitous in *The Vampire Diaries*. Thus, in the season one episodes "Fool Me Once" and "There Goes the Neighborhood," when Jeremy starts to believe in vampires, he does an internet search for them and then spends time in an internet chat room talking to others about vampires and vampirism. A savvy internet user, Jeremy realizes that much of the internet research is fictional. Prior to Jeremy's use of the internet, when Elena confronts Stefan about vampires in "Lost Girls," she says, "When you Google *vampire*, you get a world of fiction" and proceeds to grill Stefan about the different vampire lore she has collected in her research, most of which are myths.[23] And prior to that episode, in "You're Undead to Me," Elena uses new digitized records from the local television station to locate a report about vampires — including a picture of Stefan — from 1953. While internet is important in the first season, other written technology becomes important in later seasons. In particular, text messaging acts both as an aid and as a trap in several episodes. As with all of the more traditional texts, technology does not ensure reliability, and the characters must negotiate truth from fiction in their findings.

Finally, oral storytelling also plays a role in *The Vampire Diaries*. Because Stefan, Damon, and most of the other vampires are quite old,[24] numerous flashbacks occur in the series to explain current events and/or to give background information about characters. While some flashbacks are triggered by journal reading — as in the episodes "The End of the Affair" and "1912" — more often the flashbacks come with one of the characters telling his or her story. A voiceover will lead to the flashback and, quite often, remove characters from the flashback. This method of presenting a flashback, not uncommon in films or television programs,[25] ties the visual shift to the present, acting as a seamless transition but also, in many cases, demonstrating point of view. For example, in season one, both Damon and Stefan tell parts of their life before and directly after meeting Katherine, and each time they tell their story, the scene moves into a flashback. Similarly, in season three, Klaus reminds Stefan of their time in Chicago in the 1920s in "End of the Affair," and Rebekah tells Elena her perspective on the Original family in "Ordinary People." With *The Vampire Diaries*, the use of stories emphasizes the importance of first-hand knowledge — as has, to a lesser extent, the Council, whose knowledge has been passed through the generations of Mystic Falls' Founding Families.

Writing, reading, and storytelling — particularly first-hand accounts of events — have a powerful role in *The Vampire Diaries*. In each of the three completed seasons thus far, characters rely on the written word. It doesn't have any magical power, but the power it does possess is in its information. Much like *The Spiderwick Chronicles*, the journals and stories of *The Vampire Diaries* contain dangerous information that, in the wrong hands, wreaks havoc. The written and spoken word contains power. Stefan's warning to Elena after she confronts him in "Lost Girls" that "knowing this [that vampires exist] is dangerous" proves true, and the more Elena and her friends in Mystic Falls learn about the supernatural, the more endangered they become. Perhaps more than any other series or film, *The Vampire Diaries* demonstrates the dangers and power of knowledge, whether gained through journals or storytelling or library or internet research. From the moment Elena knows what Stefan and Damon are, she loses all chance of having a normal life. Every attempt she makes to find a balance, to find a moment of "normal"—whether it is at a school dance or a romantic date with Stefan—fails, unlike most texts and films that allow characters to strike a balance. As Mendlesohn notes in her discussion of intrusion fantasies, the intrusion fantasy "has as its base the assumption that normality is organized, and that when the fantastic retreats the world, while not necessarily unchanged, returns to predictability—at least until the next element of the fantastic intrudes" (xxii). Given the serial nature of *The Vampire Diaries*—and the writers' tendency to end episodes (and even seasons) with cliff hangers—normal is constantly just out of reach for the characters.

Unlike the dark drama of *The Vampire Diaries*, the original Disney film *Bedtime Stories* is a light-hearted comedy about the power of children's storytelling. Like the film *Enchanted*, *Bedtime Stories* begins with a pop-up book opening and a narrator setting up the story. The narrator in this case is Marty Bronson (Jonathan Pryce), the late father of the main character Skeeter (Adam Sandler) and his sister Wendy (Courteney Cox). He begins the main part of his narrative, "I'm gonna tell you a story now" and then offers some reflection on storytelling: "As any good storyteller knows, one must first be sure the audience is prepared." He gives background on how Skeeter came to be the handyman at the hotel that Marty used to own. The introductory narrative also reveals how Marty used to tell Skeeter stories when he was a child, stories that present Skeeter as the main character. When the main time frame of the film begins, Wendy asks Skeeter to babysit her children, Patrick (Jonathan Morgan Heit) and Bobbi (Laura Ann Kesling) while she goes for a job interview in Arizona, necessitated by the closing of the school at which she is the principal. The introductory narrative shows that Wendy and Skeeter were very different children, and adulthood has only emphasized the contrast. When Skeeter goes to Wendy's house for Bobbi's birthday, the party is something of a disaster because Wendy, a socially conscious health-food nut, serves gluten-free wheatgrass cake for the party. Reading material for bedtime stories is similarly socially conscious as Skeeter discovers when he goes through their books, which include the titles *Rainbow Alligator Saves the Wetlands* and *The Organic Squirrel Gets a Bike Helmet*, to read to the children on the first of the four nights of his babysitting stint. His reaction to the books — "I'm not reading these communist books to you guys! Don't you have any real stories?" — leads to him asking if the children would like him to tell a real story "like my old man used to do for me. Maybe I could be good at this." This first story about "Sir Fix-A-Lot" is a medieval telling of Skeeter's life as the handyman and his problems with Kendall (Guy Pearce), renamed "Sir Butt-Kiss" for the story. In all of the stories that Skeeter tells the children, as the narrative is presented, the events of the story play out visually for the film audience, each one using the same actors as those from real life. This effect is similar to the use of flashbacks in *The Vampire Diaries*, allowing the audience to become more engaged in the story through visuals. As he relates the story to the children, they begin to offer adjustments, beginning with the addition of their mother's friend and the daytime babysitter Jill (Keri Russell). Then when Skeeter ends the story initially with Sir Fix-A-Lot dying alone and in disgrace, the children refuse to accept it because as Patrick says, "It's not happy." Despite Skeeter's response — "There aren't happy endings in real life. The sooner you guys know that the better" — the children reshape the ending, giving Sir Fix-A-Lot a chance to prove himself and, amid the celebrating, making it rain gumballs because "it's a bedtime story. Anything can happen," says Patrick. Skeptical, Skeeter replies, "I wish it was like that in real life."

The next day at work, events narrated in the story begin to come true: Skeeter is given a chance to propose a theme for the new hotel and, if it is accepted, he will become the manager. Then, on his way to watch the children, when he is stopped at a traffic light, it begins to rain gumballs, thanks to a tractor trailer accident on the overpass above him. Excited by the possibility that the stories he is telling are coming true, Skeeter tells another story to the children that night, this one a western in which the character based on him is given a free horse named Ferrari. The children again resist his story and retell it to have him save a damsel in distress, who rewards him at the end with a kiss. The next day, Skeeter waits for events to happen as narrated and discovers that only what the children narrate comes true: he does not receive a Ferrari, but he does help a damsel — Violet Nottingham (Teresa Palmer), the daughter of the hotel owner (Richard Griffiths) — and receives a kiss as a reward.

On the third night, Skeeter, knowing the children have control over what comes true, tries to get them to create a story called "The Great Hotel Idea Story" so that he will have something to bring to Mr. Nottingham. They reject his suggestion, asking instead to hear a story of action and romance. Skeeter then tells them a "romaction story" about Ancient Greece featuring Skeetacus, the inventor of the X Games. Bobbi and Patrick create parts of the story containing a series of unlikely events, including meeting all of the girls who were mean to Skeetacus at a tavern and having them do the Hokey Pokey. Skeeter is not pleased with the story and demands, "What, is this a joke to you? What the heck's the matter with you?" His reaction alienates the children, who refuse to finish the story. Then next day, each event comes true again, though the final one, the appearance of Abraham Lincoln, reveals how literal interpretations do not always work with the stories: instead of the actual Abraham Lincoln or someone dressed like him, a penny falls through the crack in the dock under which he and Jill — who he has belatedly realized is the "fairest maiden in the land" — are standing. This absurd event foreshadows the way in which the final story plays out.

This story, a science fiction one, turns Skeeter into an alien, Skeeto Bronsonnian, "who talks like a goofy alien." He and General Kendallo, the Kendall character, battle, and Skeeter's character wins. However, having taken Skeeter's comments about life not always having happy endings to heart — and perhaps wanting to retaliate for his negative comments the previous night — the children declare that Skeeter's character is incinerated at the end of the story and refuse to change it, telling him, "You said happy endings don't really happen. We want our story to be real." Because Skeeter is taking the story literally, he prepares himself against being set on fire. His fear of the ending grows as he is stung on the tongue by a bee, making his speech nearly incomprehensible as he makes his presentation — so much so that his friend Mickey (Russell Brand) translates for him. Skeeter wins the competition and is awarded the manager post but is so afraid of catching fire that he douses Mr. Nottingham and his birthday cake with a fire extinguisher, leading to his being fired. His reaction — "Fired! Oh! That's how it connects" — reveals a late comprehension of the way the story is adapted from the telling to the real world.

At this point in the film, Jill, the children, and Wendy are all mad at Skeeter, Jill and the children because they think he knew the new hotel site is their old school, and Wendy because he told the children "that in real life there are no happy endings." Alone in his room at the hotel, Skeeter hears his father narrating and comments, "Great ending, huh?" Marty's response shows that he is not impressed: "That was your ending, son? I thought this was just a sad part and you were about to make it better." He explain how his stories to Skeeter used to work, moving forward when the hero does something "unexpected and courageous to beat the bad guys, save the day and get the girl." Marty reminds Skeeter, "It's your story, not mine," and encourages him to get moving and "go get 'em, son!" Whereas prior to this moment only the children's stories came true, now Skeeter, acting rather than dreaming, scrambles to counteract the plans to destroy the school, succeeding easily with the paperwork but then having to race to the demolition site when he cannot contact the demolition crew by phone. As he races to the site on a motorcycle with Jill, scenes from the previous stories appear of him racing on other transportation — two different horses and a spaceship. His success leads to a happy ending and the narrator returns, revealing how each character's story ends, the pages of the pop-up book reappearing as they did in *Enchanted*.

Despite framing the film with a book, however, *Bedtime Stories* is about storytelling and the power of children's belief and hope rather than books. The stories the children narrate come true because they believe that "anything could happen" not just in stories but in life. When Skeeter's own belief that happy endings cannot happen influences the children, their stories shift from carefree and happy to tragic in the end. Only Skeeter's determination at the end — his new-found belief in happy endings — allows him to embrace the optimism of childhood and succeed. Without childlike hope, without the belief in happy endings, characters fail, the film demonstrates. Love of stories with happy endings reinforces the optimism of childhood. Fantasy becomes reality, thanks to the storyteller's belief paired with actions.

Quite often the film and television programs with children and young adult protagonists parallel their written counterparts. Books as artifacts of power remain dangerous and characters must strive for balance between reading and action. Interactive books allow characters to overcome fears and gain confidence. The exception is the writer/storyteller-focused films, which instead of focusing on the blurring of reality and fantasy or on emphasizing the fictional nature of the text, vary in message. Some reveal the importance of first-hand accounts of information and the dangers of possessing certain knowledge, while others emphasize the importance of hope. The visual nature of films allows action to overshadow books, but books and reading still play an important role in many films and television series for children or young adult audiences.

PART II: SPECIFIC SERIES

6

Harry Potter, Book Learning, Adolescent Scribbling and Self-Reliance

In J.K. Rowling's *Harry Potter and the Sorcerer's Stone*, the first book of the *Harry Potter* series, Harry meets his first Defense Against the Dark Arts teacher, Professor Quirrell, in the Leaky Cauldron in Diagon Alley, where Hagrid has taken Harry to buy his school supplies. After meeting the trembling, stuttering professor, Harry asks Hagrid, "Is he always that nervous?" (70). Hagrid replies, "Oh, yeah. Poor bloke. Brilliant mind. He was fine while he was studyin' outta books but then he took a year off ter get some first-hand experience.... They say he met vampires in the Black Forest and there was a nasty bit o' trouble with a hag — never been the same since" (70–1). This reply offers Rowling's first comment in the series about the contrast between book learning and experiential learning, a comment that would seem to favor book learning over experiential since Quirrell's "first-hand experience" seemingly changed him into a stuttering, nervous wreck.[1]

The end of *Sorcerer's Stone*, however, presents the opposite view. As Harry and Hermione are about to part after passing through several practical physical and mental tests, Hermione to get help and Harry to face Quirrell (though he thinks he will be facing Professor Severus Snape), Hermione, in response to Harry's comment that he is not as good a wizard as she is, makes the oft-quoted comment, "Me! ... Books! And cleverness! There are more important things — friendship and bravery" (287).[2] Here Rowling stresses the importance of qualities besides book learning, underscoring previously implied favoring of other types of learning — notably Harry and Ron's reactions to Hermione and their refusal to accept her until after she breaks the school's rules and lies to their teachers to protect Harry and Ron. Hermione's comment, rather than Hagrid's observation about Quirrell,[3] drives the attitude about books and learning throughout the series. Indeed, Harry, Ron, and Hermione have just undergone numerous practical tests, only one of which puts classroom learning into practice (Hermione's defeat of the Devil's Snare), though the other skills—flying, playing chess, and completing a logic problem—are demonstrated if not acquired earlier in the story as well. In fact, Hermione, the most bookish of the characters, often leads the charge away from book learning at critical junctures of the series, most notably when she spearheads the secret Defense Against the Dark Arts club in the fifth book in the series, *Harry Potter and the Order of the Phoenix*. Better than anyone else in the series, Hermione understands that while books are useful tools, they have their limits and they can also be dangerous, whether because they are imbued with magic of their own or because their content can be misleading.

One of the primary things that the three main characters learn throughout the series is the importance of being critical readers and of relying on more than the written word. To this extent, the series fits within Sanders's arguments about books and readers in metafiction for children and the way in which these novels emphasize critical reading, though *Harry Potter* is not a heavily metafictional series. Several aspects of books, reading, and writing contribute to that knowledge. First, Harry, Ron, and Hermione encounter books that in and of themselves represent danger as artifacts of power. Secondly, in their Defense Against the Dark Arts classes, they experience different pedagogical techniques that demonstrate to them what effective teaching and learning should be. Thirdly, they encounter the ways in which authors can and do manipulate information, in class and out. Finally, they encounter the lasting power that even adolescents can wield in their own writing. By the close of the series, Harry, Ron, and Hermione have learned self-reliance largely as a result of negotiating the dangers of books and other written texts and the adult authority associated with them.

Books as Artifacts of Power

Many books in *Harry Potter* possess magical properties, though the vast majority of books are of a more traditional variety: written texts used for reference or entertainment. Even the entertaining books in *Harry Potter* are generally non-fiction. There is little reference to fiction aside from the comic Ron collects, *The Adventures of Martin Miggs, The Mad Muggle* in *Chamber of Secrets*, and later to *The Tales of Beedle the Bard* in *Deathly Hallows*. One of the most innocuous books with magical properties is *The Monster Book of Monsters*, which Hagrid assigns for his Care of Magical Creatures class in the third novel of the series, *Harry Potter and the Prisoner of Azkaban*. Veronica

6. Harry Potter, *Book Learning, Scribbling and Self-Reliance* 113

L. Schanoes, in "Cruel Heroes and Treacherous Texts: Educating the Reader in Moral Complexity and Critical Reading in J.K. Rowling's Harry Potter Books," calls the *Monster* book "more a wild animal than a written text" (137). The book even attempts to escape from Harry when he receives it for his birthday, biting his hand when he first tries to recapture it, and Harry must resort to fastening it closed with a belt. Prior to the school year, he goes to the Diagon Alley bookstore, Flourish and Blotts, to buy the rest of his books. After breaking up a fight between two of the *Monster* books in their cage, the store manager tells Harry, "I'm never stocking them again, never! It's been bedlam! I thought we'd seen the worst when we bought two hundred copies of the *Invisible Book of Invisibility* — cost a fortune, and we never found them" (53). Only once class starts do the students learn how to handle the books: "Yeh've got ter *stroke* 'em," Hagrid tells the class (113, emphasis in original). Hagrid's amusement at the book is not shared by the students, and it represents a poor start to his teaching. Had the book been assigned by another teacher, it might have put the students off books in general, but Hagrid's predilection for dangerous creatures — "wild animals" — and objects makes the book seem unique to him. Hagrid does not have the same level of authority as other adults in the series, a fact made clear by the way in which he is addressed — by last name only — compared to the other adults — title and last name.

A more sinister book in the series is Tom Riddle's diary. This diary is first encountered in the second book, *Harry Potter and the Chamber of Secrets*. Though Harry and Ron have seen Ron's sister Ginny writing in a diary prior to their discovery of Riddle's diary in the girls' bathroom, they do not recognize the diary as the same one she had been using. However, Ron is cautious of it, fearing it may be dangerous. In response to Harry's incredulity at the thought of a book being dangerous, Ron says, "Some of the books the Ministry's confiscated — Dad's told me — there was one book that burned your eyes out. And everyone who read *Sonnets of a Sorcerer* spoke in limericks for the rest of their lives. And some old witch in Bath had a book that you could *never stop reading*!" (230–1, emphasis in original). The potential dangers of these books — as well as many other artifacts that have been enchanted — and his father's experience dealing with them as part of the Misuse of Muggle Artifacts Department of the Ministry of Magic have made Ron wary of any unknown object, including Riddle's diary. The diary, however, appears benign upon examination by Harry, Ron, and Hermione. Only when Harry writes in the diary does its magical property reveal itself, for it writes back to Harry, filling him in on information about the Chamber of Secrets when it first opened fifty years prior to Harry's time at Hogwarts. The diary is stolen before Harry can question it further, and it is not until the end of *Chamber of Secrets* that Harry discovers the truly sinister nature of the diary when he attempts to rescue Ginny and encounters Tom Riddle—the wizard who would grow to become Voldemort in his adult years—who has emerged from the diary and nearly been restored to life by his draining Ginny's life to restore his own. The magic of the book is so strong that only piercing it with a basilisk fang destroys it. Later in the series Harry learn that the diary was a Horcrux, an item containing a piece of Voldemort's soul. This book is far more menacing than Hagrid's *Monster Book of Monsters*, yet because it was the only one of its kind and destroyed, Harry, Ron, and Hermione do not associate all books as dangerous. The memory of Riddle's diary is revived in the sixth book of the series, *Harry Potter and the Half-Blood Prince*, when Harry becomes fascinated by the Half-Blood Prince's Potions book and Hermione and Ginny suspect it of being akin to Riddle's diary, though their spells to test its safety reveal nothing unusual about the book.

Aside from the two individual books that are artifacts of power, one of the most important collections of powerful books appears frequently in the series. The Restricted Section of the Hogwarts library, introduced in *Harry Potter and the Sorcerer's Stone*, is separated from the rest of the library by a rope, which would not seem to be much of a deterrent for curious students with a penchant for sneaking. In *Sorcerer's Stone*, Harry sneaks into the Restricted Section and senses the books are different from other books:

> Their peeling, faded gold letters spelled words in languages Harry couldn't understand. Some had no title at all. One book had a dark stain on it that looked horribly like blood. The hairs on the back of Harry's neck prickled. Maybe he was imagining it, maybe not, but he thought a faint whispering was coming from the books, as though they knew someone was there who shouldn't be [206].

Despite his nervousness, Harry perseveres with his research — trying to discover who Nicholas Flamel is — and opens a book. As soon as he does so, "a piercing, bloodcurdling shriek split the silence — the book was screaming! Harry snapped it shut, but the shriek went on and on, one high, unbroken, earsplitting note" (206). Though it is not clear whether the book itself is enchanted or if there is a spell on all the restricted books to trip an alarm when someone unauthorized is using them, the effect is similar — Harry flees the library without having found the information he wants. Only later in the novel does Harry discover the information for which he has been searching — on the back of a Chocolate Frog card about Dumbledore.

Harry, Ron, and Hermione later gain access to the Restricted Section legally, if only through tricking Professor Lockhart in *Harry Potter and the Chamber of Secrets*, so that they can brew a Polyjuice Potion. The book they borrow, *Moste Potente Potions*, is not magical; however, "it was clear from a glance why it belonged in the Restricted Section. Some of the potions had effects almost too gruesome to think about, and there were some very unpleasant illustrations, which included a man who seemed to have been turned inside out and a witch sprouting several extra pairs of arms out of her head" (164). This book and others in the Restricted Section represent some of the dangers of magic if used for nefarious purposes, and what is interesting about Harry, Ron, and Hermione's use of the book is that it is rule-conscious Hermione's idea. Ron notes, "I never thought I'd see the day when you'd be persuading us to break rules" (166). Prior to Hermione's suggestion to use the book, all her rule-breaking comes as a result of Harry and Ron's influence — for example, her sneaking out at night to find the Sorcerer's Stone in the first novel. Though still revolving around books and schooling, Hermione's comfort zone, her rule-breaking in *Chamber of Secrets* marks a change in her straight-laced personality.

The books in the Restricted Section are just one aspect of dangerous books at Hogwarts. In *Harry Potter and the Half-Blood Prince*, even this section does not help Hermione when she begins researching Horcruxes. She tells Harry,

> I haven't found one single explanation of what Horcruxes do! ... Not a single one! I've been right through the restricted section and even the most *horrible* books, where they tell you how to brew the most *gruesome* potions — nothing! All I could find was this, in the introduction to *Magick Moste Evile*— listen —"Of the Horcrux, wickedest of magical inventions, we shall not speak or give direction..." I mean, why mention it then? [381, emphasis in original].

This book, when she closes it, "let out a ghostly wail" (381), reminiscent of Harry's encounter with the restricted book his first year. Later, when Harry retrieves Professor Horace Slughorn's memory of a conversation with Tom Riddle, he learns that Horcruxes are "a banned subject at Hogwarts" (499), which is why there are no books available on the subject in the library. However, the books do exist at Hogwarts, and in the seventh book, *Harry Potter and the Deathly Hallows*, Hermione reveals that "Dumbledore removed them all [from the library], but he — he didn't destroy them" (101). Following Dumbledore's death, Hermione performs a summoning charm to retrieve them from his office. Having known they would not return to school, Hermione says, "It just occurred to me that the more we knew about [Horcruxes], the better it would be" (102). As with getting the book in *Chamber of Secrets*, Hermione's rule-breaking here is to further her knowledge, to gather more books for research that they desperately need on their quest to find and destroy the remaining Horcruxes. These books are not magical the way some

Restricted Section books are, but they clearly represent a dangerous subject. Much like the books in *The Spiderwick Chronicles* (see Chapter 2), it is the information contained within books that is the threat more that the books themselves. The variety of dangerous books, many coming early in the series, make characters wary of books in general. Even Hermione, the avid reader of the series, is repulsed by the texts, though she knows they can be useful and never stops using them. They are her best and most dangerous tools in many ways, and her careful use of them separates her from Voldemort and other dark wizards who use the books to gain power over others.

Defense Against the Dark Arts Class

Something else Harry, Ron, and Hermione learn early in the *Harry Potter* series is that information is easily manipulated and that book learning is not always enough to prepare them for the world. One of the main places this manipulation and realization occurs is in Defense Against the Dark Arts classes. In each of Harry, Ron, and Hermione's six years at Hogwarts, they have a different Defense Against the Dark Arts instructor: Professor Quirrell in *Sorcerer's Stone*, Gilderoy Lockhart in *Chamber of Secrets*, Remus Lupin in *Prisoner of Azkaban*, Alastor "Mad Eye" Moody/Barty Crouch Junior in *Goblet of Fire*, Dolores Umbridge in *Order of the Phoenix*, and Severus Snape in *Half-Blood Prince*. While most of their classes at Hogwarts combine book learning with practical exercises,[4] the disjointed nature of Defense Against the Dark Arts, thanks to the many different instructors, reveals contrasting teaching styles. On the first day of class in *Sorcerer's Stone*, though students are eager to attend Defense Against the Dark Arts,

> Quirrell's lessons turned out to be a bit of a joke. His classroom smelled strongly of garlic.... His turban, he told them, had been given to him by an African prince as a thank-you for getting rid of a troublesome zombie, but they weren't sure they believed this story. For one thing, when Seamus Finnigan asked eagerly to hear how Quirrell had fought off the zombie, Quirrell went quite pink and started talking about the weather.... [134].

From their first Defense Against the Dark Arts class, then, Harry, Ron, and Hermione question the validity of the teacher and the information he presents. This is the only reference to Quirrell as an instructor as well, though other classes—Potions, Charms, Transfiguration—are discussed more frequently. The questionable nature of Quirrell's class—even though he is not a malevolent instructor like Snape—can be seen to foreshadow Quirrell's role as a villain. He is untrustworthy and should be under suspicion, yet his outward demeanor as the stuttering, bumbling professor makes him seem less of a threat than he is, something he articulates when Harry confronts him at the end of the novel: "Severus [Snape] does seem the [villainous] type, doesn't he? So useful to have him swooping around like an overgrown bat. Next to him, who would suspect p-p-poor, st-stuttering P-Professor Quirrell?" (288).

In *Chamber of Secrets*, the second Defense Against the Dark Arts instructor, Gilderoy Lockhart, also proves to be an ineffective teacher, more interested in self-promotion than instruction. Harry, Ron, and Hermione's first class with him is a disaster, starting with a pop quiz that asks students to recall specific details about Lockhart — "*What is Gilderoy Lockhart's favorite color?*"; "*When is Gilderoy Lockhart's birthday, and what would his ideal gift be?*" (100) — before moving on to a practical exercise dealing with Cornish pixies, who wreak havoc on the classroom when Lockhart proves incapable of handling them. Harry, Ron, and Hermione are left to clean up his mess, Hermione defending him with the claim, "He just wants to give us some hands-on experience" (103). When Harry points out that Lockhart didn't know what he was doing, Hermione disputes the claim, pointing out "all those amazing things he's done" according to his books, leading Ron to be the first one suspicious of Lockhart's veracity: "He *says* he's done" (103, emphasis in original). As with Quirrell, Lockhart's stories about his exploits come into question, and his reliability becomes more and more suspect as the novel continues, for he constantly interferes and makes situations worse while claiming he knows better than others how to fix things — whether Professor Sprout's doctoring of the Whomping Willow (90), fixing Harry's arm after it is broken in a Quidditch match (173), or claiming to know how to deal with the Heir of Slytherin (294). At the end of *Chamber of Secrets*, he admits his fraudulence to Harry and Ron, who confront Lockhart with information they have about the Chamber of Secrets and the Heir of Slytherin, expecting that Lockhart plans to enter the Chamber and rescue Ginny Weasley, despite their past experience with him. When they confront Lockhart with what he says he has done in his books, he says, "Books can be misleading," explaining, "My books wouldn't have sold half as well if people didn't think *I'd* done all those things. No one wants to read about some ugly old Armenian warlock, even if he did save a village from werewolves. He'd look dreadful on the front cover" (297, emphasis in original). Lockhart understands marketing and is unscrupulous enough to take advantage of others, demonstrating to Harry, Ron, and Hermione (who was as enthralled by Lockhart as most of the other girls in the novel[5]) that books can be unreliable. The questionable nature of Defense Against the Dark Arts instructors, begun with Quirrell, is only emphasized with Lockhart, so it might be natural to expect all Defense Against the Dark Arts teachers to be as unreliable and ineffective.

However, in *Prisoner of Azkaban*, the best Defense Against the Dark Arts instructor the students will encounter joins the Hogwarts staff. Unlike the stuttering Quirrell and the egomaniacal Lockhart, Remus Lupin almost immediately establishes his reliability to Harry, Ron, and Hermione. Their first encounter with Lupin comes on the train to Hogwarts, when the train is stopped by Dementors searching for Sirius Black. Lupin shows his own defensive skills by driving away the Dementor attacking Harry and then knowing how to counteract the Dementor's effects. This unpleasant but ultimately positive first meeting establishes Lupin as a practical, competent Defense Against the Dark Arts teacher. His first class cements his skills when, upon his arrival in the classroom, he tells the students, "Would you please put all your books back in your bag. Today's will be a practical lesson. You will need only your wands" (130). The class is surprised, for "they had never had a practical Defense Against the Dark Arts before, unless you counted the memorable class last year when their old teacher had brought a cageful of pixies to class and set them loose" (130). This practical exercise proves both popular and worthwhile for the class, for Lupin understands how to teach students at their level, and the exercise, followed by an assignment to "read the chapter on boggarts [the creature they learned to banish] and summarize it for me" is met with no resistance (139). Lupin has successfully balanced practical learning with book learning and engaged his students in the process. His effective teaching methods are only highlighted on the day that Snape substitutes for him. Hoping that at least one student will realize that Lupin is a werewolf, Snape drills the class on werewolves, though they haven't yet covered the subject in class, then assigns them to read the section of the text in class and write two rolls of parchment about the subject for homework.[6] As they read in class, he goes around the room criticizing Lupin and his instructional methods. Snape's actions serve only to underscore Lupin's strength as a teacher, something emphasized when he cancels Snape's homework assignment upon his return to class. It is only after Snape has exposed Lupin as a werewolf at the end of *Prisoner of Azkaban* that the highly competent Lupin is removed as an instructor at Hogwarts after only one school year.

On the heels of Lupin comes another fairly effective Defense Against the Dark Arts instructor in *Harry Potter and the Goblet of Fire*: Barty Crouch Junior, disguised as Alastor "Mad-Eye" Moody. The first mention of Moody in the novel comes after an incident at Moody's home. Because Moody is thought to be paranoid, the news report on him mocks him and Mr. Weasley, who is sent to deal with the incident. The initial negative report, which works to make the students wary of Moody as a teacher, is mitigated shortly before Harry, Ron, and Hermione's first Defense Against the Dark Arts class, for

6. Harry Potter, Book Learning, Scribbling and Self-Reliance 119

Moody defends Harry against a curse Draco Malfoy is planning to send Harry's way while his back is turned. The fact that Moody humiliates Draco by turning him into a ferret and bouncing him around the hallway only makes the non–Slytherin students like Moody more. Then, like Lupin, Moody starts the class by saying, "You can put those away, ... those books. You won't need them" (210), further exciting the students, who had enjoyed Lupin's practical classes the previous year and hope for more of the same kind of instruction. Moody takes note of Lupin's work with the students, then says, "You're behind — very behind — on dealing with curses" (211) and proceeds to teach the class about the three Unforgivable Curses even though,

> according to the Ministry of Magic, I'm supposed to teach you countercurses and leave it at that. I'm not supposed to show you what illegal Dark curses look like until you're in the sixth year. You're not supposed to be old enough to deal with it until then. But Professor Dumbledore's got a higher opinion of your nerves, he reckons you can cope, and I say, the sooner you know what you're up against, the better [211–2].

Following the lesson, which negatively affects Neville Longbottom, Moody tells Harry, Ron, and Hermione, "You've got to know. It seems harsh, maybe, *but you've got to know.* No point pretending" (219, emphasis in original). Moody's lessons thereafter include making the students try to break the Imperius Curse — a curse that forces them to do anything the caster wills. While the lessons are practical in nature and allow the students to learn information they will need sooner than they perhaps should need to know it, Moody is not as effective an instructor as Lupin was. Like his name, he is moody and unpredictable, which makes the students nervous around him in a way they never were with Lupin. It also makes the students and adults alike accept any possible inconsistencies of character, allowing Barty Crouch Junior to play the role successfully for the entire school year. As a result, he is able to influence the Triwizard Tournament, first by entering Harry's name into the cup, then by seeing Harry through the first tests, and finally by turning the trophy into a Portkey that transports Harry and Cedric Diggory to Voldemort's side. Moody/Crouch only comes under scrutiny when Harry returns to Hogwarts with Cedric's body and he spirits Harry away against Dumbledore's wishes, something the real Moody would never do. No one questions that he is Mad-Eye Moody until the very end of the novel, and perhaps the knowledge that they were duped by him makes the students more suspicious of their fifth Defense Against the Dark Arts teacher when she arrives.

Dolores Umbridge, assigned by the Ministry of Magic to teach Defense Against the Dark Arts in *Harry Potter and the Order of the Phoenix*, immediately sets herself up as an officious, cloying person when she is introduced at the welcome banquet and gives a speech that only Hermione and the other Hogwarts professors seem to understand indicates that "the Ministry's interfering at Hogwarts" (214). Prior to her appearance at Hogwarts, Harry encounters her at his Ministry hearing about his use of magic outside of school — something strictly forbidden for underage wizards. At the hearing, when he first sees her, Harry "thought she looked just like a large, pale toad. She was rather squat with a broad, flabby face, as little a neck as Uncle Vernon, and a very wide, slack mouth. Her eyes were large, round, and slightly bulging. Even the little black velvet bow perched on top of her short curly hair put him in mind of a large fly she was about to catch on a long sticky tongue" (146). Off-putting as her appearance is, it is Umbridge's clear dislike of Harry and Dumbledore that truly alienates Harry at this meeting. Her classroom manner justifies Harry's and most of the other students' loathing of her and makes the students question her suitability as a teacher, for after forcing them to practice chorusing a greeting to her, she tells them, "Wands away and quills out, please" (239). The students think, "The order 'wands away' had never yet been followed by a lesson they had found interesting" (239). Their concern is justified when they learn they won't be practicing any defensive spells, as Umbridge tells the class, "I can't imagine any situation arising in my classroom that would require you to *use* a defensive spell" (242, emphasis in original). Instead, they are assigned to read their textbook in class. As Tracy L. Bealer points out in "Militant Literacy: Hermione Granger, Rita Skeeter, Dolores Umbridge, and the (Mis)use of Text," "Professor Umbridge ... politicizes her Defense Against the Dark Arts classroom to promote the Ministry's version of the current wizarding sociopolitical atmosphere. Because, according to the Ministry, the world outside Hogwarts is utterly benign, there is no reason to teach the students practical defenses against the Dark Arts" (179). When Hermione, having already read the book, questions the author's premises about defensive magic, a class-wide debate ensues, revealing Umbridge to be a controlling, rigid instructor unwilling to entertain alternative points of view about her pedagogy or the ideas presented in the text. As Bealer indicates, "Umbridge establishes a strict hierarchy in her classroom, designed to situate herself as unquestioned and unquestionable leader and her students as passive receivers of the 'knowledge' her chosen textbook applies" (180). From that class on, the students spend all of their time reading the textbook while Umbridge sits at the front of the room, yet the entire class realizes, thanks to Hermione's questioning of the text, that, as Leslee Friedman says, "even if the text that Umbridge has chosen is a quality one, its use to the class, without practical engagement of its ideas, is completely invalid" (199).

Driven by the desire to learn the information she needs to pass her Ordi-

6. Harry Potter, *Book Learning, Scribbling and Self-Reliance* 121

nary Wizarding Levels exams (OWLs) and to face the increasing threat of Voldemort, Hermione hatches the plot to create a Defense Against the Dark Arts club, named Dumbledore's Army, or the D.A., in which the members will learn and practice defensive magic. Thanks to his experience using defensive magic, Harry is voted to become the leader of this group. Even though Umbridge has banned all non-approved clubs, the threat of the consequences of getting caught does not stop the group's activities. Once the members of the D.A. have secured the Room of Requirement as a place to meet and have it set to their specifications, including the "presence of hundreds of books [that] had finally convinced Hermione that what they were doing was right" (390),[7] Harry begins teaching everyone the basics, starting with the disarming spell, Expelliarmus. Like Lupin, the best of the official Defense Against the Dark Arts instructors, Harry builds the skills the group members need to know, taking them from the basic disarming spell to the very advanced Patronus charm for repelling Dementors. Bealer observes, "One of the interesting elements of Rowling's depiction of the students' acts is that their rebellion consists of enacting an adequate education" (182). Harry's teaching proves quite fruitful for all of the OWL students, who are the only ones to pass the practical portion of the Defense Against the Dark Arts OWLs with comparative ease.[8] Furthermore, the practical magic they've learned in the D.A. makes a difference when several group members travel with Harry to the Ministry of Magic at the end of *Order of the Phoenix* to face off against numerous Death Eaters. Without the rebellious questioning of the authority and problematic teaching methods of Umbridge, they would have been unprepared for the trials they faced. At this point in the series, Harry, Ron, and Hermione and many other students are taking control of their education and learning to become self-reliant, something that will become more important with each confrontation with Voldemort and his Death Eaters.

The final Defense Against the Dark Arts instructor, Severus Snape, takes over the position in *Harry Potter and the Half-Blood Prince*. For the first five novels of the series, Snape has been Potions professor at Hogwarts and loathed by all of his students except those in Slytherin, for which he is Head of House. Snape is an exacting teacher who balances practical applications — the brewing of potions — with book learning, and in fact most of the time spent in Potions class is at the cauldron creating different potions. This teaching method, so similar to the majority of other popular instructors at Hogwarts, should make Snape a good teacher; however, Snape's badgering and mocking of all but his Slytherin students make his classes a miserable experience for everyone not in his favor — particularly Harry. Since his introduction to the series, Snape has demonstrated that normally effective pedagogy does not trump an unpleasant personality. It should be no surprise, then, that Harry, Ron, and Hermione dread attending his Defense Against the Dark Arts classes. Yet Snape starts the class in a similar manner to Lupin and Moody, the two best Defense Against the Dark Arts teachers: "I have not asked you to take out your books" (177). The difference is in his approach to the class; all three start class without books, but only Snape makes it sound as if the students have done something wrong by having their books out and ready, and he goes so far as to mock Hermione's knowledge of the information in the texts by all but accusing her of plagiarism: "An answer copied almost word for word from *The Standard Book of Spells, Grade Six*" (178–9). Though the class moves to a practical exercise, practicing nonverbal spells, Snape's presence is off-putting for many students, as is his impatience with them. Only Hermione seems able to see past Snape's manner to the type of instruction he is giving and his approach to the subject. Much to Harry's shock, Hermione compares Snape's speech to Harry's comments "when you were telling us what it's like to face Voldemort": "You said it wasn't just memorizing a bunch of spells, you said it was just you and your brains and your guts — well, wasn't that what Snape was saying? That it really comes down to being brave and quick-thinking" (181). Schanoes points out that from the beginning of the series, Hermione is the only one of the three main characters who can get past her dislike of Snape to trust him: "As early as book I [*Sorcerer's Stone*], Hermione argues for Snape's innocence: she admits that 'he's not very nice' but asserts that he wouldn't betray Dumbledore. By separating Snape's lack of 'nice-ness' from his behavior in a larger conflict between good and evil, Hermione offers the reader the opportunity to do the same" (133). Harry and Ron never like Snape's class, but they do attempt to learn from him, even if they disagree with Hermione's assessment of his teaching style, and they begin to master the nonverbal spells as the novel progresses.

All of the Defense Against the Dark Arts teachers at Hogwarts offer students the opportunity to think critically about what they're learning and who is doing the teaching. They learn that there is more to education than book learning and they learn to see how different instructors disseminate information and which methods are most effective. Teachers liked and respected — like Lupin and Moody — undergo less scrutiny than those disliked; however, this limited scrutiny is something that leads to problems in *Goblet of Fire* when no one suspects Moody of sabotaging the Goble of Fire and manipulating Harry throughout the tournament. It is equally problematic in *Chamber of Secrets* for Hermione, who has a crush on Lockhart throughout the novel and refuses to question his teaching skills. The questioning, and realizing the need for questioning, does, however, start Harry, Ron, and Hermione on the road to questioning other elements of adult authority, notably the press and government offices. As with questioning of Defense Against the Dark Arts instructors, questioning the reliability of these other authority figures allows students to gain self-reliance.

The Manipulation of Information

The *Daily Prophet*, the Wizarding World's primary media outlet, is introduced in *Sorcerer's Stone*, when Hagrid receives a copy the morning after he finds Harry, though little is made of the paper. An article about the break-in at Gringotts bank is referred to later, helping to feed Harry's suspicion of Snape, but there is no critical reading of the article; it is just a collection of facts, and as such, there are no further references to the paper in the novel. In *Chamber of Secrets*, the *Daily Prophet* comes up when Harry, Hermione, and the Weasleys are at Flourish and Blotts buying school books. Gilderoy Lockhart is at the store signing copies of his autobiography and capitalizes on Harry's presence to increase his publicity, saying, "Together you and I are worth the front page" (60). Lockhart spins the accidental meeting to his favor by announcing his new post as Defense Against the Dark Arts instructor, and when a fight breaks out between Mr. Weasley and Mr. Malfoy, Fred Weasley overhears Lockhart "asking that bloke from the *Daily Prophet* if he'd be willing to work the fight into his report — said it was all publicity" (63). Though Lockhart's media spinning seems relatively harmless at the start of the novel, his focus on shaping what the media shows for his benefit represents the start of much more sinister manipulation of texts as the series progresses. In fact, his own manipulation is revealed to be less than innocuous at the end of *Chamber of Secrets* when he admits he has wiped the memory of the others who actually did the great feats for which he claims credit in his books.

Aside from Lockhart's manipulation of *Daily Prophet* in *Chamber of Secrets*, Harry and Ron run into their own trouble with media when they are spotted flying to Hogwarts in Mr. Weasley's magically-altered Ford Anglia and it is reported in the *Evening Prophet*, leading to an inquiry at Mr. Weasley's workplace. A later report in the *Daily Prophet*, which Draco Malfoy shows the disguised Harry and Ron, reports that Mr. Weasley has been fined for "bewitching a Muggle [non–Magical person] car" (221), allowing Mr. Malfoy to lobby publicly again the Muggle Protection Act that Mr. Weasley supports (222). As with Lockhart, Malfoy is using the press as a platform to manipulate readers. Draco also indicates his surprise that attacks on students at Hogwarts have not been reported, speculating, "I suppose Dumbledore's trying to hush it all up" (222), something never corroborated, though certainly a possibility:

Dumbledore knows how to spin events as well as the antagonistic characters do, both publicly and privately.[9]

While *Sorcerer's Stone* and *Chamber of Secrets* show relatively small ways in which media can be manipulated and gives students reason to question media for bias, the third book of the series, *Prisoner of Azkaban*, shows how a government can use media channels both to keep the public informed and to whitewash details that might alarm the public. Initially the *Daily Prophet* is used in *Prisoner of Azkaban* to inform the public about the search for Sirius Black, who has escaped from Azkaban Prison. The Ministry of Magic is so concerned about Sirius's threat to society that they inform the Muggle Prime Minister so that the Muggle population can be informed of the danger, though in terms Muggles can understand: "Muggles have been told that Black is carrying a gun (a kind of metal wand that Muggles use to kill each other)" (38). The goal of this first *Daily Prophet* article is to keep the public informed and calm, as are other articles published during Harry's stay in Diagon Alley before school starts. However, Mr. Weasley tells Mrs. Weasley the night before the kids leave for Hogwarts, "It's been three weeks, and no one's seen hide nor hair of [Black], I don't care what Fudge [the Minister of Magic] keeps telling the *Daily Prophet*, we're no nearer capturing Black than inventing self-spelling wands" (65). Mr. Weasley makes it clear here that Fudge is manipulating the *Daily Prophet*. There is greater focus on reading the *Daily Prophet* in this novel, and rumors of Sirius Black sightings abound, though they're all speculative (cf. 126). Late in the novel, the importance of the *Daily Prophet* comes clear when Sirius reveals he discovered Peter Pettigrew — the man who betrayed Harry's parents to Voldemort — was alive and at Hogwarts by reading an article in the *Daily Prophet* about Ron's family that included a photograph of the Weasleys, including Peter disguised as Scabbers the rat. The article gave Sirius the strength to escape from Azkaban in the hopes of protecting Harry and seeking vengeance against Pettigrew. At the conclusion of the novel, before he realizes Black has escaped again, Fudge says, "I can't tell you how much I'm looking forward to informing the *Daily Prophet* that we've got [Black] at last" (417) because "This whole Black affair has been highly embarrassing" (416). His capture will allow the Minister of Magic to create a positive spin on his office through the manipulation of media. Once Black escapes again, however, Fudge thinks, "The *Daily Prophet*'s going to have a field day! We had Black cornered and he slipped through our fingers yet again! All it needs now is for the story of the hippogriff's escape to get out, and I'll be a laughingstock!" (420). At this point in the series, Fudge does not control the media, though he is able to manipulate it to a small extent, and Harry, Ron, and Hermione's exposure to Fudge's frustration with and attempts to manipulate

6. Harry Potter, *Book Learning, Scribbling and Self-Reliance*

Phoenix, the Dumbledore-led group fighting Voldemort and his Death Eaters, he learns the truth. Hermione explains that his name does appear in the *Daily Prophet* but not on the front page: "I'm not talking about big articles. They just slip you in, like you're a standing joke" (73). Much of the negative attention given to Harry is based on the final article Rita Skeeter wrote about him in *Goblet of Fire*, even though Skeeter herself isn't writing now thanks to Hermione's threat. Hermione tells Harry, "She laid the foundation for what they're trying to do now" (73): "They're writing about you as though you're this deluded, attention-seeking person who thinks he's a great tragic hero or something.... They keep slipping in snide comments about you. If some far-fetched story appears they say something like 'a tale worthy of Harry Potter'..." (74). Though the people immediately surrounding Harry — his closest friends and the Order of the Phoenix members — believe him, the majority of the Wizarding World does not. To add to the problem, "the Ministry's leaning heavily on the *Daily Prophet* not to report any of what they're calling Dumbledore's rumor-mongering, so most of the Wizarding community are completely unaware anything's happened, and that makes them easy targets for Death Eaters if they're using the Imperius Curse" (94). Fudge's unwillingness to accept that Voldemort is back because he doesn't want to admit there is trouble has led to the smear campaign against Harry and Dumbledore so that Fudge can secure his political base. The problems continue at Hogwarts with the appointment of Umbridge, first as Defense Against the Dark Arts instructor, then as Hogwarts High Inquisitor, and finally as Headmistress. Bealer notes,

> Minister of Magic Cornelius Fudge's use of the magical community's mainstream press (a flurry of stories in the *Daily Prophet* branding Harry a delusional liar and Dumbledore a senile relic), judiciary (seating the full Wizengamot to try Harry for a minor offense in an attempt both to discredit and to expel him), and educational system creates the political equivalent of images in the Mirror of Erised — a carefully manufactured reality in which the Minister's deepest desire, that Lord Voldemort has not come back, looks true [177].

By taking control of the media and the judicial and educational systems, the Minister of Magic attempts to control the information being spread, and very few people in the Wizarding community read deeply enough to challenge the system — students and adults alike.

Because formerly reliable channels are closed to them for revealing the truth about Harry's encounter with Voldemort, Hermione decides to take matters into her own hands. Not surprisingly, Hermione, the most book-savvy of the students, devises a plan to allow Harry to get his story to the general reading public through an unlikely means. The character Luna Lovegood and her father's magazine, *The Quibbler*, are introduced early in *Order of the Phoenix* when Harry, Ron, Hermione, Neville Longbottom, and Ginny Weasley join her in a compartment on the Hogwarts Express. Hermione dismisses *The Quibbler* as "rubbish, everyone knows that" (193) because of its speculative articles — the Wizarding equivalent of the *Weekly World News* or *The National Examiner*; however, she isn't above arranging for Rita Skeeter to write an article about Harry for *The Quibbler* because, as Hermione says, "the *Prophet* won't print it because Fudge won't let them" (567). Skeeter agrees with this comment, but elaborates on the issue: "Fudge is leaning on the *Prophet*, but it comes to the same thing. They won't print a story that shows Harry in a good light. Nobody wants to read it. It's against the public mood. This last Azkaban breakout [of many of Voldemort's Death Eaters] has got people quite worried enough. People just don't want to believe You-Know-Who's back" (567). Hermione's retort, "So the *Daily Prophet* exists to tell people what they want to hear, does it?" elicits the response, "The *Prophet* exists to sell itself, you silly girl" (567), something Hermione undoubtedly knows. As Chantel M. Lavoie notes in "The Good, the Bad, and the Ugly: Lies in Harry Potter" after pointing out the homonymic connection between *prophet* and *profit*, "What sells is sensationalism, hyperbole, reassurance (when the truth is too objectionable) and downright falsehood" (80). Hermione's argument with Rita Skeeter shows her understanding of the machinations of both the *Daily Prophet* and the Minister of Magic, and she dismisses Skeeter's defense of the current line held by the *Daily Prophet*. Skeeter's disbelief that people will believe Harry if he is published in *The Quibbler* prompts Hermione to say, "Some people won't [take him seriously] ... But the *Daily Prophet*'s version of the Azkaban breakout had some gaping holes in it. I think a lot of people will be wondering whether there isn't a better explanation of what happened, and if there's an alternative story available, even if it is published in ... an *unusual* magazine — I think they might be keen to read it" (568, emphasis in original). Hermione's assessment of the public's desire for information proves correct when *The Quibbler* article is released and Harry receives many supportive letters.[10] The release of the article also prompts Umbridge to enact Educational Decree Number Twenty-seven, which bans students from having copies of *The Quibbler*. Rather unexpectedly, Hermione argues in favor of the decree: "If she could have done one thing to make absolutely sure that every single person in this school will read your interview, it was banning it!" (582). Once more, Hermione shows she understands what motivates people and how to manipulate them, and it is clear that Umbridge has no such understanding — she expects people to obey authority figures without question and punishes those who do not, not realizing that her actions will likely evoke a

6. Harry Potter, *Book Learning, Scribbling and Self-Reliance* 129

response opposite to that anticipated. Friedman notes that "this decree again brings to the forefront Umbridge's fear of what reading can accomplish. As with the Slinkhard book [her chosen text for Defense Against the Dark Arts class], where she limits reading and its practical applications, here she attempts to completely shut down reading as a path to uncontrolled knowledge" (201). Umbridge is unsuccessful in both cases because she believes in an absolute authority that the students—and indeed many adults—do not. Though publication of the article does not legitimize Harry—the Ministry of Magic still controls the *Daily Prophet*—it does bring the Minister of Magic under greater scrutiny. The appearance of Voldemort himself inside the Ministry of Magic at the end of *Order of the Phoenix* forces Fudge to acknowledge publicly that Voldemort has returned, though he continues to attempt to downplay the danger. In addition, *The Quibbler* article on Harry is bought and reprinted by the *Daily Prophet*, thus legitimizing it.

What is perhaps most important in *Order of the Phoenix* in terms of negotiating media outlets is that Harry, Ron, and Hermione move from being receivers of published data to manipulators of the system that had been controlling them: they gain power from their actions and use that power, small as it is, to encourage the school-wide rebellion, minus Slytherin House, over Umbridge and the Ministry of Magic. Though they never control the *Daily Prophet* or *The Quibbler* following their validation, they learn the lesson not to trust print media to present unbiased information. The role of the *Daily Prophet* in particular becomes smaller in the remaining two novels in the series, *Harry Potter and the Half-Blood Prince* and *Harry Potter and the Deathly Hallows*. In *Half-Blood Prince*, the references to the *Daily Prophet* now generally revolve around characters criticizing it—"The *Prophet* is bound to report the truth occasionally ... if only accidentally," Dumbledore says (357); "The *Prophet's* behind the times," Tonks tells Harry (466). In addition, Harry, Ron, and Hermione consult it every day to see if anyone they know has died or disappeared. The Ministry of Magic poses the larger problem for Harry now: Rufus Scrimgeour, the new Minister of Magic, wants to use Harry as a spokesperson for the Ministry of Magic, to assure the Wizarding community that the Ministry of Magic is handling the Voldemort crisis well. However, Harry's newly developed skill for understanding how both media and government can and do manipulate facts makes him wary of the Ministry of Magic, especially when he sees reports about the capture of people such as Stan Shunpike who he believes are innocent. Harry continually refuses Scrimgeour, who accuses Harry of being "Dumbledore's man through and through" (348) because, as Dumbledore did, Harry expects more of the Ministry of Magic than a pretense of success against Voldemort.

Early in *Deathly Hallows*, prior to Voldemort and the Death Eaters taking over the Ministry of Magic, the *Daily Prophet* is still largely controlled by the Ministry of Magic. Once the Ministry falls to Voldemort's forces, the *Daily Prophet* is even more tightly controlled by the government, which begins spreading propaganda about Muggle-born witches and wizards, accusing them of stealing Wizard magic. To deal with the Muggle-born witches and wizards, the new government creates the Muggle-born Register, which is a front for the removal of all non-pure-blood Wizards from the community. The *Daily Prophet* as a cover for Voldemort's regime becomes even less reliable, and *The Quibbler* takes its place publishing truths about the goings-on in the Wizarding World until the Death Eaters hold Luna Lovegood hostage and force her father, Xenophilius Lovegood, to publish their propaganda in return. The only media outlet that offers content not controlled by the new regime is the pirate radio station run by Lee Jordan, a recent graduate of Hogwarts, which is forced to change its signal for each broadcast and to password-protect its contents. This radio station reports on the Order of the Phoenix's activities as well as on the deaths and captures of Witches and Wizards, many of whom are Muggle-born. Print media is no longer reliable; only verbal reports can be trusted.

Rather than media being the focus of questionable writing in *Deathly Hallows*, two books become focal points: *The Life and Lies of Albus Dumbledore* by Rita Skeeter and *The Tales of Beedle the Bard*, the collection of stories that Dumbledore bequeaths to Hermione. Because Rita Skeeter has been established as a malevolent, unreliable writer who doesn't like Dumbledore,[11] her tell-all biography of him naturally comes under great scrutiny. However, even with the knowledge Harry has of Skeeter's writing, he is unable to dismiss some of her claims about Dumbledore's past, especially as they are accompanied by copies of letters Dumbledore exchanged with Gellert Grindewald, a wizard infamous for his anti–Muggle sentiments. Of all of the writing that he has to negotiate in the series, this biography poses the greatest challenge to Harry, for he reveres Dumbledore and has difficulty reconciling the man he knew as headmaster of Hogwarts with the man portrayed in Skeeter's book. Learning that the man he trusts and admires above all others has a questionable past forces Harry to realize that people can and do change — something that helps prepare him for entering Snape's memories and learning the final piece of information that Dumbledore withheld from him: Harry is the "seventh Horcrux, ... the Horcrux [Voldemort] never meant to make" (709). Driven by his reading of Skeeter's book, Harry's acceptance of Dumbledore, flaws and all, allows him to walk into the Forbidden Forest and sacrifice himself for the benefit of the Wizarding World.

The other book that plays an important role in *Deathly Hallows* is *The*

Tales of Beedle the Bard. Neither Harry nor Hermione is familiar with this collection of wizard folktales, which, like Muggle folktales, have been adopted as children's literature, but Ron is quite familiar with them, having heard them since childhood. The key story from the collection is "The Tale of the Three Brothers," which contains the origins of the Deathly Hallows: the Elder Wand, the Resurrection Stone, and the Cloak of Invisibility. In the edition of the book that Dumbledore leaves to Hermione is the symbol of the Deathly Hallows, and a good part of *Deathly Hallows* revolves around them trying to figure out the significance of the book and this symbol to their search for Voldemort's remaining Horcruxes. In bequeathing the book to Hermione, Dumbledore anticipated her fixation on the book's significance, as well as her ability to uncover that significance. He tells Harry, "I am afraid I counted on Miss Granger to slow you up" in the quest for the Hallows rather than telling Harry about them directly so that Harry would "possess them safely" unlike the previous owners of the Hallows (720). Dumbledore's tactic works well: he knows Hermione's devotion to books and her ability to analyze them, and he uses those qualities to manipulate Harry, Ron, and Hermione until they are prepared to face Voldemort with all of the information they need about the Hallows. Though *The Tales of Beedle the Bard* appears to be a simple collection of children's stories, it, like the other texts that Harry, Ron, and Hermione must negotiate in the *Harry Potter* series, also comes under scrutiny for its accuracy. Rather than searching for the lies in the truth, however, with *The Tales of Beedle the Bard*, the search is for the truth among the fiction. Of the three main characters, Hermione has the most difficulty believing that the Hallows are anything but a story, though the Invisibility Cloak that Harry possesses and reports of the Elder Wand help to convince her of the possibility that they do exist.

All of the texts that Harry, Ron, and Hermione encounter in the series — particularly the media — teach them to negotiate the adult world of information manipulation, whether it is in what is revealed by the press, how the information is shaped and controlled by government agencies, or how something as innocuous as a children's story can hold deeper truths. Harry, Ron, and Hermione become strong, critical readers by the time they leave school in *Deathly Hallows* to embark on their quest to find and destroy the Horcruxes, and they continue to learn new ways to approach texts on their quest.

Adolescent Writing

In addition to negotiating texts written for them by adults, the students of Hogwarts School of Witchcraft and Wizardry are also learning to find their own voice through the writing they do. While most of the writing done by Hogwarts students is for classes, some students use writing as a means of rebelling against the strictures of their boarding school education. From Tom Riddle, to Harry's father and his friends, to many of Harry's fellow students during his fifth year at Hogwarts, even to a young Albus Dumbledore, many characters in the *Harry Potter* series use writing in various forms to challenge the system. This writing, often infused with magic, demonstrates a questioning of the official curricula and a magical skill beyond the classroom, and is a means to subvert authority. For most characters, the adolescent rebellion diminishes as they grow older, but it also reflects their later place in wizarding society.

The first significant piece of adolescent writing in the *Harry Potter* series is Tom Riddle's diary in *Chamber of Secrets*. This diary, planted by Lucius Malfoy in the Weasleys' purchases for school, finds its way into Ginny Weasley's hands. When Ginny later discards the book, Harry and Ron find it in the girls' bathroom where they and Hermione have been brewing Polyjuice Potion so that they can spy on Draco Malfoy. Harry soon discovers that this fifty-year-old magical diary is interactive. When he writes in it, he enters into a conversation with Tom Riddle, its creator, and is led to believe that Hagrid is the Heir of Slytherin.[12] At the end of the novel, Harry enters the Chamber of Secrets to rescue Ginny, who has, unbeknownst to him, reclaimed the diary. He meets the sixteen-year-old Tom Riddle and learns that this Riddle is "a memory.... Preserved in a diary for fifty years" (308). Ginny has poured out her heart to the diary, which has allowed Riddle to "leave its pages at last" (313). It is during his conversation with Riddle that Harry learns that Tom Riddle is the childhood name of Lord Voldemort, and only Harry's quick and desperate thinking to stab the diary with a basilisk fang destroys the diary and stops Voldemort from fully returning.

Though the diary is referenced several time as the series progresses, only in the sixth book in the series, *Harry Potter and the Half-Blood Prince*, does Dumbledore reveal that the diary was not just a dangerous, enchanted book but a Horcrux—an item containing a piece of Voldemort's soul—and that Voldemort has in fact created seven Horcruxes so that he can escape true death. Even as a sixteen-year-old, Voldemort's fear of death motivated him to explore taboo magical realms in an attempt to preserve himself forever, and he is willing to kill people to accomplish his goals, a necessity in the production of a Horcrux.

Tom Riddle, in his creation of this diary, is clearly rebelling against the magical restrictions of school and of wizard society. He wants to explore magic beyond that taught in school, for he cannot find the information he needs about Horcruxes in the library as it is a banned subject. After not being able to find the information he wants in the books at school, Riddle approaches Horace Slughorn, his Head of House, to learn as much as he can about Horcruxes before, one assumes, he finds even more information about Horcruxes later and begins creating them, starting with his diary. Not surprisingly, Riddle's rebellion against the strictures of Hogwarts and of wizard society involves Dark magic, and this youthful rebellion sets the stage for the adult Voldemort's plans. He continues to push the boundaries of magic, refusing ever to accept the rules of his society because he believes his skills as a wizard should not be limited. Following the creation of the first Horcrux, Voldemort creates six more and attempts to take over wizarding society. When he and the Death Eaters overtake the Ministry of Magic in the final book in the series, they also take over Hogwarts, and Voldemort seeks to impose his own curriculum upon the students — a curriculum that includes the teaching of the Dark Arts. Rather than coming around to mainstream wizarding society, Voldemort has attempted to recast society to his ideals and remains willfully ignorant of any objections to his plans.

Unlike Voldemort's refusal to fit in with wizard society, most of the adolescent writers in the series use writing as a youthful rebellion but later lose much of that rebellion as they mature. A second example of adolescent writing that has a significant impact on the series is the Marauder's Map, the enchanted map that Harry's father James and James's friends Sirius Black, Remus Lupin, and Peter Pettigrew created to help them sneak around Hogwarts when they were in school. This map, introduced in *Prisoner of Azkaban* when Fred and George Weasley give it to Harry, is an interactive map of Hogwarts, including all of the secret passages, and allows the user to see everyone who is in the school. Though how James Potter and his friends created the map is never revealed, the skill to create such a map would have been far beyond the scope of most Hogwarts students, just as their development of Animagi shows a skill beyond their years and their failure to register the Animagi breaks wizard law. It is clear that the map is used to help them break school rules, to subvert authority. Fred and George, and later Harry, Ron, and Hermione, all use it for the same purposes, though by the end of the series, the map is also used as an aid to fighting Voldemort and other evil — or at least antagonistic — characters, showing that even subversive items have their mainstream uses.

Though less is known about James, Sirius, Remus, and Peter than about other characters in the series, it is clear from some of the memories Harry enters into that all of them enjoyed flouting the rules, particularly the leaders of the foursome, James and Sirius. In fact, Sirius expresses his disappointment that Harry isn't more willing to break school rules like his father had been, saying, "You're less like your father than I thought.... The risk would've been what made it fun for James" (*Order* 667). Yet all four creators of the map settle into acceptable roles in the wizarding world and join the original Order of the Phoenix. Though Peter Pettigrew turns traitor, the others remain positive characters (and even Peter helps Harry in the final book of the series, partially redeeming himself in the process).

Despite their place in society, however, James and Sirius do not completely lose their taste for danger and their desire to resist society's confinements. When James is forced into hiding because Voldemort and his Death Eaters are after James, Lily, and Harry, Lily writes to Sirius that "James is getting a bit frustrated shut up here, he tries not to show it but I can tell — also, Dumbledore's still got his Invisibility Cloak, so no chance of little excursions" (*Deathly* 180). The implication that James would risk being caught to go on a "little excursion" sounds similar to his behavior at Hogwarts and validates Sirius's comment about the risk being the fun for James. In both cases, he is rebelling against the confines of his life. Similarly, Sirius, despite thirteen years in the prison at Azkaban, retains a wicked, rebellious streak. He encourages Harry's rule-breaking and longs to leave hiding to help Harry in *Goblet of Fire* and the Order in *Order of the Phoenix*. Unlike Voldemort, however, neither James nor Sirius's activity is criminal, aside from their continued use of an unregistered Animagus form, in school or out, but merely mischievous and occasionally cruel, particularly when dealing with Severus Snape.

Perhaps one of the least inherently rebellious of the main characters, Hermione Granger also knows how to manipulate writing to her advantage. When Hermione organizes Dumbledore's Army in *Order of the Phoenix,* she requires new members to sign a piece of parchment that swears them to secrecy. Later, when one of the members, Marietta, turns traitor, the spell Hermione put on the parchment causes her face to be "horribly disfigured by a series of close-set purple pustules that had spread across her nose and cheeks to form the word 'SNEAK'" (612). As Friedman notes, "Hermione consciously uses the written word — and the act of others' reading — to punish, and to make an example of what comes of betrayal" (200), and this is evident by the fact that the pustules on Marietta's face have not disappeared by the next book in the series. Though the creation of a cursed piece of parchment would not have been taught at Hogwarts, Hermione is advanced enough to create it. She also creates a method of communication between D.A. members with a Protean Charm. The charm allows her to send messages about meeting days and times through fake galleons (wizarding coins). When she changes the information on one galleon, it changes on all galleons, with the coins warming to let their holder know there is a message.[13] Her rebellious actions are infrequent, but when Hermione does rebel, it is because she perceives an injustice. She is ruthless in her pursuit of right, even if it means subverting authority. Hermione's efforts at protecting the D.A. are much more effective than her efforts with her Society for the Promotion of Elvish Welfare, or S.P.E.W., but both reflect her activist leanings, something she is considering pursuing past her schooling at Hogwarts.

Other instances of Hogwarts students rebelling against Umbridge's regime through reading and writing are clear in *Order of the Phoenix*. When the article containing Harry's interview with Rita Skeeter appears in *The Quibbler*, Umbridge bans the magazine with her issuance of Educational Decree Number Twenty-seven. Despite the ban, all of the students in the school have a copy of the contraband magazine, and no student is expelled, for "the students were several steps ahead of [Umbridge]. The pages carrying Harry's interview had been bewitched to resemble extracts from textbooks if anyone but themselves read it, or else wiped magically blank until they wanted to peruse it again" (582). The magical blanking of the pages is similar to the enchantment on the Marauder's Map, which becomes a blank piece of parchment when the user taps it with a wand and says, "Mischief Managed," and is unlikely to be taught in school.[14] The rebellion expressed by the students of Hogwarts against Umbridge is replicated during their ultimate rebellion against Voldemort, when his Death Eaters take over Hogwarts in *Deathly Hallows*, though that rebellion occurs through action rather than writing.

Umbridge's lack of understanding of adolescents and their ability to evade authority is clear in her many Educational Decrees, and Fred and George Weasley take the rebellion to the highest level when they determine that Umbridge has overstepped her authority. Though always pranksters and practical jokers, the twins, as Fred says, "have always stopped short of causing real mayhem" until the final weeks of their time at Hogwarts (627). One way in which they cause mayhem is through setting off their Weasleys' Wildfire Whiz-Bangs fireworks. These fireworks, which multiply when typical spells are used to get rid of them, include "sparklers [that write] swearwords in midair of their own accord" (632). This use of taboo language as a form of rebellion is common among adolescents, and Fred and George clearly know how to use it effectively. They adapt magic they have learned from their lessons for their unsanctioned purposes — before they set off their fireworks, they are seen trying to sell Skiving Snackboxes, Headless Hats, and various other items, much to Hermione's dismay. The joking nature of the Weasley twins carries through their life after Hogwarts, for they open their own joke shop in Diagon Alley, yet when Harry visits the shop in *Half-Blood Prince*, he learns that their best sellers are the non-joke items, hats and cloaks that repel some curses, among other items, even though these items start off as jokes like the rest of their products. The jokesters become mainstream and extremely successful.

Like his contemporaries with their Marauder's Map, Severus Snape does his own writing as an adolescent, and similar to James, Sirius, Remus, and Peter, Snape's authorship is not revealed until the end of the novel. Rather than creating a magical document, however, Snape annotates his copy of *Advanced Potion-Making*. These annotations include adjustments to the instructions by the author of the book as well as spells in the margins of the book. Harry first encounters this book in *Half-Blood Prince*, when he adds Potions unexpectedly to his schedule and has to borrow a textbook. At first, he is irritated by the annotations: "To his annoyance he saw that the previous owner had scribbled all over the pages, so that the margins were as black as the printed portions" (189). That annoyance quickly turns to fascination when the suggestions made by the "Half-Blood Prince," as the owner names himself, elicit potions that exceed even Hermione's efforts, much to Hermione's disgust. When Hermione and Ginny, suspicious of the book and fearing it is like Riddle's diary, test it for malicious magic, they learn that "it really does seem to be ... just a textbook" (193).

Harry becomes fascinated with the book and with the Half-Blood Prince, and he, Ron, and Hermione speculate on the identity of the mysterious Prince. At one point, Harry even wonders if the Prince might be his father, James, though this theory is quickly dismissed. The fascination with the book lasts until Harry uses an incantation that he has found labeled "For Enemies" in the margins of the book (447–8). This spell, Sectumsempra, which Harry uses against Draco Malfoy when Malfoy attempts to cast an Unforgivable Curse on Harry, slashes Malfoy open, nearly killing him. When Harry sees the results of this spell, he is "stunned; it was as though a beloved pet had turned suddenly savage; what had the Prince been thinking to copy such a spell into his book?" (525). This incident, however, is foreshadowed when Harry uses another unknown incantation, Levicorpus, on Ron early in the book (238–9). Though this incantation, which hoists the victim into the air, doesn't injure Ron, who finds it amusing once Harry learns the counter curse, it is a clear warning that performing unknown incantations is potentially dangerous.

Harry is horrified when he learns that Snape is the Half-Blood Prince at the end of the novel, yet as with other young writers, Snape's annotations show his rebellion against the curriculum, for he alters the standard potions, adapting them successfully in a more mainstream manner than Fred and George adapt their lessons. His annotations are a reflection of who he becomes later. He is an excellent Potions master, even if his teaching style leaves much to be desired for the non–Slytherin students. Further, there is a darkness to his character—evident in how he treats Harry, and in how he treated James Potter and, on occasion, even Lily Potter—that explains some of the incantations that Harry discovers. Snape might be on the right side, but he is not likeable, and his textbook annotations reflect that duality.

Perhaps the most surprising adolescent writer of the series is Albus Dumbledore. Dumbledore's writing is revealed in *Deathly Hallows* and, like Snape's, is not imbued with magic. Instead, his writing, presented by Rita Skeeter in her biography of him, reveals some of his youthful ideas exchanged in letters with Gellert Grindewald, a dark wizard with whom Dumbledore dueled many years prior to the rise of Voldemort. The letter that Rita Skeeter prints in her book *The Life and Lies of Albus Dumbledore* shows clearly that he and Grindewald had exchanged ideas about wizards' superiority and dominance over Muggles, and Dumbledore argues in his letter, "*Yes, we have been given power and yes, that power gives us the right to rule, but it also gives us responsibility over the ruled*" (357). He further argues that they should use force to "*seize control FOR THE GREATER GOOD,*" by violent means if necessary (357). Though Harry knows that Rita Skeeter is an unreliable source, and though he also knows how the elder Dumbledore showed a lack of bias against Muggles, this information about the youthful Dumbledore disillusions Harry, who has put Dumbledore on a pedestal since they first met. Hermione points out that Dumbledore was very young when he wrote the letters, to which Harry replies, "They [Dumbledore and Grindelwald] were the same age as we are now. And here we are, risking our lives to fight the Dark Arts, and there he was, in a huddle with his new best friend, plotting their rise to power over the Muggles" (361). As a direct result of Dumbledore's adolescent writings, Harry spends much of this final book in the series wondering how much he really knew about Dumbledore and what the truth about his idol is.

Harry realizes eventually that Dumbledore did indeed reject these youthful writings—which contributed in part to the death of Dumbledore's sister Ariana—something that Dumbledore confirms when he and Harry speak after Voldemort tries to kill Harry again. Dumbledore, like Voldemort, had been rebelling against the common practice for dealing with Muggles but this rebellion is short-lived, and Dumbledore spends the rest of his life trying to atone for his youthful exchanges with Grindewald. It is, in fact, the fallout from his youthful ideas that makes Dumbledore the person he is throughout the series, and he represents the opposite end of the spectrum from Voldemort, who never changes from his youthful ideas.

Yet, though Dumbledore rejects the idea of "For the Greater Good" in relationship to dealings with Muggles, the motto does seem to apply to his dealings with the Ministry of Magic and, more importantly, with Harry. When dealing with the Ministry of Magic, Dumbledore presents a reasonable front, yet when his ideas are rejected, rather than work within the system, he forms his own society, the Order of the Phoenix, to do what he thinks the Ministry should be doing for the greater good of wizard society. This tendency is most noticeable in *Order of the Phoenix* when Marietta is brought forward to confirm the existence of the D.A. and Harry's part in it. Rather than let Marietta speak her mind, Kingsley Shaklebolt, an Auror working with the Order of the Phoenix, modifies her memory, prompting Dumbledore to say just before his escape from Hogwarts, "He was remarkably quick on the uptake, modifying Miss Edgecomb's memory like that while everyone was looking the other way — thank him for me, won't you, Minerva?" (621). The fact that this memory modification was applied to a student in his care does not bother Dumbledore; her memory needed to be modified for the greater good of Harry and Dumbledore and the Order of the Phoenix, regardless of casualty. Lavoie, in her analysis of lying in *Harry Potter*, comments on Dumbledore's lies: "As a model up to the point of his death, Dumbledore accords truth the dignity which giver and recipient deserve. He tells outright lies to the Ministry when necessary, for instance, and every lie he tells seems to be a good one — that is necessary for the greater good" (83). The fact that Dumbledore is usually seen as a sympathetic figure makes his lies and other actions that would normally be viewed negatively more acceptable. "For the greater good" is a matter of point of view. Dumbledore also grooms Harry throughout the series to sacrifice himself — or so Dumbledore thinks — to defeat Voldemort, knowing that Harry's death will be for the greater good of wizarding society — and Harry, "Dumbledore's man through and through," buys into the plan. Though Dumbledore has altered his vision of relating to Muggles, his belief in doing things "for the greater good," regardless of individuals affected by them, remains.

Adolescent writing can be seen both as an act of rebellion against the strictures of school and wizard society and as a foreshadowing of how students will mature. Though most of the adolescent scribblers outgrow the rebellion and become functional members of society, remnants of their rebellion and the ideas reflected in their writing can be seen in the adults these youths become. The unsanctioned adolescent writing itself lasts much longer than the sanctioned writing from classes. Class writing holds a large place in the series while Harry, Ron, and Hermione are attending Hogwarts, yet this writing does not last: students receive their assignments, complete them under duress — often copying each other's work, or allowing their work to be copied, including Hermione — receive their grades, and then forget the writing. Only the unsanctioned writing endures, which represents students' attempts to show their own power and their ability to rely on their own voices. Hogwarts students negotiate a world full of powerful books, questionable authority figures, and problematic writing. Those successful at negotiating these elements, like Harry, Ron, and Hermione, become self-reliant at the end of their journey.

7

Inkheart and the Rejection of Literacy

While the books in the *Harry Potter* series can be imbued with magic when wizards and witches put spells on them, most books in the series are tools and, though sometimes dangerous, are used as resources for schoolwork rather than for pleasure reading. Even bookworm Hermione reads to gain knowledge rather than for the sheer joy of reading.[1] *Inkheart*, the first novel in Cornelia Funke's *Inkheart* series, focuses on the pleasure that books bring to their readers. The main character Meggie Folchart often thinks of books as "familiar voices, friends that never quarreled with her, clever, powerful friends" (15). They are her home away from home, her reminders of places she has visited and her comfort, and she goes nowhere without taking at least one book with her.

Claudia Nelson, in her essay "Writing the Reader: The Literary Child in and beyond the Book," argues that fantasies[2] such as *Inkheart* "that contain characters who engage with others designated within the text as 'fictional'" (223) emphasize the benefits and delights of reading: "Among their defining traits is a shared emphasis on the delight associated with immersing oneself in a story, a delight that the complexity of their construction seeks to replicate for the reader" (226). In her discussion of *Inkheart,* Nelson indicates that "*Inkheart* waxes lyrical about both the emotional comfort that Meggie derives from books ... and the ability of Meggie's father, Mo, to read" in a manner that captivates audiences (227).[3] For Nelson the benefits of reading are explored in all of these books, even those with reluctant readers, though in the case of *Inkheart,* there is no reluctance. She argues that "if even the reluctant readers within the world of the novel can find themselves happily immersed in a moment that they understand to be fictional, by implication the reader outside the world of the novel can, and should, do the same" (228). Chapter 3 argues that Nelson's claim that "one of the standard messages of

7. Inkheart *and the Rejection of Literacy*   141

children's metafiction is simply 'Read!'" (228) is problematic because action is as important if not more important than reading, and her claim remains problematic in relation to the *Inkheart* series as well.

The *Inkheart* series revolves around certain characters' abilities to read aloud. In particular, Meggie's father Mo, Meggie herself, a secondary character called Darius, and a villain named Orpheus read so well that they can bring characters (or other things) out of a story as well as send people from their world into a story. Like the texts discussed in Chapter 3, the *Inkheart* series presents a world in which, to return to David Lewis's comments, "the medium itself — language — becomes invisible as we read or listen" (135). Mo, Meggie, Darius, and Orpheus are the means by which the medium becomes invisible. Though any well-written story can be transformed in this manner, the focal text of the series is a novel called *Inkheart* written by Fenoglio. The first of Funke's novels takes place in the real world, the second in a combination of the real world and Inkworld (the land of the fictional *Inkheart*), and the final novel almost entirely in Inkworld. Meggie, the main character, as well as her father Mo and Great Aunt Elinor and many other characters in the series are avid readers, and throughout the series, books, reading, and storytelling all play an important role. However, an examination of several different characters in the series reveals not just the problems with reading, especially obsessive reading, but also ultimately a rejection of literacy.

Elinor

The first character of the series placing the importance of reading into question is Meggie's Great Aunt Elinor. Elinor is a character whose obsession with books isolates her from the rest of the world: late in *Inkheart*, Mo shares his belief that Elinor "couldn't cope with the world except between the covers of a book" (426). When she is introduced in *Inkheart*, she reveals her priority immediately, telling Meggie that "some of [the books in her study] are so valuable that I wouldn't hesitate to shoot you if you dared to touch them" (36). Her house, to which Mo has brought Meggie, is overcrowded with books. Upon entering the house, Meggie sees that "where other people have wallpaper, pictures, or just an empty wall, Elinor had bookshelves" (37). Elinor's obsession with books is well known in her community, and she observes, "Everyone living around this lake thinks I'm crazy," which makes getting the aid of the police to help find Mo when he is taken hostage impossible and leads to Elinor's comment that "a passion for books is extremely unhealthy" (86). Her passion for books has also endangered Mo, for Elinor has taken the book he asked her to hide out of its place so that she can read it. As a result, when Mo is kidnapped, he takes the book she replaced it with instead of the one the kidnappers want.

Later in the novel, Elinor's obsession with books shows when she discovers that Capricorn, the villain of both the novel and of the fictional *Inkheart* in the story, has sent his henchmen to destroy parts of her library. She mourns the loss of the books, thinking of them as her children (386). The mockery to which other characters subject her[4] calls into question the importance of avid reading in the series, and the other two books in the series, *Inkspell* and *Inkdeath*, serve to emphasize the problem with an obsession with books.

In the beginning of *Inkspell*, Elinor is quite contently living with Meggie, Mo, and Meggie's mother Resa, whom Mo had read into the fictional *Inkheart* by accident and who was restored to the main world of the novel by Darius, though without her voice. Elinor has both her books — she is restoring her depleted collection — and her family. She, like Meggie, is fascinated by Inkworld, the land described by the fictional *Inkheart*, and she longs to experience it as Resa did, even knowing it is not an ideal world. When Meggie, Mo, and Resa disappear into Inkworld, Elinor is distraught, yet she seems torn between anxiety over them — particularly Mo and Resa, who were dragged into Inkworld by one of the villains of the series — and jealousy. At several points during *Inkspell* she wishes she were with them, and toward the end of the novel, she thinks,

> *I want to be with them.... They're my family: Resa and Meggie and Mortimer. I want to see the Wayless Wood and feel a fairy settle on my hand again, I want to meet the Black Prince even if it means smelling his bear, I want to hear Dustfinger talking to fire even if I still can't stand the man! I want, I want, I want ...* [621].

Though she starts her thought with her family, she quickly shifts to all of the exciting aspects about the fictional Inkworld she has heard about, underscoring her obsession with what she has read.

In *Inkdeath*, the final novel of the series, Elinor is so depressed that she is missing out on what her family is experiencing in Inkworld that she convinces Darius to read them into Inkworld to join the others, even knowing he is not as adept at reading as Mo is (and that he was responsible for Resa being mute on her return to the primary world of the series). Once they arrive in Inkworld, Elinor's expectations are soon dashed, for the world has changed since Mo read out many of the characters. She and Darius track down the author of the book, Fenoglio, and Elinor spends much of the remainder of the novel bickering with Fenoglio over aspects of the world she doesn't like, as well as trying to convince him to rewrite the story a satisfactory ending. Her obsession with books, and with *Inkheart* in particular, makes Elinor an unsympathetic character much of the time, one mocked by others and even by herself.

Elinor's character as a whole puts reading, at least reading obsessively, into question. Books have led to her being isolated from her community and labeled crazy. The worlds of her books are more real to her than her own world, and this is not a positive thing. She is mocked for her obsession, leading to a negative impression of reading.

Orpheus

A second character who serves as a warning against reading obsessively is Orpheus, who does not appear in the series until the second book, *Inkspell*. Orpheus has the same ability as Mo, Meggie, and Darius to read characters from books and people into books, but unlike Mo, Orpheus has both embraced and honed his skill until he can manipulate the contents of a story however he desires. He has also taken his skill a step farther by discovering that he can rewrite passages from a book using the author's words. Upon reading these revisions, he can alter the events and characters of a story. This rewriting also gives him the ability to insert new people into a story at will. When Dustfinger learns of this talent, he hires Orpheus to read him back into Inkworld. The only thing Orpheus cannot achieve with his reading and rewriting talent is to insert himself into the stories, something that upsets him greatly, as the one thing he wants more than anything else is to enter *Inkheart*, his favorite novel. He becomes jealous of Meggie when he learns that she has succeeded in reading herself and Farid into Inkworld, and this jealousy makes him more than happy to read Mo, Basta, and Capricorn's mother Mortola into Inkworld, knowing that Mortola means to kill Mo.

Though Orpheus, like Elinor, is an avid reader, he does not treat books well. When he is at Elinor's home, holding her and Darius hostage after reading Mo, Resa,[5] Basta, and Mortola into Inkworld, he alternates between trying to read himself into Inkworld and amusing himself by reading aloud from Elinor's books. When he is finished with a book, he tosses it wherever he likes, infuriating Elinor. For Orpheus, books are tools not treasures, and he does not care what happens to any of them except *Inkheart*, which he guards jealously as he tries to enter its pages. At the end of *Inkspell*, when Meggie, at Farid's behest, reads Orpheus into Inkworld, he refuses to believe she was responsible for his appearance, instead attributing it to his final reading attempt.

In *Inkdeath*, the problems with Orpheus's obsession with reading *Inkheart* become visible. He has promised Farid that he will try to read Dustfinger back to life, but while he is gathering information and ideas about how to accomplish that task, he also uses his talents to make himself comfortable as well as to change aspects of Inkworld that he does not like. His creation of new kinds of fairies and unicorns for the ruler to hunt, among other changes, infuriates Fenoglio, *Inkheart*'s author, but Orpheus is set on recreating Inkworld to his specifications. Orpheus's obsession with Inkworld and his ego over his talents is such that he thinks he can improve upon the author's creation that he loved as a child.

Upon the return of Dustfinger, which Orpheus attributes to himself, his obsession with the story, and with Dustfinger's character in particular, turns ugly. Because he believes it is his words that have brought Dustfinger back to life, he expects Dustfinger to be grateful and to befriend him, something he longs for as Dustfinger is Orpheus's favorite character from the novel. When Dustfinger disdains Orpheus and further insults him by stealing the last copy of *Inkheart*, which Orpheus has in his home, Orpheus's love for Dustfinger turns to hate, and he spends the remainder of the novel trying to get revenge on Dustfinger as well as Mo, to whom Dustfinger credits his return from the dead. His vengeance is such that he writes and reads a passage that nearly drives Mo mad at the end of the novel. Not only has Orpheus shown through his previous acts that reading is dangerous, but he has also shown how an obsession with books (or a particular book in this case) can lead to problems. In his case the problems are villainous as opposed to Elinor's more benign obsession with books, but both act as an indictment against reading.

Fenoglio

By contrast with Elinor and Orpheus, the character Fenoglio, the author of the focal book *Inkheart*, is not an obsessive reader, though it is clear that he is well-read. When Mo and Meggie first seek him out in *Inkheart* in search of a copy of his book, Capricorn having collected and destroyed most copies of it, Mo references a common attitude about authors: "It's a funny thing about writers. Most people don't stop to think of books being written by people much like themselves. They think that writers are all dead long ago.... They know their stories but not their names, and certainly not their faces. And most writers like it that way" (233). This idea of the anonymous author filters through the series and leaves Fenoglio torn between two primary positions, for unlike "most writers," he would like to be acknowledged for his work, particularly once he starts interacting with his characters. Often, particularly early in the series, Fenoglio has a god complex. He is fascinated to meet Dustfinger, one of his characters, and even delighted when he meets the villain Capricorn, at least initially, until Capricorn proves to be as villainous as Fenoglio wrote him, even out of Inkworld. Though he justifies writing such a villain, Fenoglio does not hesitate to write a passage for Meggie to read aloud that will defeat Capricorn and his men when they imprison Fenoglio and Meggie. When she comments on the shortness of his final passage, a mere page, he tells her, "No more is needed. As you'll see. The words just have to be the right ones" (477). His ability to find the "right" words is something he takes pride in, and in the rest of the series, during which Fenoglio lives in Inkworld, he becomes known as Inkweaver. In Inkworld, Fenoglio earns his living by writing a variety of things, including love poetry for the guards to recite to the women they are courting, and stories for the Motley Folk, the traveling performers of Inkworld. Some of these stories include ones about the Bluejay, a Robin Hood-type character modeled physically on Mo. When Fenoglio sees the world acting as he expects and desires, he demands credit for his success.

However, more often than not, Fenoglio is more like a parent than a god, and he despairs of how the child he has created — Inkworld — is growing. Upon his arrival in Inkworld, he discovers that the characters he created have continued living and dying beyond his writing and that changes wrought by Mo's readings have affected the world. In particular, the premature death of Cosimo the Fair has led his father's nickname to change from the Laughing Prince to the Prince of Sighs and for his kingdom of Ombra to change into a less pleasant land, events that upset Fenoglio greatly and make him wish to reshape the world into his ideal again. When Meggie arrives in Inkworld and finds him, Fenoglio sees his chance to return Inkworld to the form he desires and writes passages for her to read. Yet nearly every new passage has unforeseen, often negative, consequences. Thus when he creates a new Cosimo to replace the one who has died, the new Cosimo is a violent adulterer who wants to wage war against his father-in-law, the Adderhead, a plan that ends with the slaughter of Cosimo and nearly all of the men under his command — most of the able-bodied males in Ombra. In this way, Fenoglio's changes resemble Orpheus's, though they are made without malicious intent. Indeed, some of Fenoglio's writings do make positive differences, as when he writes a passage that allows Meggie to save Mo (*Inkspell* 329), or a passage to find safe shelter for the children of Ombra (*Inkdeath* 465). Each success gives Fenoglio back his confidence and the idea that he is in charge of Inkworld,[6] which tends to lead to overconfidence and the next failure. Despite his efforts, Fenoglio has little control over his story, and his god complex repeatedly shatters.[7]

Fenoglio, like Elinor, is often portrayed as a buffoon. While Elinor's fault is an obsession with books, Fenoglio's fault is his belief that he can control the world he created. He does not want to be the invisible author the book requires. Though his ability to write stories for the Motley Folk is admired in Inkworld, this largely oral culture is even more ignorant of the author than the world from which Fenoglio has come, for it is the storytellers, not the authors, who earn the admiration of audiences.[8] There are few readers in Inkworld to admire Fenoglio, something he uses to his advantage by plagiarizing writers from his world for some of his clients, and his bragging about his skills serves to separate him negatively from others, much as Elinor's reading separates her from others in the real world and her abrasive, know-it-all attitude does in Inkworld. In addition, because this society is largely illiterate, many people are suspicious of the written word. The diminished role that Fenoglio plays in Inkworld underscores the lack of importance of reading by the end of the series. By the final chapter of *Inkdeath*, told in future tense from the point of view of Meggie's brother, who is born following the end of the main events of the series, Fenoglio is reduced to "a lazy old man" who is "getting more forgetful every day" (663), not the creator of Inkworld or the person who can write a passage to return the Folchart family to their world, not even the originator of the Bluejay stories.

Mo

Unlike Elinor, Fenoglio, and Orpheus, all of whom are subject to contempt by other characters and who are often dislikeable, Mo Folchart, Meggie's father, is always an admirable character and in fact could be seen as a protagonist in the final book of the series, *Inkdeath*. It is Mo's skill as a reader of text that initiates the events of the series. Nine years prior to the opening action of *Inkheart*, when Meggie was three, Mo read aloud from *Inkheart*, inadvertently pulling Dustfinger, Capricorn, and Basta from it and sending Meggie's mother, Resa, into its pages. Nine years later, Capricorn wants Mo to do more reading for him to release the Shadow, wanting to recreate Inkworld in the real world. Mo's skills as a reader have earned him the nickname Silvertongue, though he has never read aloud to Meggie since the incident, instead telling her stories without reading or encouraging Meggie to be an independent reader. However, Mo has not rejected books or reading in the first novel — quite the opposite. Still a bookbinder, or "book doctor" as Meggie calls him, Mo has a reverence for books that he has shared with Meggie, and their home is cluttered with books, albeit not to the same extent as Elinor's house. He travels around frequently to repair books for different people, often taking Meggie with him. Though he initially attempted to get Resa back from *Inkheart*, following an incident in which the mail carrier was accidentally transported into the book in exchange for a character whom he read out, Mo stops his attempts, believing them too dangerous. Only when Capricorn has captured Meggie and Elinor and threatens them does Mo read aloud again, demonstrating his skill with *Treasure Island* and *Tales from the Thousand and One Nights*, this second reading calling Farid from the pages in exchange for one of Capricorn's men.

As the series progresses, Mo's role as Silvertongue diminishes — the last time he reads aloud is at the end of *Inkheart* when he completes Meggie's reading of Fenoglio's passage and kills Capricorn and his henchmen. With his transportation to Inkworld by Orpheus, Mo takes on a new identity, one given to him by Fenoglio: the Bluejay. This new identity initially saves his life, for when Mortola shoots him upon their arrival in Inkworld, the White Women, who come to take him to the land of the dead, call him the Bluejay, a name that he does not yet own, and without his real name, they cannot claim him. Meggie's reading of Fenoglio's passage also helps to keep Mo alive. Once Mo is on the mend, however, Inkworld residents constantly mistake him for the Bluejay because Fenoglio has described him so well, including a scar from a dog bite. When he is brought to the Castle of Night, home of the Adderhead, he thinks about his identity: "He wasn't choosing his own way through this story, that much was certain. It had even given him a new name — the Bluejay. Sometimes he felt as if the name were really his. As if he had been carrying it around him like a seed that only now had begun to grow in this world of words" (420). Only Meggie, reading Fenoglio's words, can again change Mo's fate, for she reads a passage introducing the idea of a White Book, which will keep its owner alive "as long as that book exists ... as long as the book remains intact" (499). Mo's skills as a bookbinder allow him a reprieve from execution and come to haunt the Adderhead when Mo creates a book that is rotting slowly, leading the Adderhead to mirror that rotting. The third and final book of the series, *Inkdeath*, revolves in large part around the Adderhead's desire for a new, pristine White Book to save and heal him, and the plan to kill Mo with the old one.

Inkdeath also presents Mo with a strong sense of duality. At the end of *Inkspell*, when the Black Prince offers Mo a Bluejay mask, Mo rejects it, though already he is attracted to the persona: "In silence, Mo turned the mask this way and that in his hands. For a strange moment he felt an urge to put it on, as if he had done so many time before. Oh yes, Fenoglio's words were powerful, but words they were, nothing but words — even if they had been written for him. Any actor, surely, could choose the part he played?" (615). The lure of Fenoglio's words become stronger in *Inkdeath*, and at the beginning of the novel the Bluejay identity has become as much a part of him as Mo Folchart: he has sword fighting skills he never learned and spends much of the early part of the novel performing feats as the Bluejay. What is interesting here is that the reading aloud of Fenoglio's Bluejay stories has not initially caused the influence on him. Instead, because Fenoglio has written Mo as the Bluejay in this world, that identity has taken him over, germinating like a seed as Mo thinks in *Inkspell*. Further, because there is little need for Mo to be Mo the bookbinder (or Silvertongue), that identity slips farther away from him, allowing both Meggie and Orpheus to use the Bluejay name to affect Mo's actions — Meggie to protect him and Orpheus to harm him. Yet Mo is able to foil Orpheus's attempt to defeat him with overwhelming fear by clinging to the remnants of his identity as a bookbinder at the end of *Inkdeath*, with Dustfinger's help. As Mo is suffering, Dustfinger tells him, "So Orpheus read the words, but you are making them come true!" (581), reminding Mo, "It's not a pleasant feeling to read the words that guide your actions. No one knows that better than I do, but they didn't come true for me, either. They have only as much power as you give them" (582). These words help Mo to resist Orpheus as do his self-reminders that he "was not the Bluejay, not Silvertongue, just Mortimer. Orpheus had written nothing about the bookbinder" (591). Touching and examining books helps ground Mo whereas touching his sword brings back Orpheus's words, and Mo uses the Adderhead's desire for a new White Book to aid his resistance, telling Dustfinger, whose daughter has been captured, "Lead them [the Adderhead's soldiers] here! ... It's time my hands bound a book again — even if the job must never be finished. Let them capture the bookbinder, not the Bluejay. They won't notice the difference. And I'll banish the Bluejay forever, bury him deep in the dungeon cell below, with the words Orpheus wrote" (593). As he works on the new White Book, he becomes more and more in touch with his original identity: "The only reason for every move he made was to bring back Mortimer Folchart, the bookbinder who could not be bound by Orpheus's words. Mo hardly felt them anymore. All the despair that had seeped into his heart in that dark cell, all the rage and hopelessness had faded as if his hands had washed them out of his heart" (615). With the successful defeat of the Adderhead, and Orpheus's departure, Mo is able to retire the Bluejay, who was used as a means to resist and defy an oppressive prince. However, the songs about the Bluejay still remain part of the lore of Inkworld, and Dustfinger wonders "whether they [Mo and the Bluejay] were only two sides of the same man" (651). Certainly Mo has come to love Inkworld as much as Resa and Meggie, and the choice to remain in Inkworld means Mo will have little bookbinding work, despite the new ruler's love of books and prior references to a lack of a good bookbinder in the kingdom (*Inkspell* 256). One of the most sympathetic characters and avid readers — as well as the primary authority figure in Meggie's life — Mo has rejected the real world and its literacy.

Dustfinger and Violante

Unlike all of the other characters discussed thus far, all of whom originate in a world outside of *Inkheart*, Dustfinger, Violante, and the majority of the secondary characters in the *Inkheart* series come from inside Fenoglio's book. These characters exist in a world that is largely illiterate. Literate characters include the royals and a few other people, primarily scribes and people employed to manage the royal library. Women are forbidden to learn to read and write. Most of the average folk in Inkworld are not just illiterate but suspicious of the written word. Thus in *Inkspell*, when Resa writes a note for Dustfinger, the messenger Cloud-Dancer and other members of the Motley Folk, are suspicious of her both because she is a female who can write and because they don't believe that Dustfinger can read. When she explains that she taught Dustfinger to read, Cloud-Dancer still insists that she tell him what the note says, saying, "You'd better tell me what you've written, so that I can tell him the words even if your note gets lost. Which can easily happen with written words, much more easily that with words in your head" (232). Cloud-Dancer's attitude toward the written word is common among the average Inkworld citizen, though he is more accepting of Resa's skill than most of the Motley Folk.

Dustfinger himself, though literate now, learned only to communicate with Resa, who is mute when restored to her world and a captive of Capricorn and Mortola. Since reading does not come easily for Dustfinger, he feels "a fresh sense of pride every time those spindly symbols finally fitted together into words and he could get their secret out of them" (*Inkheart* 328). He does not truly enjoy reading and does not read for pleasure like most of the characters who can read. Knowing he has emerged from a book does not encourage him to read it, and Dustfinger informs a shocked Meggie that he does not want to know how his story ends. He tells Meggie and Mo that he does not want to meet Fenoglio in *Inkheart* because "he might tell me how my story ends" (241), something that confuses Meggie until he asks if she wants to know how *her* story will end. Only after he is told that Fenoglio has written his death in *Inkheart* does Dustfinger finally read the book. Unlike characters who have learned to rely on the written word, Dustfinger refuses to let the words control him, though he does fear their power throughout the first two books of the series, as evidenced by his desire to leave his marten Gwin behind when he returns to Inkworld because Gwin is partly the cause of his death in *Inkheart*. Dustfinger has little use for the written language. His main reliance on writing comes in *Inkspell* when he hires Orpheus to write and read a passage to return him to Inkworld. Following Dustfinger's death in *Inkspell* and his return to life in *Inkdeath*, his fear and anxiety over the written word disappear, and he is dismissive of both Fenoglio and Orpheus's desire to "improve" Inkworld (*Inkdeath* 253). This lack of fear of what is written allows Dustfinger to help Mo overcome Orpheus's words, as discussed above. Of all the characters in the *Inkheart* series, Dustfinger seems to have the most practical attitude toward reading and writing: it is a tool not to be trifled with, but not something that brings joy. However, his rejection of writing is also the most vocal of all the characters, something that makes sense given his negative experiences with the written word.

A contrast to Dustfinger is Violante, the Adderhead's daughter, who married Cosimo the Fair in an arrangement between their ruling parents. Known as Her Ugliness because of a birthmark on her face, Violante resembles a younger, more powerful Elinor in her obsession with books. Because it is illegal for women to read, Violante must bribe those in charge of the castle's library to allow her to take books to read, something she does willingly. Her obsession with books and reading is such that, despite her increasingly poor eyesight, she reads to the point of neglecting her son, Jacopo. Though she turns out to be an ally for Mo in the attempt to overthrow her father in *Inkdeath*, her obsession with books, reading, and the stories her mother told her make Violante susceptible to trickery — she, like Elinor, gets lost in books to the distraction of all else. Citizens of Inkworld have little respect for her, though they do accept her as their leader at the end of the series, and under her reign, the lion emblem of Ombra has a new addition: the lion's paw "was laid on a book with blank pages, and his mane was made of fire" (655–6). Though this emblem could be read as a symbol that books, reading and writing will become prominent in Ombra, it is more likely to symbolize Ombra's (the lion) defeat of the Adderhead, represented by the blank or white book, with the fire a symbol of Dustfinger, who is also known as Fire-Dancer for his ability to manipulate fire and who is an integral part of the defeat. It will take more than Violante's love of books — and the likely removal of the prohibition of women reading — to turn illiterate Ombra literate, particularly given the distrust of literacy, the lack of books, and the lack of access to education in Inkworld.

Meggie

Perhaps the most important character of the *Inkheart* series is Meggie Folchart, Mo's daughter and the focal character of *Inkheart*, though her role diminishes slightly in the later books, especially in *Inkdeath*. Given that she is the focal child character of the series, Meggie's relationship to books and

7. Inkheart *and the Rejection of Literacy*

reading should be the most telling of all the characters. In *Inkheart*, there is no doubt that books and reading are paramount for Meggie. The novel opens with her in bed, a book under her pillow. Unable to sleep, she takes out the book and plans to break her father's rule about lighting candles by which to read. This plan is foiled when she spies a stranger — who turns out to be Dustfinger — outside the house. This first interruption in Meggie's reading sets the stage for the rest of the series, in which real life inserts itself into Meggie's reading, disrupting it and gradually drawing her away from the world of books.

Not surprisingly, this first, brief interruption from reading does not alter Meggie's attitude to books, and throughout much of *Inkheart,* her thoughts revolve around her love of books, gained from her father, and books' importance to and influence on her. In fact, she frequently compares events going on in her life with her reading experiences, as when she first sees Elinor's gate: "It looked alarming, with sharp ashen-gray spikes, a gate made of spearheads just waiting to impale anyone who tried to clamber over it. It reminded Meggie of one of her favorite stories, the tale of the Selfish Giant who wouldn't let children into his garden. This was exactly how she imagined his garden gate" (30–1).[9] Later she compares her memory to "a picture in a book" (103). She spends a great deal of time thinking of the comfort books offer her, how they are like friends, yet she also encounters a new experience with books in *Inkheart*: fear. After her father is kidnapped and she learns Elinor has the copy of *Inkheart* that Mo had hidden, Meggie takes the book, planning to read it and find out what the secrecy surrounding this book, which her father has kept hidden from her, is. However, she has difficulty initially opening the book:

> She didn't usually hesitate so long before opening a book, but she was afraid of what was waiting for her inside this one. That was a brand-new feeling. She had never before been afraid of what a book would tell her. Far from it. Usually, she was so eager to let it lead her into an undiscovered world, one she had never been to before, that she often started to read at the most unsuitable times [90].

Meggie's love for books, her fascination and obsession, is slowly being undermined by the events of real life. Books are becoming dangerous rather than a safe place to which she can escape.

Once Meggie witnesses her father reading aloud for the first time, her interest in books shifts: she wants to be able to read aloud like Mo, to read so eloquently that her voice entices characters from their texts, even though she knows Mo will not approve because his skill has cost him Resa. Meggie does not possess this same fear and, since she was just three at the time her mother was read into *Inkheart*, she does not feel the loss of Resa as acutely as

Mo does — particularly since "there were hardly any mothers in her favorite stories" and fairy tales primarily featured "wicked stepmothers" (285). Like Mo, however, Meggie's newly-developed reading skill leads to trouble, for Capricorn learns of her ability and decides to use her to read out the Shadow since Mo has escaped. While she is imprisoned with Fenoglio, Meggie starts to understand the problem of removing characters from books, for she reads out Tinker Bell and the Steadfast Tin Soldier, both of whom fare poorly in the new world, particularly Tinker Bell, who is captured by Basta. Meggie feels shame for "luring this fragile little creature out of her book" (370). The Steadfast Tin Soldier has a slightly better fate because Fenoglio experiments with Meggie's reading abilities by rewriting part of the soldier's story, which allows Meggie to return him to his rightful place, something none of the other readers presented in *Inkheart* can do. The action foreshadows the changing role of reading aloud, of reshaping stories, that occurs later in the series. At the end of *Inkheart*, when Meggie is reading Fenoglio's passage to kill Capricorn and his henchmen, her innocence comes to the fore, for she is unable to complete reading the passage that will kill the others and it falls to Mo, who has come to rescue her, to complete the reading. At the conclusion of *Inkheart*, Meggie, Mo, Resa, and Elinor return to Elinor's home and to their safe, individual reading. Meggie has decided on her future vocation: "She wanted to learn to make up stories like Fenoglio. She wanted to learn to fish for words so that she could read aloud to her mother without worrying about who might come out of the stories and look at her with homesick eyes. So Meggie decided words would be her trade.... As Mo had said: writing stories had a kind of magic, too" (534).

This plan, however, does not materialize, and in *Inkspell*, Meggie, still an avid reader at the start, has become obsessed with Inkworld, though she has never read the entire novel, Dustfinger having stolen it at the end of *Inkheart* before she could read it all. Her writing consists of notebooks full of descriptions of Inkworld garnered from Resa's stories of living there, and Meggie, along with Elinor, develops a desire to experience Inkworld in person as her mother did. When Farid arrives on their doorstep after Orpheus has read Dustfinger back into Inkworld without him, he begs Meggie to read the passage he has stolen from Orpheus so that he can join Dustfinger. Meggie agrees, but only if she can go as well, though neither knows if she will be able to transport herself into the story, as the reader usually cannot travel with others. In preparation for the trip, Meggie packs numerous items, including one book, "a collection of stories set near the lake that lay close to Elinor's house. That way she would be taking a little bit of home with her — for Elinor's house was her home now, more than anywhere else had been. And who knew, maybe Fenoglio would be able to use the words in it to write her back again, back into her own story" (98). However, not long after her arrival in Inkworld, Meggie tries reading the book, but "she couldn't get past the first page, and had finally forgotten the book and left it lying as she sat beside a stream with swarms of blue fairies hovering over it. Did your hunger for stories die down when you were in one yourself? Or had she just been too exhausted?" (150). Within just a couple of days of being in Inkworld, Meggie has left her most potent connection to her world behind, abandoning both her single book and her best means of finding a return to her parents and Elinor. Though she wonders at her lack of interest in the stories, she never thinks again of the abandoned book, even at moments when she longs to return to her world. She does keep the blank notebook Mo has made her, but even that does not move her, for she puts off her plan to record her experiences in Inkworld. To a great extent, she has rejected books, the very things she treasured most in her world.

As *Inkspell* progresses, Meggie varies between enjoying Inkworld to the exclusion of everything else and feeling homesick. She has a chance to visit the Castle of Ombra's library and see the illuminated manuscripts collected there, though she is not afforded a chance to read them. Reading in Inkworld for Meggie becomes about necessity rather than pleasure; she reads passages Fenoglio writes to save her father from death and to make changes to Inkworld that Fenoglio desires, though she is often skeptical about these changes. Reading becomes a practical matter. Pleasure in stories now comes from oral rather than written tales[10] and in Meggie's experiences, which she attributes to Fenoglio: "With every new day his story was spinning a magic spell around her heart, sticky as spiders' webs, and enchantingly beautiful too" (238). Though painfully real at times, Inkworld is a story to Meggie for much of *Inkspell* rather than just another world, and she embraces this story, not wanting to "play our old game" with Mo and "imagine we're in another story" (519). Inkworld is her story of choice now. Though at the end of *Inkspell*, after Mo and Resa have escaped from the Adderhead and Dustfinger dies by exchanging his life for Farid's, Meggie tells Mo, "I want to go home," Mo's knowing response "No, you don't" is accurate (603), for Meggie, like her parents, loves Inkworld and wants to return home only in moments of tragedy or horror.

The final book of the series, *Inkdeath*, continues this trend. Afraid for her father's safety, Meggie tries to convince Mo to return to their world, where he is not an outlaw with a price on his head. As in *Inkspell*, Meggie's experience with reading in *Inkdeath* largely revolves around the practical: she reads Fenoglio's words to save the Black Prince, to find shelter for the children of

Ombra, and to protect her father. Words are a tool rather than a joy, and so it remains for the duration of the novel. At the end of *Inkdeath*, Meggie has fully accepted her place in Inkworld, having fallen in love with Doria, about whom, Fenoglio tells her, he wrote a short story: "He builds castles and city walls. He even invents a flying machine, a clock to measure time, and ... a printing machine for a famous bookbinder" (488). Fenoglio further informs Meggie, "It gets even better! This Doria has a wife who is said to be from a distant land, and she often gives him his ideas in the first place" (488). This story about an older Doria, like Fenoglio's Bluejay stories, calls into question how much choice Meggie actually has regarding her role in Inkworld. Has she arrived just to fulfill the role as Doria's future wife? Was her arrival in Inkworld thus inevitable? There is no clear answer to these questions, and unlike Mo, who rejects the Bluejay role at the end of the series, at least on the surface, Meggie is not shown questioning her place in Inkworld. What is clear is that Meggie and her family remain in Inkworld, eschewing the chance to return home and embracing Inkworld and its lack of books. Like Seth and Justin in *Malice*, Meggie and her family do not complete the home/away/home structure common to children's literature at the conclusion of *Inkdeath*, a marked difference from the first book in the series, which is a clear home/away/home story. Though Mo remains a bookbinder and literacy still exists for a very few in Inkworld, by choosing to remain in this world where orality dominates, Meggie, Mo, Resa, Elinor, and Fenoglio are essentially rejecting books and literacy for living.

There is an argument to be made that the Folchart family and Fenoglio are lost in a book, in the beauty of a story, and that this experience is positive because early in the series being lost in a book was the goal of a positive reading experience. However, given the increasingly negative portrayal of characters — particularly Elinor and Violante — who are voracious readers, as well as the knowledge that the Folcharts have no interest in returning to their world, getting lost in a book is not a positive thing but a refusal to cope with reality, a refusal for Meggie, Mo, Resa, Elinor, and Fenoglio to live their own story. Of all the interactive books discussed in Chapter 3 and here, the *Inkheart* series has the most negative message about books, readers, and reading.

8

Living Characters and Life Behind the Scenes in *The Sylvie Cycle*

In *Rhetorics of Fantasy*, after she discusses her four classifications of fantasy, Farah Mendlesohn turns to books she calls "the irregulars": "a few works that appear to break my 'rules,' novels that do not fit comfortably into my design" (246). One of the novels she discusses is Roderick Townley's *The Great Good Thing*, the first novel of *The Sylvie Cycle*. The entire series, in fact, does not seem to fit into any of the categories Mendlesohn discusses. Similarly, it is separate from the children's fantasy examined in this book. There are no books acting as artifacts of power; there is very little movement between Sylvie's fictional world and the outside world of her Readers; and there is little focus on writer-characters. Like the *Inkheart* series and the books discussed in Chapter 3, Roderick Townley's *The Sylvie Cycle* contains characters from the real world and from the world of a book, in this case *The Great Good Thing*, a fictional small-run book published in 1917. However, by contrast with the other texts discussed, Townley's trilogy focuses on the characters from the world of the book and how they exist both when the book is closed and when it is being read. Also unlike *Inkheart*, in which characters continue to evolve beyond what is written, Sylvie and her fellow characters in *The Great Good Thing* understand that they are characters in a book, and they do not physically age. Instead, they act as they are written while they wait for their next Reader[1] to open the book, and in fact, the trilogy questions what it means for a character to be "written," exploring fate versus free will in the process. Not all Readers are viewed equally, and the trilogy frequently discusses types of Readers. While Readers play a critical role in some ways throughout the trilogy, as with the other books discussed thus far, reading itself and books — with the exception of the one in which Sylvie and her fellow characters reside —

do not play much of a role in the series. The ultimate message of *The Sylvie Cycle* does not encourage reading or a love of books. Instead, the focus is on action, in this case upon performing a "Great Good Thing."

The Workings of the Fictional World

Princess Sylvie and the other fictional characters in *The Sylvie Cycle* all live within the confines of their book, *The Great Good Thing*, a small-run book with few Readers. Their book was published in 1917, though the outside world setting is some time after 1917. The first book of the trilogy, *The Great Good Thing*, begins with a description of the lack of Readers and how Sylvie's "amazing life" is not great because "she didn't get to live it very often" (1). Characters are aware that they live in a book, and the narrative makes reference to their navigation through the text, as when

> Sylvie disappeared in the direction of page 6.
> She found a comfy spot on the left-hand margin beside the seventh paragraph and rested her head on "grandiloquent," the largest adjective in sight [6].

Later in the book, the illustrations are also referenced (23). When Readers open the book, the characters, who roam freely when it is closed, must rush to the page the Reader has chosen and must begin performing the story for the Reader. These performances resemble live dramatic performances, and any miscue or other problem the characters have is perceptible to the Reader. Thus, when Sylvie rushes late to a scene, hurries her dialog, and knocks over a suit of armor when a new Reader, Claire, starts the book (10), Claire believes this action belongs in the story and later searches in vain for the "funny part" (19). Because Sylvie and the others rarely make errors of this sort, however, Claire never finds the funny part again.

In *Into the Labyrinth*, the second book of the trilogy, *The Great Good Thing* has been republished and becomes popular. The fictional characters, used to few Readers, must adjust to an onslaught of new Readers and each time an edition of the book opens, they race to their places to perform, soon becoming run off their feet from the number of performances they must do. Then the book is uploaded to the internet, and the characters must adjust to new ways of moving through the story.[2] Whereas they could walk across pages in the print versions, in the online version, they must walk down the page as the Reader scrolls through the text. Because the book is now both in print and online, characters must also move between the two media, and their performances, especially online, are problematic until they adjust to the different formats. Later in *Into the Labyrinth*, a virus enters their book and affects the story: from altering words to eating chunks of text to inserting characters from other books — notably Benjamin Gunn from *Treasure Island* and the Tin Woodman from *The Wonderful Wizard of Oz*. All of these problems affect the characters' reality, which is based on the text. Thus when small *d*s are removed from a passage, the queen changes into an ear when the king's endearment *dear* becomes *ear*, and a fog enters the text when *midst* becomes *mist*.

In addition to the medium affecting characters' performances, external, Reader-based elements can affect the characters. The first Reader presented in the trilogy, for example, Ricky, drops "a gob of strawberry jam" into the book "just two words in front of Sylvie, spattering her blue shoes" (*Great* 4) and disrupting the flow of the story. Then without cleaning off the jam, he closes the book and throws it, flinging all the characters about. Claire, Ricky's sister, later scares the characters when she cleans off the jam and "then began looking for where she'd left off. That took a while. It always takes Readers time when the characters aren't where they belong" (15). Further, the pace at which a Reader reads affects performances. When *The Great Good Thing* is first becoming popular again in *Into the Labyrinth*, an overview of the pacing of the reading is given:

> It started with a librarian in Cleveland reading through most of Part One faster than Sylvie had ever known Readers could read. Whoever librarians were, they sure could zip through a book! The characters kept up as best they could, but the king's knights were sweating as they raced around in heavy armor pursuing Riggeloff [the fictional story's villain] and his thieves. In the midst of this madness, a very young girl in Maine opened the book with soft fingers and began sounding out the words of Chapter One: "'Father,' said Princess Sylvie, 'I cannot marry Prince Rig. Rigga.' Mommy, what's this word?" [12].

While the characters' performances determine content, Readers determine pacing. Other places where the external world affects the characters in the story include when the computer virus is introduced to the online version of the story in *Into the Labyrinth* and in *The Constellation of Sylvie*, the final book of the trilogy, when the space craft on which *The Great Good Thing* has been placed takes off, forcing the characters to learn to cope with no gravity. Further, when the book is flung across one of Jupiter's moons in *The Constellation of Sylvie*, the characters must cope with extreme cold. Laurel, the Author of the story, who is made into a character in *The Great Good Thing*, explains the "different realities" of Readers and characters: characters "don't eat Reader food or breathe Reader air," but "because the book gets cold," the characters feel the external cold as well (*Constellation* 108).

The most dramatic external effect of *The Great Good Thing*, however, occurs in the first book of the trilogy when Claire's brother Ricky sets fire to the book, destroying it and the safe, unchanging home Sylvie and the other characters have known. They survive only in Claire's mind, which they can enter thanks to Sylvie's previous forays into Claire's dreams. Their experiences in Claire's mind are different from those in their book, for they perform only when Claire is thinking of them, and then without the written script they are used to. As Claire ages, she gradually outgrows the story, forcing the characters to retreat further into her mind with other neglected memories. When Claire is trying to recall the story for her daughter, the physical separation between character and Reader vanishes for the first time, for, in an attempt to save the story, the girl with the dark blue eyes — revealed as Laurel, the Author, in *Into the Labyrinth*— escorts Sylvie out of Claire's mind and into her home. Though Claire cannot see Sylvie because, as Laurel explains, Sylvie doesn't exist "out here," out of her book, Claire can hear Sylvie "if she's very quiet" (*Great* 129). Sylvie is able to tell Claire the entire story, which Claire repeats to her daughter Lily. Later in *The Great Good Thing*, Sylvie again leaves Claire's mind and returns to her home where Claire is on her deathbed. Sylvie aids Lily, now an adult, as she did Claire, allowing Lily to tell the story to her mother. Once Lily falls asleep, Sylvie waits for a chance to enter Lily's mind, hoping to reestablish the story there. She is successful beyond her hopes, for Lily records the story and it is republished, leading to the events of *Into the Labyrinth*. These non-book interactions with characters are done to keep the story alive, and the only other time Sylvie exits her realm is in *The Constellation of Sylvie* when she enters Wink's mind to ease his death.[3]

Something Sylvie discovers during her interactions with Laurel, Claire and Lily is the difference between being a storybook character and a Reader. When she is first in Claire's mind, she learns that Readers do not know how their story will end (*Great* 31). Mendlesohn notes of this event that Sylvie's "realization that the Reader (Claire) doesn't know [how her story ends] ... destabilizes Sylvie's understanding of her own world. Even though Sylvie has been aware of how her world works, she has not been aware that its workings are specific to itself" (256–7). It is a difficult concept for Sylvie to grasp. In addition, when she sees Claire in her first foray outside Claire's mind, she believes Claire is disguised, for now she is "a large, comfortable-looking lady" rather than the little girl she knew (*Great* 127). Still later, she believes Claire is wearing a different disguise when she is an elderly woman. Because Sylvie does not age, she has difficulty understanding the concept of aging, even when Laurel explains Readers: "They start little, then they get big, then they disappear" (179–80). Even when she does start to understand death, she is unimpressed: "Personally, Sylvie didn't see the point of it [dying]. In her story, the villains might be turned into crickets and eaten by the owl, but they were fine again when the next Reader opened the book" (198–9). Sylvie has similar difficulties throughout the trilogy with concepts unfamiliar to someone from "the Middle Ages" (*Constellation* 8), and she must rely on Laurel, Fangl, and Rosetta, all of whom originate in the real world before being written into the new edition of the book by Lily, to explain modern concepts.

The characters too can interfere (or attempt to) with the story. In *The Constellation of Sylvie*, Pingree the Jester attempts to blackmail Sylvie into marriage by stealing the three helper animals. Sylvie fears their loss because they play a substantial role in parts of the story and without them the story cannot function. Fortunately, the primary Reader of *The Great Good Thing* in *The Constellation of Sylvie*, the astronaut Kara, does not read the book completely during the animals' absence. Also during *The Constellation of Sylvie*, the characters, who have grown fond of Kara and Matt, the other sympathetic astronaut, use their book to aid the astronauts twice: once when their air is failing and again when that same air dramatically reverses the astronauts' age. In both cases, the characters of *The Great Good Thing*, led by Sylvie and her tutor Fangl, who has figured out the problems, physically rearrange the text in their book to give messages to the astronauts. The result is a message amid garbled text. The first message reads, "'**breathe moon water**,' cried Sylvie. 'ind ve cninud icss **Sylvi I a ae f is**'" (115). Though Kara at first thinks she is going crazy, focusing on the garbled part only, almost immediately she returns to the message and implements the suggestion to save her and the other astronauts. The second message, occurring after the air they have been breathing has reduced their ages significantly and has in fact killed Wink, the third, antagonistic, and youngest astronaut, also brings results, and both Kara and Matt think "it's a message from God" (157) saving them. Though attributing the message to God, Kara and Matt treasure *The Great Good Thing*, to the point that they have a passage read at their world-televised wedding ceremony, leading Laurel to comment, "I have a feeling ... that our book is going to be popular again" (191).

Fate Versus Free Will and "Written" Characters

Because Sylvie and the others in *The Great Good Thing* are fictional, written by someone else, one of the focuses of *The Sylvie Cycle* is how much they are limited by the way in which they are written and whether they have free will. Also prevalent in the *Harry Potter* and *Inkheart* series, as well as other children's fantasy series discussed, the exploration of fate versus free will is particularly noticeable in Princess Sylvie's character, but it is a factor for many of the secondary characters as well. Sylvie's mother, Queen Emmeline, for example, does not adapt well to changes, whether they are being in Claire's mind, adapting to the internet version of *The Great Good Thing*, dealing with a flood of new readers, or seeing the night sky in *The Constellation of Sylvie*. As the queen tells Sylvie at the beginning of *Into the Labyrinth*, when they are dealing with a massive readership, "a queen likes to sit on her throne and reign, not scamper about like a ... like a ... whatnot!" (9). Though the way the queen is written is not mentioned directly, her reactions to changes show that she is not adaptable. Other characters' personalities are more overtly referenced. Pingree the jester, for example, though a character enjoyed by Readers, acts as a secondary villain in each novel of the trilogy. In *The Great Good Thing*, he ousts the king from power when the characters retreat deep into Claire's mind. In *Into the Labyrinth*, though his role is smaller, he spies on Sylvie and tries to disrupt her actions. In *The Constellation of Sylvie*, his villainy is strongest, for he steals the helper animals from the story and attempts to blackmail Sylvie into marriage, threatening to "make them [the animals] disappear. Forever" (85). When Sylvie threatens Pingree with physical injury, he calls her bluff. The ensuing discussion overtly comments on characterization:

> "Why this sudden show of bravery? You're a cowardly, lowly creature and always have been. It's the way your character is written."
> Pingree smiled. "All true, I'm afraid," he said. "But you leave out one quality that the Author gave me in abundance."
> "Ugliness?"
> "Intelligence. I suddenly realized in the midst of my cowardly squirming just now, that I had nothing to fear."
> "Do you see this knife?"
> "Yes, but I know how *your* character is written. There's not a touch of cruelty in it. You could no more cut off my nose than you would cut off your own" [87, emphasis in original].

Pingree's intelligence, given to him by the Author, does indeed allow him to understand Sylvie, for she does not harm him because it is not in her nature. Later in *The Constellation of Sylvie*, Laurel, the Author, explains Pingree as she and Sylvie travel to rescue the animals: "I thought I'd give him just a touch of greed to make him interesting.... I didn't realize that a little goes a long way" (164). This character trait written by his Author explains Pingree's actions throughout the series: he is greedy and uses every means at his disposal to get wealth when no one is reading the book. That he is also written to be intelligent helps him.

Another character who chafes at his given role in the story is Prince

Godric, though for different reasons than Pingree. Within the fictional world of *The Great Good Thing*, Prince Godric is one half of two characters, the other being the Keeper of the Cave, a villainous, disfigured, and ill-tempered man whom Sylvie transforms into Prince Godric with a kiss. Though Godric would like to believe that the Keeper of the Cave is not him, they cannot "appear on the same page together. They were like strong magnets sharing the same field. Turned one way, they repelled each other. Turned the other way, they *became* each other" (*Constellation* 137, emphasis in original). As the Keeper of the Cave, he helps Pingree hide the helper animals in *The Constellation of Sylvie* because Pingree promises him, "when he gets power, he'll change the story and let me out of here" (99). The Keeper of the Cave, like Pingree, uses the skills he was written — strength and the ability to build anything — in an attempt to change his role. However, his being the other half of Prince Godric makes success impossible, for they share a body, and though each hates the story, they are tied to it.

A different type of character from Pingree and Prince Godric/the Keeper of the Cave is Rosetta Stein. Introduced into the trilogy in *Into the Labyrinth*, she is an addition to *The Great Good Thing* placed in the book at Sylvie's request. Lily the Writer adds Rosetta, a yoga instructor in the real world, to help the overworked characters cope with their stress, but Rosetta herself has difficulty coping with her new setting. She is written in as a shepherdess but retains her knowledge of the outside world, including her belief that all people are equal. As a result, she does not like the way that Pringe Riggeloff treats her or think it acceptable behavior. The ensuing conversation between Sylvie and Rosetta articulates the fate versus free will issue well:

"I didn't care for the way he spoke to me."
"I can't believe Prince Godric would speak to you disrespectfully."
"No," Rosetta said, "the other prince."
"Oh!" Sylvie smiled. "You have to remember Riggeloff's just behaving the way his character is written."
"He was insulting."
"He's got nobility in him, too, but he can be very bad. He *has* to be bad."
"I keep forgetting," said Rosetta recklessly, "I'm not out in the real world where people have free will" [70, emphasis in original].

Though Rosetta eventually adapts to *The Great Good Thing*, she struggles with her new role and the belief that the characters, including her now, do not have free will. Because the characters are "written" certain ways, they cannot have free will from Rosetta's perspective.

How much of Sylvie's and other characters' actions are their own and how much they are written, determined by how the Author shaped her characters as she wrote *The Great Good Thing*, is debatable. Claudia Nelson, in her article "Writing the Reader: The Literary Child in and beyond the Book," believes that "Sylvie in *The Great Good Thing* is admirable not because the original author wrote her that way but because she has written *herself* that way" (234, emphasis in original).[4] Similarly, Mendlesohn notes that when Sylvie is dictating the story to Lily in *The Great Good Thing*, "Sylvie is *writing her own world*" (259, emphasis in original). In fact, she is rewriting it, for she adds characters to the story — Laurel and Fangl. At one point in *The Constellation of Sylvie*, when Laurel and Sylvie argue over whether Sylvie should risk herself to relieve Wink's suffering, Sylvie tells Laurel, "It's the way I was written. You of all people should know this" (141).[5] Sylvie attributes her actions here, and in previous books, to the way Laurel created her: she is a brave and active heroine who must do great good things, whether they are in the world of *The Great Good Thing* or in the external world saving her story or easing Wink's suffering. Much like the characters in *Inkheart*, characters in *The Great Good Thing* have traits given to them by the Author, but these traits, while shaping personalities, do not necessarily determine actions, though they may predispose characters to acting certain ways. Thus in *The Constellation of Sylvie*, when Sylvie longs to explore the universe like Kara, Fangl observes, "You were written to do great good things, not watch other people do them" (45). Though he understands her anxiety, he tells her, "You're the heroine of your story, Princess. You have to let this young woman be the heroine of hers" (45). Sylvie chafes at her observer role in Kara's life because her personality, as written by Laurel, demands *she* be the heroine. Yet Laurel downplays her role as Author at times — though she dislikes the adjustments Sylvie and Lily have made to her story when it is republished. When she reveals that she is the Author, she tells Sylvie, "I always felt this book was a gift. It came to me somehow, and I just wrote it down" (*Labyrinth* 171). She, like Fenoglio in *Inkheart*, has limited control over her characters once she has written them. They are shaped by her descriptions, but have freedom to choose subsequent actions and do so, even when their Author disapproves.

Imaginative Readers and Hostile Readers

In each book in *The Sylvie Cycle*, the fictional characters and their story come under threat from Readers who do not appreciate imaginative literature, and in each novel the characters overcome the threat. Claudia Nelson comments that Townley's novel *The Great Good Thing* "identifies readers ready to internalize story as fundamentally different from readers hostile to the world of imagination" (229). In *The Great Good Thing*, the "hostile" Reader Ricky contrasts greatly with his sister Claire, who is eager to "internalize [the] story." Ricky, the first Reader introduced, earns the characters' ire by dropping jam in the book and, calling it a "dumb story," throwing the book across the room. His mistreatment of the book leads to a conversation among the characters, who long for a "real Reader," one who will "[pay] attention" to the performance (5). Even the potential escape from the boredom of being unread cannot make up for an inattentive, unappreciative, and destructive Reader. While Ricky has no interest in the imaginative story in the fictional *The Great Good Thing*, Claire loves the book and returns to reread it often. She enjoys the book so much that she begins to dream about it, which allows Sylvie to move from the pages of *The Great Good Thing* to Claire's mind during Claire's dreams, something the other characters frown upon. However, Sylvie's illicit forays into Claire's mind become important when Ricky burns the book in an attempt to make the pages look old (21). The destruction of the book would have meant the end of Sylvie and the other characters had not Claire internalized the story, and they are all able to enter Claire's mind after the fire. In *The Great Good Thing*, the hostile Reader represents the destruction of the book while the imaginative Reader is its salvation.

This theme continues in *Into the Labyrinth*. Though there is not a single focal imaginative Reader in this novel, because the book is so popular, imaginative Readers abound, keeping Sylvie and the other characters busy. The threat to *The Great Good Thing* comes again in the form of a hostile reader, this time Ricky's grandson, also named Ricky, who seems to have inherited his grandfather's malevolence. Though it is unclear if Ricky has actually read *The Great Good Thing*, he is responsible for launching the computer virus that threatens *The Great Good Thing*, and his hostility is extreme. When the virus fails, he has a temper tantrum that escalates when his parents order him to visit with Aunt Lily and stay off his father's computer. He is so enraged that he "brought back his booted foot, and gave the computer a tremendous kick" (242). This Ricky's behavior is more extreme than his grandfather's, for while the first Ricky did not mean to destroy *The Great Good Thing*, this Ricky clearly does.

The third book of the trilogy again contrasts an imaginative and a hostile Reader. The reading relationship between Kara and Wink in *The Constellation of Sylvie* parallels the relationship between Claire and Ricky in *The Great Good Thing*. *The Great Good Thing* ends up on a space ship heading for Jupiter when the President's daughter, who loves the now-out-of-print book, replaces Einstein's *Special Theory of Relativity* with it in the capsule set to be placed on one of Jupiter's moons. Kara discovers the shift when she opens the capsule planning to reread the Einstein's book for "fun" (20). She is delighted to have something fictional to read, despite the disdain Wink shows for it, calling it "just a silly kids' book" (21) and labeling Einstein "the greatest storyteller who ever lived" (27). Wink poses as great a threat to *The Great Good Thing* as Ricky in the first book does, for he steals it from Kara, threatening to throw it out the compactor; tosses it onto the surface of Jupiter's moon; and then rips a page from it. After each of these actions, Kara, now an adored Reader, rescues the book. Though she is a scientist, she retains a love of imaginative stories that Wink does not, and her enthusiasm for the story wins the affection of the fictional characters.

As with the other books in the trilogy, *The Constellation of Sylvie* displays a marked contrast between imaginative and hostile Readers. In each book, the hostility is seen as unnatural, and all three antagonistic Readers seem to have something wrong with them that contributes to their dislike of imaginative fiction: Ricky in *The Great Good Thing*, a generally unlikable character, is constantly playing with matches; Ricky in *Into the Labyrinth*, though a less prominent character, clearly has significant problems controlling his temper; and Wink in *The Constellation of Sylvie* has "late-onset bipolar disorder" (59). The implication of these personality problems is that normal people, people without these problems, would never think to harm or reject an imaginative book. Reading imaginative stories is thus considered a normal pastime to be encouraged in the trilogy, even though none of the fictional characters is portrayed as a Reader. Laurel, the Author, is also the first Reader, though she is never shown reading in the trilogy. Fangl, Claire's old geometry teacher who is written into *The Great Good Thing* by Lily (via Sylvie, who wants to save his memory) is the closest to a Reader among the fictional characters, though he is more often shown writing ideas down than reading.

The Role of Reading

While there is some focus on imaginative and hostile Readers in *The Sylvie Cycle*, the trilogy does not, in fact, promote reading or books. Instead, the focus of the trilogy is on action. Though Sylvie and the other characters in both *The Great Good Thing* and *The Constellation of Sylvie* appreciate imaginative Readers, they want them only to escape the boredom of not performing. When the book is popular in *Into the Labyrinth*, Readers are more of a burden than a blessing. There is no balance. Sylvie herself, though literate, is not a reader, no doubt in part because of her story being set in the Middle Ages. Rather, she is a character of action, striving to complete great good things in her story and out of it. Reading plays no role in these actions. As a result, the reader sees Sylvie in *The Great Good Thing* save her story by venturing into the real world and telling it first to Claire and then to Lily. In *Into the Labyrinth*, she saves the electronic version of her story by venturing into the internet and destroying a computer virus. And in *The Constellation of Sylvie*, she saves Kara and Matt, with the help of other characters, which in turn saves her story. *The Constellation of Sylvie* offers the most book-based action since she and others rearrange the physical makeup of the story to send a message to astronauts.

Reading is important for passing on the story, yet even that importance is tempered by the idea that Readers do not actually read: "The truth is, no one reads a story; one *overhears* it; and if the characters aren't there, living and suffering on the page before you, nothing make sense" (*Labyrinth* 67–8, emphasis in original). Though this quote is focusing on problems Sylvie and the others have keeping up with Readers early in *Into the Labyrinth*, the idea that Readers do not read but overhear calls into question the role of reading in the trilogy. While it could make readers of *The Sylvie Cycle* rethink how they view reading in a positive sense — reading is really overhearing performers and catching the nuances of each performance — the passage also underscores the secondary nature of reading in the trilogy. The characters seem more like the toys in *Toy Story* and its sequels, desperately trying to get their owners to play with them and give their life meaning. They want to survive, and to do so, Sylvie and the characters must pass the story on. Their good Readers, Claire, Lily, Kara, and Matt, help them live. The hostile Readers find no redemption, the most extreme case being Wink's death in *The Constellation of Sylvie*. Further, both Claire and Kara, the two primary good Readers, like Sylvie, long to do great good things of their own, and both accomplish it in their own way. For Claire, keeping the story alive is her great good thing, while for Kara, it is her space exploration, though she will also be better known to the characters of *The Great Good Thing* for her help keeping the story alive. They keep it alive via word of mouth, much like Bastian in *The Neverending Story* does at the end of that novel. Despite *The Sylvie Cycle*'s presentation of life behind the scenes of a fictional book, reading itself isn't key. *Story* and the passage of story is, and these are done through action rather than reading.

Conclusion

Didacticism and subversion. Reading and experience. Authority and self-sufficiency.

All of the children's and young adult fantasy discussed in this book contain these elements. While the balanced framework that Perry Nodelman references when he speaks of the current critics' belief that "ideally, children's literature ought to teach without seeming to do so" (158) appears to some degree in each text, the didactic element is not always what might be expected in children's literature prominently featuring books and reading. Far from books being, to use Joe Sutliff Sanders's descriptions, "ennobling" and "safe" with "the reader-book bond [being] sacrosanct" (351), often they are frightening, dangerous, and subject to intense scrutiny and even outright rejection. In addition, books can even be used by young protagonists to manipulate the very authority figures that the books represent, not necessarily an "ennobling" use of books. Even the most avid of youthful readers—Ella from *Ella Enchanted*, Claire from *The Morganville Vampires*, Meggie from *Inkheart*, and Hermione from *Harry Potter*—move away from books as their stories develop and they mature. Though all four of these characters retain a fondness for books and continue to use them, particularly in Claire and Hermione's cases, books move from being central to their identities to secondary. Furthermore, the more ambivalent and reluctant readers featured in the children's fantasy discussed here are often even more eager to distance themselves from books. Harry and Ron in *Harry Potter*, Devin and Frankie in *Cracked Classics*, and Henry in *Faerie Wars* never embrace books, and even the positive experiences that Devin and Frankie have with their entrance into classic literature do not make them avid readers. Other characters who embrace books learn to be wary of them because of the dangers they pose. Such is the case with the Grace children in *The Spiderwick Chronicles*, Sophie and Josh in *The Secrets of the Immortal Nicholas Flamel*, and Seth and Kady (among many others) in

Malice. Other characters such as Harold and George in *Captain Underpants* and Artemis in *Artemis Fowl* use books to manipulate authority figures.

Since books represent adult authority, these different presentations of books in children's fantasy are subversive to varying degrees. The reader-book bond is certainly not "sacrosanct" in many of the children's fantasy novels discussed (*Libyrinth* is the primary exception), and in books and series in which the bond does seem sacrosanct (*Artemis Fowl, Septimus Heap*, and *Captain Underpants* to a lesser extent), the books are used either to manipulate authority figures and/or as a direct response to being forbidden to read a book—certainly subversive actions. Yet though the presentation of books may be subversive in children's fantasy, the novels themselves remain didactic in other ways. From realizing the importance of family (*Artemis Fowl, The Spiderwick Chronicles, Beyond the Spiderwick Chronicles*), to learning to overcome one's fears (*The Pagemaster, The Neverending Story*), to learning to question authority (*The Secrets of the Immortal Nicholas Flamel, Harry Potter, Libyrinth, The Secret Circle*), these children's and young adult fantasies contain lessons for their young protagonists and readers. The message that dominates, however, is that experience matters more than books and reading. Only when the young characters step beyond the protection of adult authority can they make their own decisions. These decisions will naturally be influenced by what the characters have already learned from adults, but until they proceed on their own, until they make their own mistakes, the characters cannot truly learn. The children who step outside the realm of adult authority, whether that authority is represented by a person or a book, must learn to fend for themselves and negotiate the world of adults without guides. Perhaps the ultimate message of these children's fantasy novels is that adult authority—whether personal or represented by books—can take children and young adults only so far. Eventually they need to explore beyond the safety of school and books and, using the knowledge they have gained from adults, learn to be self-sufficient.

This message ultimately matters far more than any message about the importance of books and reading, for if children cannot learn self-sufficiency, they cannot transition successfully to adulthood. As Jeanne Murray Walker notes, "adulthood is the valued goal" of the children's fantasy protagonist (73). Children cannot reach this goal if they blindly rely on books, if they remain forever lost in a book.

Chapter Notes

Chapter 1

1. Dominant elements of literature (or art or linguistics) are called *unmarked*; non-dominant elements are *marked*. For a fuller discussion of markedness in children's literature, see my article "Junie B. Jones and the Language Police: Language Attitudes and the Marked Child Narrator."

2. Exceptions to closure are more apt to happen at the end of a novel that is part of a series. For example, the first novel of *The Morganville Vampires* series ends with one of the characters in the midst of being stabbed. Even the early *Harry Potter* novels do not have full closure, for the main threat, Voldemort, is always a presence until his final defeat in *Harry Potter and the Deathly Hallows*.

3. The argument over what constitutes not just quality fantasy but quality children's literature is a major issue in children's literature studies, particularly as it relates to encouraging and engaging young readers.

Chapter 2

1. Mandy refuses to use "big magic" to help Ella, particularly at the end of the novel when Ella is planning to go to the balls in honor of Prince Char, because using big magic can have unexpected consequences, as with the gift of obedience that Ella receives from Lucinda at the start of the novel — and that leads to much of the trouble Ella encounters in the novel.

2. References to Magyk in the *Septimus Heap* series, whether it is the word *Magyk* itself or to aspects of Magyk, are presented in a different font from the rest of the text in the series and are represented here by bolding the words presented in the different font in direct quotes.

3. Writing in the *Septimus Heap* series is as important as reading, and there are several notable diaries presented throughout the series: Septimus's; Marcellus Pye's in *Physik*; Princess Esmeralda's in *Physik*; Syrah Syara's in *Syren*. In addition, letter writing and other types of written messages are referenced frequently in the series.

4. Notable near-sentient objects include the door into the Heaps' old room and the door to the ExtraOrdinary Wizard's chamber, both of which open more easily for some characters than others and that can bar unpleasant people from entering. Similarly, the floor of the Wizard Tower writes messages to different characters as they enter the building.

5. The rest of the series does not focus on the book, though there is always a code at the bottom of the pages for the reader to decrypt. Most of the series is more focused on technologies than on books and reading. The first novel itself, however, is presented as if it is a report filed by one of the fairies brought in to psychoanalyze Artemis.

6. This contrast of book learning (Nick) and idealizing (Laurie) compares in some ways to Mary Pope Osborne's *The Magic Tree House* series in which Jack is very concerned about planning and having all the facts from books on hand before acting while his sister Annie prefers to jump into the fray and explore the worlds to which the books in the tree house take them.

7. Danu Talis is Scott's representation of Atlantis.

8. Some of the Immortals besides the Flamels and John Dee that Sophie and Josh encounter are Joan of Arc, Shakespeare, Billy the Kid, Niten (Miyamoto Musashi), Palamedes (the Saracen Knight), Black Hawk, and Virgina Dare. Elders include Hekate, Mars Altor (Huitzilopochtli), Anubis, Bastet, Aten, Odin, Hel, and Prometheus. Children of the Elders born after the fall of Danu Talis, such as Scathach and her twin Aoife, are called the Next Generation. Prior to the Elders were

beings called Great Elders, Archons, and Earthlords.

9. Both Josh and Sophie, as well as other characters, also frequently reference popular culture, particularly films, in the series. Josh uses the opening five notes to the theme of *Close Encounters of the Third Kind* as the trigger whistle for his air magic. Billy the Kid and Machiavelli discuss the "red shirts" in *Star Trek* at one point in *The Enchantress*, with Billy revealing that Black Hawk (another Immortal) is a true Trekkie and Machiavelli acknowledging that he prefers *Star Wars*.

10. They can, however, read photographs of the pages in the book (*Glass Houses* 190).

11. This ability is explained at the end of the novel when she discovers the bodies of her parents, who became lost in the Libyrinth and died there. Nod, one of the imps who live amid the books and help clean and maintain the Libyrinth, "gave her some of Nod's own code. That made her strong. Nod surrounded her, kept her warm, fed her on Nod's own bodies so she would grow and live, and hear the stories and then tell them to Nod. When she got big enough, Nod took her to the crèche" (290).

12. When Gyneth first sees printed type, he believes he will go blind, for that is what he has been taught.

13. *Libyrinth* is the first novel in the *Libyrinth* trilogy. The other two novels, *The Boy from Ilysies* and *The Book of the Night*, shift focus from books as artifacts of power to an exploration of gender roles as well as how the characters' world was created.

Chapter 3

1. Pantaleo sees the metafictive elements as instructive for young readers: "Child's text, like other postmodern picture books with metafictive devices, contributes to readers' visual literacy competence, literary understanding, and literary development" (36).

2. The font used to represent The Lack's speech in the text differs from the standard font of the rest of the novel. Each of the Six, including Tall Jake, has a different font to represent his/her speech.

3. None of them has memory loss following this departure from Malice because of the way in which they depart the world.

Chapter 4

1. The remaining novels do not clearly indicate consonant self-narration, though given that the narrative style is similar in all five novels, it seems likely they are also consonant self-narrations.

2. Other examples include transitional tags like "now" (cf. *Sea* 25, 70, 98, 170, 210, 212; *Titan's* 99, 129, 150, 216, 254; *Last* 5, 31) and "anyway" (cf. *Titan's* 83; *Battle* 216), and addresses to the reader such as "imagine" (cf. *Lightning* 300; *Last* 135) and "believe me" (cf. *Battle* 242, 254, 256).

3. Riordan's follow-up series to *Percy Jackson & the Olympians*, *The Heroes of Olympus* employs a more traditional third person limited narrative that moves between three different characters in the three books of the series published thus far (including Percy Jackson in the second book of the series). This different technique removes the immediacy of the first person narrative used in the first series and removes emphasis from storytelling.

4. Her difficulty with reading sets her apart from other bookish female sidekicks such as Hermione Granger in the *Harry Potter* series, though the parallels between the three main characters in *Percy Jackson & the Olympians* (Percy, Annabeth, and Grover) to those in *Harry Potter* (Harry, Hermione, Ron) are undeniable, and in fact led one group in a Children's Literature class that I taught to argue that Harry Potter was the main character of *The Lightning Thief*. Riordan, at the end of *The Lightning Thief*, makes a veiled reference to *Harry Potter*: the security guard at the Empire State Building is reading "a huge book with a picture of a wizard on the front" (336). Percy also notes that "I wasn't much into fantasy" (336), another way in which he ties his narrative to reality. In *The Last Olympian*, the final book of the series, the guard is reading "a big black book with a flower on the cover" (144), an oblique reference to *New Moon* from the *Twilight Saga*.

5. They do, however, remark on how startling it was for them to discover that gods and magic are real and that they are descended from the pharaohs of Egypt and that their parents were magicians (cf. *Red* 4–5, 15, 60, 71–2).

6. There is a reference at the end of Sadie's narrative of a possible run-in with other magics and gods, hinting at a crossover with Riordan's other series.

7. The Secrets series also engages the reader like this, but the emphasis on that series is the fictional nature, and the creation of fiction, rather than the reality of the situation.

8. The use of brackets is consistent in *The Red Pyramid*, where they are used only for exchanges between Sadie and Carter that don't relate to the main narrative but often focus on storytelling. However, in *The Throne of Fire*,

the brackets, while usually used for exchanges between Sadie and Carter, also are sometimes used for addresses to the implied listener. Further, in *The Throne of Fire*, exchanges between Sadie and Carter occasionally occur outside of the brackets. The usages in *The Serpent's Shadow* return to the consistency of *The Red Pyramid*.

Chapter 5

1. For a full discussion of the novel, see Chapter 2.

2. Much later in the season, Nick's death is proved false, for he returns still possessed by a demon.

3. A similar message is learned by Harry in *Harry Potter and the Half-Blood Prince* when he uses a spell against Draco Malfoy that he finds in his potions book. See Chapter 6 for a full analysis.

4. I believe one reason the series failed was that the adult characters often felt intrusive in what was billed as a series about teen witches. By contrast, the teens dominate the action in *The Vampire Diaries*, the CW's successful counterpart to *The Secret Circle*, and adults play a very secondary role.

5. Like *The Secret Circle*, *Buffy the Vampire Slayer*'s audience is broader than young adults. It has, in fact, generated a cult following among adults of all ages as well as a considerable body of academic research, including conferences such as Slayage.

6. Though there is only supposed to be one Slayer, Buffy's death at the end of season one activates Kendra as the next Slayer despite the fact that Buffy is revived a short time later.

7. There is also a chapter book adapted from the film by Jordan Horowitz.

8. The name of the land in *The Neverending Story* is changed from Fantastica in the book to Fantasia for all of the films.

9. One significant difference between the written and the film version is that in the film version, Bastian gives the Childlike Empress his mother's name, whereas in the novel, the name is of his own making.

10. In the novel, because the point of view is Bastian's alone, Mr. Coreander's reaction to the theft is never revealed, though at the end of the novel when Bastian admits to the theft—and that he has lost the book—Mr. Coreander is not upset.

11. The use of the same actor to play Mr. Coreander and the Old Man of the Wandering Mountain makes sense given that in the real world of the film Mr. Coreander acts as the keeper of *The Neverending Story* just as the Old Man of the Wandering Mountain is the keeper of *The Neverending Story* in Fantasia.

12. For example, Disney's *Cinderella*, *Snow White*, and *Sleeping Beauty* all begin with a book opening and a narrator reading the opening as the pages turn. *Beauty and the Beast* also opens with a narrative about the Beast, though the illustrations are from a stained glass window. In addition, *Shrek* opens with a book, though the opening narrative is soon subverted when it is revealed that Shrek is reading the story while using the bathroom—and that he uses pages from the book as toilet paper. Similarly, *Shrek 2* also subverts the opening narrative technique: it begins with a book opening and Prince Charming (Rupert Evert) reading his own narrative, but the prince soon discovers that Princess Fiona is "on her honeymoon" and that the big bad wolf, dressed as a grandmother, is in her place in the bed.

13. As with *The Secret Circle*, *The Vampire Diaries* is aimed at a youthful audience, though it is not limited to young adults.

14. The term *journal* is used more often than *diary* in the series despite the series name.

15. "Lost Girls" gives an abbreviated version of the passage she writes in "You're Undead to Me."

16. The use of diaries and journals is different in the written series, where Elena's diary, like *The Field Guide* in *The Spiderwick Chronicles*, is dangerous, though her diary becomes less important in the third book of the series.

17. Alaric also has his own journal, first referenced in "Bloodlines," though it does not feature prominently in the series.

18. Though Jonathan Gilbert's journal is the main family journal of the series, Logan Fell (Chris J. Johnson), another descendent of the Founding Families, makes reference to journals kept by the founding fathers and passed to children in the episode "Turning Point." To this extent, the journals, like the Books of Shadows in *The Secret Circle*, represent the authority of past generations.

19. Partway through the first season, Elena learns that she was adopted by her parents. She later learns that the man she thought of as Uncle John, her father's brother, is actually her birth father.

20. Klaus, unlike the other Original vampires, was born of a human/witch mother and a werewolf father after his mother had an affair with a werewolf. The other Original vampires had the same human father.

21. Luka tells Bonnie that males who work witchcraft prefer to be called warlocks.

22. The Lockwoods are one of the Founding Families and descended from werewolves.

23. In the world of *The Vampire Diaries*, garlic, crosses, mirrors, and holy water cannot harm vampires. Sunlight is deadly, but the prominent vampires in the series possess daylight rings — rings that have been made by a witch to protect vampires from sunlight.

24. Exceptions are a few vampires like Caroline Forbes (Candice Accola) and, at the conclusion of season three, Elena, who are turned during the series.

25. Films like *Titanic* are presented as a flashback. In *Buffy the Vampire Slayer* and its spinoff *Angel*, flashbacks are also often presented via a narrative, though they may also be part of a dream or an opening sequence to an episode.

Chapter 6

1. Earlier in the novel, when Harry is given Dudley's second bedroom, he observes that most of the toys in the room are damaged with one exception: "Other shelves were full of books. They were the only things in the room that looked as though they'd never been touched" (37–8). Dudley's lack of interest in books might be expected to be a contrast to Harry, but in fact, once Harry has the opportunity to read, he favors action over books for most of the series.

2. There has, in fact, been a backlash against this comment from many feminist critics who see Hermione's comment as more about gender than about attitudes toward education (cf. Heilman, "Blue" 224; Elster 208; Friedman 193).

3. This observation could also be read to indicate that book learning alone was not adequate to prepare Quirrell for real-life experiences. My thanks to Bianca Tredennick for her observations on this topic.

4. With the exception of History of Magic classes, which are pure lecture and traditional book learning, every other class combines reading with experience, and most of what Rowling presents for classes is the practical application: working with plants such as Mandrakes in Herbology, practicing Levitation and Summoning in Charms, changing matches into needles in Transfiguration, reading palms and tea leaves in Divination. Charles Elster's article "The Seeker of Secrets: Images of Learning, Knowing, and Schooling" explores duality in *Harry Potter*, especially the binary experiential ("real learning") and school learning, and the transcendence of that duality.

5. Schanoes argues that Hermione's fascination with (and blindness about) Lockhart stems from her relationship with books: "While Hermione, due to her intelligence and clear-sightedness, can often accurately read the situations she and her friends find themselves in ... she is without such insight within the world of *her* books. While books are the source and medium of her intellectual strength, they also form the bedrock of her knowledge, with the result that she has an extremely difficult time questioning the validity of the books themselves" (141, emphasis in original). However, as Leslee Friedman notes in "Militant Literacy: Hermione Granger, Rita Skeeter, Dolores Umbridge, and the (Mis)use of Text," "It is a mark of the fact that Hermione learns from her mistakes that by the fourth book [*Goblet of Fire*] she has learned to doubt text, to question it and adapt it to her own mean" (193).

6. His ploy works, though not as he had planned, for only Hermione makes the connection, and she keeps silent about it because Lupin is an excellent instructor. Only at the end of *Prisoner of Azkaban* does she rethink her silence, for she briefly believes that Lupin has betrayed Harry and is working with Sirius Black.

7. Though Hermione spearheads the creation of the D.A., the books in the Room of Requirement are still needed for her to fully embrace the rebellious club.

8. Each OWL, with the exception of History of Magic, has two parts: a written exam and a practical one.

9. The clearest example of Dumbledore's control of information is in his dealings with Harry. At the end of several books, most notably *Order of the Phoenix*, he tells Harry that he has kept information from him but that now that Harry is mature enough, Dumbledore will tell him everything; however, Dumbledore continues to withhold information from Harry, as Harry learns when he enters Snape's memories in *Deathly Hallows*. As Chantel M. Lavoie indicates, "Largely because of Dumbledore's circumspection, Harry labors under, and suffers because of, a number of half-truths, the other halves of which are revealed from book to book. One of the frustrations of the boy's ongoing trial (and a source of suspense for the reader) is how often a fuller comprehension of the truth might have benefited him" (84).

10. He also receives a number of letters mocking him as deluded, for many people still trust the *Daily Prophet* over *The Quibbler*. However, the article marks a critical shift in public opinion in Harry's favor.

11. In *Goblet of Fire*, there is a conversation between Dumbledore and Skeeter during which he makes reference to an article in which Skeeter called him "an obsolete dingbat" (307).

12. Early in the novel, Harry and some of his fellow students believe that Harry is the Heir of Slytherin, particularly after he reveals himself a Parselmouth, able to speak to snakes.
13. Hermione gets the idea from Voldemort's use of the Dark Mark tattoos on his Death Eaters. When Voldemort wants to call his Death Eaters, he presses his wand to the mark on one tattoo, making all of the Death Eaters' tattoos burn.
14. Many of the common jinxes students use — Jellylegs Jinx, Bat-Bogey Hex, etc. — are unlikely to be taught in school, but just as Muggle children will learn inappropriate schoolyard rhymes, so too will wizard children learn these prank jinxes.

Chapter 7

1. Hermione does have a love of knowledge, so in that respect, she has a joy of reading, particularly early in the series.
2. Nelson adapts Nicole E. Didicher's term "intrusion fantasy" for texts like *Inkheart* in which characters interact with characters they consider fictional.
3. At the time Nelson's article was published, only the first two novels in the series had been published, and the focus of her *Inkheart* analysis is on the first book in the series.
4. In *Inkheart*, for example, Dustfinger mocks Elinor for her lack of practical knowledge of snakes, saying, "Haven't you learned anything from all those clever books of yours?" (207).
5. Resa is not supposed to be transported to Inkworld (Orpheus does not include her in the passage he reads); however, she grabs hold of Mo as the passage is being read and is transported with him.
6. Shortly after writing the passage to help Mo, Fenoglio thinks, "*From now on I, and not my characters, will be telling this story again*" (*Inkspell* 337).
7. At the end of *Inkspell*, shortly after the death of Dustfinger, Fenoglio tells Meggie, "the words don't obey me anymore. Except when it suits them. They've turned against me like snakes" (306–7).
8. Meggie and Mo are a bridge of sorts between storyteller, author, and reader. They read so beautifully that they engage reader (and character), but they lack the originality of storytellers, who do not perform by rote but improvise as needed in their performances.
9. Shortly after Meggie's observations about the gate, Mo tells her that Elinor modeled the gate after a photograph in a book, though not the Selfish Giant's story (31).

10. Taddeo, a librarian at the Castle of Night, tells Meggie, "The strolling players, you see — well, they're like walking books here, where real books are so few and far between!" (551).

Chapter 8

1. Throughout the trilogy, *Reader*, *Writer*, and *Author* are treated as proper nouns.
2. The trilogy was published prior to the current proliferation of electronic readers such as Kindle and Nook, so the technology presented is web-based.
3. Though Townley is generally consistent in his separation of character and Reader worlds, there is one instance at the end of *The Great Good Thing* in which he breaks his rule of interaction. At the end of the novel, Lily opens the new edition of *The Great Good Thing* and asks Sylvie, "How do you like it?" (210). They have a brief conversation that alarms the other characters at first, for Sylvie is breaking the first rule of storybook characters — "*Never look at the Reader*" (48, emphasis in original) — as well as interacting with one, whom she introduces to the others as the Writer. Mendlesohn comments, "When Lily opens the book, it is to greet the characters and to be greeted in turn by Sylvie. The barriers between the two worlds have been *permanently* breached, and now both worlds are Real, for this moment at least" (260, emphasis in original). While this barrier breaching could be seen similar to the medium becoming invisible referenced in David Lewis's article, in fact, it feels more like a narrative inconsistency in Townley's novel, which has quite clearly established rules for how characters and Readers can interact, than evidence of a closeness between Reader and character. That closeness has existed elsewhere, most noticeably in dreams. This break in Townley's rule is one of a number of inconsistencies in the series.
4. Nelson's article examines only the first book of the trilogy, though it is applicable to all of it.
5. In *Into the Labyrinth*, Laurel knows that Sylvie is planning an expedition because "That's the way your character is written" (166). The arguments over Sylvie risking herself seem contradictory despite adding to the debate of fate versus free will. In *The Constellation of Sylvie*, Laurel tells Sylvie, "You can't die.... You're fictional" (68), yet she and Sylvie later act as if Sylvie can die when she goes to aid Wink. This contradiction is one of many inconsistencies in the trilogy.

Bibliography

Primary Children's and Young Adult Books

Abbott, Tony. *Crushing on a Capulet.* New York: Volo-Hyperion, 2003. Cracked Classics #6: Romeo and Juliet.

———. *Humbug Holiday.* New York: Volo-Hyperion, 2002. Cracked Classics #4: A Christmas Carol.

———. *Mississippi River Blues.* New York: Volo-Hyperion, 2002. Cracked Classics #2: The Adventures of Tom Sawyer.

———. *Trapped in Transylvania.* New York: Volo-Hyperion, 2002. Cracked Classics #1: Dracula.

———. *What a Trip!* New York: Volo-Hyperion, 2002. Cracked Classics #3: Around the World in Eighty Days.

———. *X Marks the Spot.* New York: Volo-Hyperion, 2002. Cracked Classics #5: Treasure Island.

Alcott, Louisa May. *Little Women.* 1868–9. Mineola, NY: Dover, 2000. Print. Dover Juvenile Classics.

Alexie, Sherman. *The Absolutely True Diary of a Part-Time Indian.* New York: Little, Brown, 2013. Print.

Atwater-Rhodes, Amelia. *Demon in My View.* 2000. The Den of Shadows Quartet. New York: Delacorte, 2009. Print.

———. *In the Forests of the Night.* 1999. The Den of Shadows Quartet. New York: Delacorte, 2009. Print.

———. *Midnight Predator.* 2002. The Den of Shadows Quartet. New York: Delacorte, 2009. Print.

———. *Shattered Mirror.* 2001. The Den of Shadows Quartet. New York: Delacorte, 2009. Print.

Baird, Alison. *The Hidden World.* New York: Puffin, 1999. Print.

Baker, Alan. *Benjamin's Book.* New York: Lothrop, 1982. Print.

Basye, Dale E. *Heck: Where Bad Kids Go.* New York: Random House, 2008. Print.

Bleddor, Frank. *The Looking Glass Wars.* New York: Dial, 2006. Print.

———. *Seeing Redd.* New York: Speak, 2007. Print. The Looking Glass Wars 2.

Bloom, Becky. *Wolf!* Illus. Pascal Biet. New York: Orchard, 1999. Print.

Blume, Judy. *Tales of a Fourth-Grade Nothing.* 1972. New York: Penguin, 2007. Print.

Bosch, Pseudonymous. *If You're Reading This, It's Too Late.* Illus. Gilbert Ford. New York: Little, Brown, 2008. Print. Secret Series Book 2.

———. *The Name of This Book Is Secret.* Illus. Gilbert Ford. New York: Little, Brown, 2007. Print. Secret Series Book 1.

———. *This Book Is Not Good for You.* Illus. Gilbert Ford. New York: Little, Brown, 2009. Print. Secret Series Book 3.

Brennan, Herbie. *Faerie Wars.* New York: Bloomsbury, 2003. Print.

Browne, Anthony. *Bear Hunt.* New York: Atheneum, 1980. Print.

Buckley, Michael. *The Sisters Grimm, Book One: The Fairy-Tale Detectives.* New York: Amulet, 2005. Print.

———. *The Sisters Grimm, Book Two: The Unusual Suspects.* New York: Amulet, 2005. Print.

_____. *The Sisters Grimm, Book Three: The Problem Child.* New York: Amulet, 2006. Print.

_____. *The Sisters Grimm, Book Four: Once Upon a Crime.* New York: Amulet, 2007. Print.

_____. *The Sisters Grimm, Book Five: Magic and Other Misdemeanors.* New York: Amulet, 2007. Print.

_____. *The Sisters Grimm, Book Six: Tales from the Hood.* New York: Amulet, 2008. Print.

_____. *The Sisters Grimm, Book Seven: The Everafter War.* New York: Amulet, 2009. Print.

_____. *The Sisters Grimm, Book Eight: The Inside Story.* New York: Amulet, 2010. Print.

Burningham, John. *Come Away from the Water, Shirley.* New York: Crowell, 1977. Print.

_____. *Mr. Grumpy's Outing.* New York: Holt, 1970. Print.

_____. *Would You Rather ...* New York: Crowell, 1978. Print.

Caine, Rachel. *Carpe Corpus.* New York: NAL Jam, 2009. Print. The Morganville Vampires Book Six.

_____. *The Dead Girls' Dance.* New York: Signet, 2007. Print. The Morganville Vampires Book Two.

_____. *Feast of Fools.* New York: Signet, 2008. Print. The Morganville Vampires Book Four.

_____. *Ghost Town.* New York: NAL, 2010. Print. The Morganville Vampires Book Nine.

_____. *Glass Houses.* New York: NAL Jam, 2006. Print. The Morganville Vampires Book One.

_____. *Lord of Misrule.* New York: NAL Jam, 2009. Print. The Morganville Vampires Book Five.

_____. *Midnight Alley.* New York: Signet, 2007. Print. The Morganville Vampires Book Three.

Carroll, Lewis. *Alice's Adventures in Wonderland.* 1897. *Alice in Wonderland.* 2nd ed. Ed. Donald J. Gray. New York: Norton, 1992. Print. Norton Critical Ed.

_____. *Through the Looking Glass.* 1897. *Alice in Wonderland.* 2nd ed. Ed. Donald J. Gray. New York: Norton, 1992. Print. Norton Critical Ed.

Child, Lauren. *Beware of Storybook Wolves.* New York: Scholastic, 2000. Print.

_____. *Who's Afraid of the Big Bad Book?* New York: Hyperion, 2002. Print.

Cleary, Beverly. *Ramona the Pest.* 1968. New York: Avon, 1992. Print.

Colfer, Eoin. *Artemis Fowl.* New York: Hyperion, 2001. Print.

Collins, Suzanne. *The Hunger Games.* New York: Scholastic, 2008. Print.

Connolly, John. *The Book of Lost Things.* New York: Simon & Schuster, 2007. Print.

Cowell, Cressida. *A Hero's Guide to Deadly Dragons.* New York: Little, Brown, 2007. Print. How to Train Your Dragon Book 6.

_____. *How to Be a Pirate.* New York: Little, Brown, 2004. Print. How to Train Your Dragon Book 2.

_____. *How to Cheat a Dragon's Curse.* New York: Little, Brown, 2006. Print. How to Train Your Dragon Book 4.

_____. *How to Ride a Dragon's Storm.* New York: Little, Brown, 2008. Print. How to Train Your Dragon Book 7.

_____. *How to Speak Dragonese.* New York: Little, Brown, 2005. Print. How to Train Your Dragon Book 3.

_____. *How to Train Your Dragon.* New York: Little, 2003. Print. How to Train Your Dragon Book 1.

_____. *How to Twist a Dragon's Tail.* New York: Little, Brown, 2007. Print. How to Train Your Dragon Book 5.

DiCamillo, Kate. *The Tale of Despereux.* Illus. Timothy Basil Ering. Cambridge, MA: Candlewick, 2003. Print.

DiTerlizzi, Tony, and Holly Black. *Arthur Spiderwick's Field Guide to the Fantastical World Around You.* New York: Simon & Schuster, 2005. Print.

_____. *Beyond the Spiderwick Chronicles Book 1: The Nixie's Song.* New York: Simon & Schuster, 2007. Print.

_____. *Beyond the Spiderwick Chronicles Book 2: A Giant Problem.* New York: Simon & Schuster, 2008. Print.

_____. *Beyond the Spiderwick Chronicles Book 3: The Wyrm King.* New York: Simon & Schuster, 2009. Print.

———. *The Spiderwick Chronicles Book 1: The Field Guide*. New York: Scholastic, 2003. Print.
———. *The Spiderwick Chronicles Book 2: The Seeing Stone*. New York: Scholastic, 2003. Print.
———. *The Spiderwick Chronicles Book 3: Lucinda's Secret*. New York: Scholastic, 2003. Print.
———. *The Spiderwick Chronicles Book 4: The Ironwood Tree*. New York: Scholastic, 2004. Print.
———. *The Spiderwick Chronicles Book 5: The Wrath of Mulgarath*. New York: Scholastic, 2004. Print.
———. *The Spiderwick Chronicles: Care and Feeding of Sprites*. New York: Simon & Schuster, 2006. Print.
———. *The Spiderwick Chronicles: Notebook for Fantastical Observations*. New York: Simon & Schuster, 2005. Print.
Drescher, Henrik. *Simon's Book*. New York: Lothrop, 1983. Print.
Druitt, Tobias. *Corydon & the Island of Monsters*. New York: Knopf, 2006. Print.
Duane, Diane. *Deep Wizadry*. 1985. The Young Wizards. New York: SFBC, 2001. Print.
———. *High Wizadry*. 1990. The Young Wizards. New York: SFBC, 2001. Print.
———. *So You Want to Be a Wizard*. 1983. The Young Wizards. New York: SFBC, 2001. Print.
———. *A Wizard Abroad*. 1993. The Young Wizards. New York: SFBC, 2001. Print.
———. *The Wizard's Dilemma*. The Young Wizards. New York: SFBC, 2001. Print.
Eager, Edward. *Seven-Day Magic*. Illus. N.M. Bodecker. New York: Harcourt, 1962. Print.
Ende, Michael. *The Neverending Story*. Trans. Ralph Manheim. New York: Firebird-Penguin, 1979. Print.
Ensor, Barbara. *Cinderella (As If You Didn't Already Know the Story)*. New York: Yearling, 2006. Print.
Estes, Eleanor. *The Witch Family*. 1960. New York: Harcourt, 2000. Print.
Felix, Monique. *The Story of a Little Mouse Trapped in a Book*. La Jolla, CA: Green Tiger, 1980. Print.
Fitzpatrick, Becca. *Crescendo*. New York: Simon & Schuster, 2010. Print. Hush, Hush Saga Book 2.
———. *Finale*. New York: Simon & Schuster, 2012. Print. Hush, Hush Saga Book 4.
———. *Hush, Hush*. New York: Simon & Schuster, 2009. Print. Hush, Hush Saga Book 1.
———. *Silence*. New York: Simon & Schuster, 2011. Print. Hush, Hush Saga Book 3.
Funke, Cornelia. *Igraine the Brave*. Trans. Anthea Bell. New York: Chicken House-Scholastic, 1998. Print.
———. *Inkdeath*. Trans Anthea Bell. New York: Chicken House-Scholastic, 2008. Print.
———. *Inkheart*. Trans. Anthea Bell. New York: Chicken House-Scholastic, 2003. Print.
———. *Inkspell*. Trans. Anthea Bell. New York: Chicken House-Scholastic, 2005. Print.
Garden, Nancy. *Prisoner of Vampires*. Illus. Michele Chessare. New York: Farrar, Straus & Giroux, 1984. Print.
Gatward, David. *Booksurfers One: Treasure Island*. London: FourteenFiftyFour, 2011. Kindle ebook file.
———. *Booksurfers Two: The Wonderful Wizard of Oz*. London: FourteenFiftyFour, 2011. Kindle ebook file.
Gerstein, Mordicai. *A Book*. New York: Roaring Brook Press, 2009. Print.
Grahame, Kenneth. *The Wind in the Willows*. 1908. Mahwah, NJ: Watermill, 1980. Print.
Hardinge, Frances. *Fly by Night*. New York: Harper, 2005. Print.
Higgins, F.E. *The Black Book of Secrets*. New York: Square Fish, 2007. Print.
Hoban, Russell. *Monsters*. Illus. Quentin Blake. New York: Scholastic, 1989. Print.
Horowitz, Anthony. *Groosham Grange*. 1988. New York: Puffin, 2009. Print.
———. *Return to Groosham Grange: The Unholy Grail*. 1989. New York: Puffin, 2010. Print.
Horowitz, Jordan, adapt. *The Pagemaster*. New York: Scholastic, 1994. Print.
Hughes, Shirley. *Chips and Jessie*. New York: Lothrop, 1985. Print.
Hughes, Thomas. *Tom Brown's School Days*.

1857. Mahwah, NJ: Watermill, 1988. Print.

Jones, Diana Wynne. *The Chronicles of Crestomanci, Volume 1: Charmed Life, The Lives of Christopher Chant*. 1977, 1988. New York: Greenwillow-Harper, 2001. Print.

Kipling, Rudyard. *The Complete Stalky & Co*. 1929. Ed. Isabel Quigly. New York: Oxford University Press, 1999. Oxford World's Classics.

Kirschner, David, and Ernie Contreras. *The Pagemaster*. Illus. Jerry Tirtilli. Atlanta: Turner, 1993. Print.

Klimo, Kate. *The Dragon in the Driveway*. Illus. John Shroades. New York: Yearling, 2009. Print. Dragon Keepers Book 2.

———. *The Dragon in the Library*. Illus. John Shroades. New York: Yearling, 2010. Print. Dragon Keepers Book 3.

———. *The Dragon in the Sock Drawer*. Illus. John Shroades. New York: Yearling, 2008. Print. Dragon Keepers Book 1.

Klise, Kate. *Dying to Meet You*. Illus. M. Sarah Klise. New York: Sandpiper-Houghton, 2009. Print. 43 Old Cemetery Road Book One.

———. *Over My Dead Body*. Illus. M. Sarah Klise. New York: Sandpiper-Houghton, 2009. Print. 43 Old Cemetery Road Book Two.

———. *The Phantom of the Post Office*. Illus. M. Sarah Klise. New York: Sandpiper-Houghton, 2012. Print. 43 Old Cemetery Road Book Four.

———. *Till Death Do Us Bark*. Illus. M. Sarah Klise. New York: Sandpiper-Houghton, 2011. Print. 43 Old Cemetery Road Book Three.

Knudsen, Michelle. *Library Lion*. Illus. Kevin Hawkes. Somerville, MA: Candlewick, 2006. Print.

Lang, Andrew, ed. *The Blue Fairy Book*. 1891. New York: Dover, 1965. Print.

Le Guin, Ursula K. *The Farthest Shore*. 1972. *The Earthsea Trilogy*. New York: SFBC, 2005. Print.

———. *The Tombs of Atuan*. 1970. *The Earthsea Trilogy*. New York: SFBC, 2005. Print.

———. *A Wizard of Earthsea*. 1968. *The Earthsea Trilogy*. New York: SFBC, 2005. Print.

Levine, Gail Carson. *Ella Enchanted*. New York: Harper, 1997. Print.

Lewis, C.S. *The Lion, the Witch and the Wardrobe*. 1950. New York: Scholastic, 1995. The Chronicles of Narnia Book 2.

Lindgring, Astrid. *Pippi Longstocking*. 1950. Trans. Florence Lamborn. New York: Puffin, 1997. Print.

MacDonald, George. *The Princess and the Goblin*. 1872. New York: Puffin, 1996. Print.

Mahy, Margaret. *Alchemy*. New York: Simon Pulse, 2003. Print.

McCaughrean, Geraldine. *A Pack of Lies*. Tarrytown, NY: Cavendish, 1988. Print.

McKinley, Robin. *Beauty: A Retelling of the Story of Beauty & the Beast*. New York: Harper, 1978. Print.

Meyer, Stephenie. *New Moon*. New York: Little, Brown, 2006. The Twilight Saga Book 2.

———. *Twilight*. New York: Little, Brown, 2005. Print. The Twilight Saga Book 1.

Miéville, China. *Un Lun Dun*. New York: Ballantine, 2007. Print.

Moore, John. *The Unhandsome Prince*. New York: Ace, 2005. Print.

Murphy, Jill. *The Worst Witch*. 1974. New York: Puffin, 2001. Print.

Nesbit, E. *Wet Magic*. 1913. Lexington, KY: Dragonwood, 2005. Print.

Nix, Garth. *Abhorsen*. New York: Eos-Harper, 2003. Print.

———. *Lirael*. New York: Eos-Harper, 2001. Print.

———. "Nicholas Sayre and the Creature in the Case." *Across the Wall: A Tale of Abhorsen and Other Stories*. New York: Eos-Harper, 2005. 3–136. Print.

———. *Sabriel*. New York: Eos-Harper, 1995. Print.

North, Pearl. *The Book of the Night*. New York: Tor, 2012. Print.

———. *The Boy from Ilysies*. New York: Tor, 2010. Print.

———. *Libyrinth*. New York: Tor, 2009. Print.

O'Brien, Robert C. *Mrs. Frisby and the Rats of NIMH*. New York: Scholastic, 1971. Print.

Oram, Hiawyn. *Angry Arthur*. Illus. Satoshi Kitamura. New York: Harcourt, 1982. Print.

Osborne, Mary Pope. *Afternoon on the Amazon*. Illus. Sal Murdocca. New York: Random House, 1995. Print. Magic Tree House #6.
———. *Buffalo before Breakfast*. Illus. Sal Murdocca. New York: Random House, 1999. Print. Magic Tree House #18.
———. *Civil War on Sunday*. Illus. Sal Murdocca. New York: Random House, 2000. Print. Magic Tree House #21.
———. *Day of the Dragon King*. Illus. Sal Murdocca. New York: Random House, 1998. Print. Magic Tree House #14.
———. *Dingoes at Dinnertime*. Illus. Sal Murdocca. New York: Random House, 2000. Print. Magic Tree House #20.
———. *Dinosaurs Before Dark*. Illus. Sal Murdocca. New York: Random House, 1992. Print. Magic Tree House #1.
———. *Dolphins at Daybreak*. Illus. Sal Murdocca. New York: Random House, 1997. Print. Magic Tree House #9.
———. *Earthquake in the Early Morning*. Illus. Sal Murdocca. New York: Random House, 2001. Print. Magic Tree House #24.
———. *Ghost Town at Sundown*. Illus. Sal Murdocca. New York: Random House, 1997. Print. Magic Tree House #10.
———. *Good Morning, Gorillas*. Illus. Sal Murdocca. New York: Random House, 2002. Print. Magic Tree House #26.
———. *High Tide in Hawaii*. Illus. Sal Murdocca. New York: Random House, 2003. Print. Magic Tree House #28.
———. *Hour of the Olympics*. Illus. Sal Murdocca. New York: Random House, 1998. Print. Magic Tree House #16.
———. *The Knight at Dawn*. Illus. Sal Murdocca. New York: Random House, 1993. Print. Magic Tree House #2.
———. *Lions at Lunchtime*. Illus. Sal Murdocca. New York: Random House, 1998. Print. Magic Tree House #11.
———. *Midnight on the Moon*. Illus. Sal Murdocca. New York: Random House, 1996. Print. Magic Tree House #8.
———. *Mummies in the Morning*. Illus. Sal Murdocca. New York: Random House, 1993. Print. Magic Tree House #3.
———. *Night of the Ninjas*. Illus. Sal Murdocca. New York: Random House, 1995. Print. Magic Tree House #5.
———. *Pirates Past Noon*. Illus. Sal Murdocca. New York: Random House, 1994. Print. Magic Tree House #4.
———. *Polar Bears Past Bedtime*. Illus. Sal Murdocca. New York: Random House, 1998. Print. Magic Tree House #12.
———. *Revolutionary War on Wednesday*. Illus. Sal Murdocca. New York: Random House, 2000. Print. Magic Tree House #22.
———. *Stage Fright on a Summer Night*. Illus. Sal Murdocca. New York: Random House, 2002. Print. Magic Tree House #25.
———. *Sunset of the Sabertooth*. Illus. Sal Murdocca. New York: Random House, 1996. Print. Magic Tree House #7.
———. *Thanksgiving on Thursday*. Illus. Sal Murdocca. New York: Random House, 2002. Print. Magic Tree House #27.
———. *Tigers at Twilight*. Illus. Sal Murdocca. New York: Random House, 1999. Print. Magic Tree House #19.
———. *Tonight on the Titanic*. Illus. Sal Murdocca. New York: Random House, 1999. Print. Magic Tree House #17.
———. *Twister on Tuesday*. Illus. Sal Murdocca. New York: Random House, 2001. Print. Magic Tree House #23.
———. *Vacation under the Volcano*. Illus. Sal Murdocca. New York: Random House, 1998. Print. Magic Tree House #13.
———. *Viking Ships at Sunrise*. Illus. Sal Murdocca. New York: Random House, 1998. Print. Magic Tree House #15.
Owen, James A. *The Dragon's Apprentice*. New York: Simon & Schuster, 2011. Print. Chronicles of the *Imaginarium Geographica* Book Five.
———. *Here, There Be Dragons*. New York: Simon & Schuster, 2006. Print. Chronicles of the *Imaginarium Geographica* Book One.
———. *The Indigo King*. New York: Simon & Schuster, 2010. Print. Chronicles of the *Imaginarium Geographica* Book Three.
———. *The Search for the Red Dragon*. New York: Simon & Schuster, 2008. Print. Chronicles of the *Imaginarium Geographica* Book Two.
———. *The Shadow Dragons*. New York:

Simon & Schuster, 2009. Print. Chronicles of the *Imaginarium Geographica* Book Four.
Packard, Edward. *The Cave of Time.* New York: Bantam, 1979. Print. Choose Your Own Adventure #1.
Park, Barbara. *Junie B. Jones and the Stupid Smell Bus.* Illus. Denise Brunkus. New York: Random House, 1992. Print. Junie B. Jones #1.
Peake, Mervyn. *Gormenghast.* 1950. *The Gormenghast Novels.* New York: Overlook, 1995. Print.
_____. *Titus Alone.* 1959. *The Gormenghast Novels.* New York: Overlook, 1995. Print.
_____. *Titus Groan.* 1946. *The Gormenghast Novels.* New York: Overlook, 1995. Print.
Pierce, Tamora. *Alanna: The First Adventure.* New York: Random House, 1983. Print. Song of the Lioness Book One.
_____. *The Imortals.* 1992–6. New York: SFBC, 2003. Print. [Contains the novels *Wild Magic, Wolf-Speaker, Emperor Mage,* and *The Realms of the Gods.*]
_____. *In the Hand of the Goddess.* New York: Random House, 1984. Print. Song of the Lioness Book Two.
_____. *Lioness Rampant.* New York: Random House, 1988. Print. Song of the Lioness Book Four.
_____. *The Woman Who Rides Like a Man.* New York: Random House, 1986. Print. Song of the Lioness Book Three.
Pilkey, Dav. *The Adventures of Captain Underpants.* New York: Scholastic, 1997. Print. Captain Underpants Book 1.
_____. *The Adventures of Ook and Gluck, Kung-Fu Cavemen from the Future.* New York: Blue Sky-Scholastic, 2010. Print.
_____. *The Adventures of Super Diaper Baby.* New York: Scholastic, 2002. Print.
_____. *Captain Underpants and the Attack of the Talking Toilets.* New York: Scholastic, 1999. Print. Captain Underpants Book 2.
_____. *Captain Underpants and the Big, Bad Battle of the Bionic Booger Boy Part 1: The Night of the Nasty Nostril Nuggets.* New York: Scholastic, 2003. Print. Captain Underpants Book 6.
_____. *Captain Underpants and the Big, Bad Battle of the Bionic Booger Boy Part 2: The Revenge of the Ridiculous Robo-Boogers.* New York: Scholastic, 2003. Print. Captain Underpants Book 7.
_____. *Captain Underpants and the Invasion of the Incredibly Naughty Cafeteria Ladies from Outer Space (and the Subsequent Assault of the Equally Evil Lunchroom Zombie Nerds).* New York: Scholastic, 1999. Print. Captain Underpants Book 3.
_____. *Captain Underpants and the Perilous Plot of Professor Poopypants.* New York: Scholastic, 2000. Print. Captain Underpants Book 4.
_____. *Captain Underpants and the Preposterous Plight of the Purple Potty People.* New York: Scholastic, 2006. Print. Captain Underpants Book 8.
_____. *Captain Underpants and the Terrifying Return of Tippy Tinkletrousers.* New York: Scholastic, 2012. Print. Captain Underpants Book 9.
_____. *Captain Underpants and the Wrath of the Wicked Wedgie Woman.* New York: Scholastic, 2001. Print. Captain Underpants Book 5.
_____. *Super Diaper Baby 2: The Invasion of the Potty Snatchers.* New York: Blue Sky, 2011. Print.
Polacco, Patricia. *Aunt Chip and the Great Triple Creek Dam Affair.* New York: Trumpet-Scholastic, 1996. Print.
Portman, Frank. *King Dork.* New York: Delacorte, 2006. Print.
Pratchett, Terry. *A Hat Full of Sky.* New York: Harper, 2004. Print.
_____. *I Shall Wear Midnight.* New York: Harper, 2010. Print.
_____. *The Wee Free Men.* New York: Harper, 2003. Print.
_____. *Wintersmith.* New York: Harper, 2006. Print.
Rees, Celia. *Sorceress.* New York: Candlewick, 2002. Print
_____. *Witch Child.* Cambridge, MA: Candlewick, 2000. Print.
Reeves, James. *The Strange Light.* Illus. J.C. Kocsis. New York: Rand McNally, 1966. Print.
Riordan, Rick. *The Battle of the Labyrinth.* New York: Disney-Hyperion, 2008. Print. Percy Jackson & the Olympians Book Four.

Bibliography—Primary Children's ... Books

———. *The Kane Chronicles Survival Guide.* New York: Disney-Hyperion, 2012. Print.
———. *The Last Olympian.* New York: Disney-Hyperion, 2009. Print. Percy Jackson & the Olympians Book Five.
———. *The Lightning Thief.* New York: Miramax-Hyperion, 2005. Print. Percy Jackson & the Olympians Book One.
———. *The Lost Hero.* New York: Disney-Hyperion, 2010. Print. The Heroes of Olympus Book One.
———. *The Mark of Athena.* New York: Disney-Hyperion, 2012. Print. The Heroes of Olympus Book Three.
———. *Percy Jackson & the Olympians: The Demigod Files.* New York: Disney-Hyperion, 2009. Print.
———. *The Red Pyramid.* New York: Disney-Hyperion, 2010. Print. The Kane Chronicles Book One.
———. *The Sea of Monsters.* New York: Disney-Hyperion, 2006. Print. Percy Jackson & the Olympians Book Two.
———. *The Serpent's Shadow.* New York: Disney-Hyperion, 2012. Print. The Kane Chronicles Book Three.
———. *The Son of Neptune.* New York: Disney-Hyperion, 2010. Print. The Heroes of Olympus Book Two.
———. *The Throne of Fire.* New York: Disney-Hyperion, 2011. Print. The Kane Chronicles Book Two.
———. *The Titan's Curse.* New York: Disney-Hyperion, 2007. Print. Percy Jackson & the Olympians Book Three.
Rowling, J.K. *Fantastic Beasts & Where to Find Them.* Vancouver: Raincoast, 2001. Print.
———. *Harry Potter and the Chamber of Secrets.* New York: Levine-Scholastic, 1999. Print.
———. *Harry Potter and the Deathly Hallows.* New York: Levine-Scholastic, 2007. Print.
———. *Harry Potter and the Goblet of Fire.* New York: Levine-Scholastic, 2000. Print.
———. *Harry Potter and the Half-Blood Prince.* New York: Levine-Scholastic, 2005. Print.
———. *Harry Potter and the Order of the Phoenix.* New York: Levine-Scholastic, 2003. Print.
———. *Harry Potter and the Prisoner of Azkaban.* New York: Levine-Scholastic, 1999. Print.
———. *Harry Potter and the Sorcerer's Stone.* New York: Levine-Scholastic, 1995. Print.
———. *Quidditch through the Ages.* Vancouver: Raincoast, 2001. Print.
———. *The Tales of Beedle the Bard.* New York: Levine-Scholastic, 2008. Print.
Sage, Angie. *Darke.* Illus. Mark Zug. New York: Tegen-Harper, 2011. Print. Septimus Heap, Book Six.
———. *Flyte.* Illus. Mark Zug. New York: Tegen-Harper, 2006. Print. Septimus Heap, Book Two.
———. *Frognapped.* Illus. Jimmy Pickering. New York: Tegen-Harper, 2007. Print. Araminta Spookie 3.
———. *Ghostsitters.* Illus. Jimmy Pickering. New York: Tegen-Harper, 2008. Print. Araminta Spookie 5.
———. *Magyk.* Illus. Mark Zug. New York: Tegen-Harper, 2005. Print. Septimus Heap, Book One.
———. *My Haunted House.* Illus. Jimmy Pickering. New York: Tegen-Harper, 2006. Print. Araminta Spookie 1.
———. *Physik.* Illus. Mark Zug. New York: Tegen-Harper, 2007. Print. Septimus Heap, Book Three.
———. *Queste.* Illus. Mark Zug. New York: Tegen-Harper, 2008. Print. Septimus Heap, Book Four.
———. *Septimus Heap: The Magykal Papers.* Illus. Mark Zug. New York: Tegen-Harper, 2009. Print.
———. *The Sword in the Grotto.* Illus. Jimmy Pickering. New York: Tegen-Harper, 2006. Print. Araminta Spookie 2.
———. *Syren.* Illus. Mark Zug. New York: Tegen-Harper, 2009. Print. Septimus Heap, Book Five.
———. *Vampire Brat.* Illus. Jimmy Pickering. New York: Tegen-Harper, 2007. Print. Araminta Spookie 4.
Sanvoisin, Éric. *The City of Ink Drinkers.* Illus. Martin Matje. Trans. Georges Moroz. New York: Dell-Random House, 2001. Print.
———. *The Ink Drinker.* Illus. Martin Matje. Trans. Georges Moroz. New York: Dell-Random House, 1996. Print.
———. *Little Red Ink Drinker.* Illus. Martin

Matje. Trans. Georges Moroz. New York: Delacorte, 2002. Print.
_____. *A Straw for Two.* Illus. Martin Matje. Trans. Georges Moroz. New York: Dell-Random House, 1998. Print.
Schulman, Polly. *The Grimm Legacy.* New York: Putnam, 2010. Print.
Scieszka, Jon. *2095.* Illus. Lane Smith. New York: Puffin, 1995. Print. The Time Warp Trio #5.
_____. *The Book That Jack Wrote.* Illus. Daniel Adel. New York: Viking, 1994. Print.
_____. *Da Wild, Da Crazy, Da Vinci.* Illus. Adam McCauley. New York: Puffin, 2004. Print. The Time Warp Trio #14.
_____. *The Good, the Bad, and the Goofy.* Illus. Lane Smith. New York: Puffin, 1992. Print. The Time Warp Trio #3.
_____. *Hey Kid, Want to Buy a Bridge?* Illus. Adam McCauley. New York: Puffin, 2004. Print. The Time Warp Trio #11.
_____. *It's All Greek to Me.* Illus. Lane Smith. New York: Puffin, 1999. Print. The Time Warp Trio #8.
_____. *Knights of the Kitchen Table.* Illus. Lane Smith. New York: Puffin, 1991. Print. The Time Warp Trio #1.
_____. *Marco? Polo!* Illus. Adam McCauley. New York: Puffin, 2006. Print. The Time Warp Trio #16.
_____. *Me Oh Maya.* Illus. Adam McCauley. New York: Puffin, 2003. Print. The Time Warp Trio #13.
_____. *The Not-So-Jolly Roger.* Illus. Lane Smith. New York: Puffin, 1991. Print. The Time Warp Trio #2.
_____. *Oh Say, I Can't See.* Illus. Adam McCauley. New York: Puffin, 2005. Print. The Time Warp Trio #15.
_____. *Sam Samurai.* Illus. Adam McCauley. New York: Puffin, 2001. Print. The Time Warp Trio #10.
_____. *See You Later, Gladiator.* Illus. Adam McCauley. New York: Puffin, 2000. Print. The Time Warp Trio #9.
_____. *The Stinky Cheese Man and Other Fairly Stupid Tales.* Illus. Lane Smith. New York: Viking, 1992. Print.
_____. *Summer Reading Is Killing Me.* Illus. Lane Smith. New York: Puffin, 1998. Print. The Time Warp Trio #7.
_____. *Tut, Tut.* Illus. Lane Smith. New York: Puffin, 1996. Print. The Time Warp Trio #6.
_____. *Viking It and Liking It.* Illus. Adam McCauley. New York: Puffin, 2002. Print. The Time Warp Trio #12.
_____. *Your Mother Was a Neanderthal.* Illus. Lane Smith. New York: Puffin, 1993. Print. The Time Warp Trio #4.
Scieszka, Jon, and Francesco Sedita. *Spaceheadz.* Illus. Shane Prigmore. New York: Simon & Schuster, 2010. Print. SPHDZ #1.
Scott, Michael. *The Alchemyst.* New York: Delacorte, 2007. Print. The Secrets of the Immortal Nicholas Flamel #1.
_____. *The Enchantress.* New York: Delacorte, 2012. Print. The Secrets of the Immortal Nicholas Flamel #6.
_____. *The Magician.* New York: Delacorte, 2008. Print. The Secrets of the Immortal Nicholas Flamel #2.
_____. *The Necromancer.* New York: Delacorte, 2010. Print. The Secrets of the Immortal Nicholas Flamel #4.
_____. *The Sorceress.* New York: Delacorte, 2009. Print. The Secrets of the Immortal Nicholas Flamel #3.
_____. *The Warlock.* New York: Delacorte, 2011. Print. The Secrets of the Immortal Nicholas Flamel #5.
Shan, Darren. *Cirque du Freak: A Living Nightmare.* New York: Little, Brown, 2001. Print. Cirque du Freak Book One.
Sierra, Judy. *Wild about Books.* Illus. Marc Brown. New York: Knopf, 2004. Print.
Silverstein, Shel. *A Light in the Attic.* New York: Harper, 1981. Print.
_____. *Where the Sidewalk Ends.* New York: Harper, 1974. Print.
Skelton, Matthew. *Endymion Spring.* New York: Delacorte, 2006. Print.
Smith, Lane. *It's a Book.* New York: Roaring Brook Press, 2010. Print.
Smith, L.J. *The Secret Circle:* The Captive, Part II *and* The Power. 1992. New York: Harper, 2008. Print.
_____. *The Secret Circle:* The Initiation *and* The Captive, Part I. 1992. New York: Harper, 2008. Print.
_____. *The Vampire Diaries:* The Awakening *and* The Struggle. 1991. New York: Harper, 2007. Print.

_____. *The Vampire Diaries: The Fury and Dark Reunion.* 1991. New York: Harper, 2007. Print.

_____. *The Vampire Diaries: The Return Vol. 1: Nightfall.* New York: Harper, 2009. Print.

_____. *The Vampire Diaries: The Return Vol. 2: Shadow Souls.* New York: Harper, 2010. Print.

_____. *The Vampire Diaries: The Return Vol. 3: Midnight.* New York: Harper, 2011. Print.

Snickett, Lemony. *The Bad Beginning.* Illus. Brett Helquist. New York: Harper, 1999. Print. A Series of Unfortunate Events, Book the First.

Steer, Dugald A. *The Dragon Diary.* Illus. Douglas Carrel. Cambridge, MA: Candlewick, 2009. Print. Dragonology Chronicles, Vol. Two.

_____. *Dragonology: The Complete Book of Dragons.* Illus. Wayne Anderson, Douglas Carrel, and Helen Ward. Cambridge, MA: Candlewick, 2003. Print.

_____. *The Dragon's Eye.* Illus. Douglas Carrel. Cambridge, MA: Candlewick, 2006. Print. Dragonology Chronicles, Vol. One.

Stein, David Ezra. *Interrupting Chicken.* Somerville, MA: Candlewick, 2010. Print.

Stewart, Trenton Lee. *The Mysterious Benedict Society.* New York: Little, Brown, 2008. Print.

Stine, R.L. *Goosebumps: Attack of the Mutant.* New York: Scholastic, 1994. Print.

Storr, Catherine. *Marianne Dreams.* 1958. New York: Puffin, 1964. Print.

Taylor, G.P. *Wormwood.* New York: Putnam, 2004. Print.

Tolkien, J.R.R. *The Fellowship of the Ring: Being the First Part of The Lord of the Rings.* 1954. New York: Houghton, 1999. Print.

_____. *The Hobbit or There and Back Again.* 1966, 1982. Rev. ed. New York: Ballantine, 1997. Print.

_____. *The Return of the King: Being the Third Part of The Lord of the Rings.* 1955. New York: Houghton, 1999. Print.

_____. *The Two Towers: Being the Second Part of The Lord of the Rings.* 1954. New York: Houghton, 1999. Print.

Townley, Roderick. *The Constellation of Sylvie.* New York: Jackson-Atheneum, 2005. Print.

_____. *The Great Good Thing.* New York: Aladdin-Simon & Schuster, 2001. Print.

_____. *Into the Labyrinth.* New York: Aladdin-Simon & Schuster, 2002. Print.

Twain, Mark. *The Adventures of Tom Sawyer.* 1876. Mineola, NY: Dover, 1998. Print.

Van Allsburg, Chris. *Bad Day at Riverbend.* Boston: Houghton, 1995. Print.

_____. *The Mysteries of Harris Burdick.* Boston: Houghton, 1984. Print.

Wilce, Ysabeau S. *Flora Segunda: Being the Magickal Mishaps of a Girl of Spirit, Her Glass-Gazing Sidekick, Two Ominous Butlers (One Blue), a House with Eleven Thousand Rooms, and a Red Dog.* New York: Magic Carpet, 2008. Print.

Wilder, Laura Ingalls. *By the Shores of Silver Lake.* 1939. New York: Harper, 1994. Print. Little House Series #5.

_____. *Little House on the Prairie.* 1935. New York: Harper, 2004. Print. Little House Series #2.

_____. *Little Town on the Prairie.* 1941. New York: Harper, 2004. Print. Little House Series #7.

_____. *The Long Winter.* 1940. New York: Harper, 2004. Print. Little House Series #6.

_____. *On the Banks of Plum Creek.* 1937. New York: Harper, 1994. Print. Little House Series #4.

Wooding, Chris. *Havoc.* Illus. Dan Chernett. New York: Scholastic, 2010. Print.

_____. *Malice.* Illus. Dan Chernett. New York: Scholastic, 2009. Print.

Yates, Louise. *Dog Loves Books.* New York: Knopf, 2010. Print.

Zusak, Markus. *The Book Thief.* New York: Knopf, 2005.

Primary Adult Books

Carey, Mike, and Peter Gross. *The Unwritten: Dead Man's Knock.* New York: Vertigo, 2011. Print.

_____. *The Unwritten: Inside Man.* New York: Vertigo, 2010. Print.

_____. *The Unwritten: Tommy Taylor and the Bogus Identity.* New York: Vertigo, 2010. Print.

Cervantes, Miguel de. *Don Quixote*. 1605, 1615. Trans. Tobias Smollett. New York: Barnes, 2004. Print.
The Epic of Gilgamesh. Trans. Andrew George. New York: Penguin, 2003. Print.
Fforde, Jasper. *The Eyre Affair*. New York: Penguin, 2001. Print.
_____. *Lost in a Good Book*. New York: Penguin, 2002. Print.
_____. *Something Rotten*. New York: Viking, 2004. Print.
_____. *The Well of Lost Plots*. New York: Viking, 2003. Print.
Harkness, Deborah. *A Discovery of Witches*. New York: Viking, 2011. Print. All Souls #1.
_____. *Shadow of Night*. New York: Viking, 2012. Print. All Souls #2.
Homer. *The Odyssey*. Trans. Robert Fagles. New York: Penguin, 2006. Print.
Kane, Stacia. *Unholy Ghosts*. New York: Random House, 2010. Print. Downside Ghosts #1.
The Mahabharata. Abr. ed. Trans. John D. Smith. New York: Penguin, 2009. Print.
Moning, Karen Marie. *Bloodfever*. New York: Delacorte, 2007. Print. Fever #2.
_____. *Darkfever*. New York: Delacorte, 2006. Print. Fever #1.
_____. *Dreamfever*. New York: Delacorte, 2009. Print. Fever #4.
_____. *Faefever*. New York: Delacorte, 2008. Print. Fever #3.
_____. *Shadowfever*. New York: Delacorte, 2011. Print. Fever #5.
Sterne, Laurence. *Tristram Shandy*. 1759–1767. Hertfordshire, UK: Wordsworth, 1996. Print.
Wells, Jaye. *Green-Eyed Demon*. New York: Orbit, 2011. Print. Sabina Kane 3.
_____. *The Mage in Black*. New York: Orbit, 2010. Print. Sabina Kane 2.
_____. *Red-Headed Stepchild*. New York: Orbit, 2009. Print. Sabina Kane 1.
White, Skyler. *and Falling, Fly*. New York: Berkley, 2010. Print.

Films and Television Series

Beauty and the Beast. Screenplay by Linda Woolverton. 1991. Disney, 2010. DVD.
Bedtime Stories. Screenplay by Matt Lopez and Tim Herlihy. Disney, 2008. DVD.
Buffy the Vampire Slayer: The Complete First Season. Created by Joss Whedon. 1997. 20th Century–Fox, 2001. DVD.
Buffy the Vampire Slayer: The Complete Second Season. Created by Joss Whedon. 1997–8. 20th Century–Fox, 2002. DVD.
Buffy the Vampire Slayer: The Complete Third Season. Created by Joss Whedon. 1998–9. 20th Century–Fox, 2002. DVD.
Buffy the Vampire Slayer: The Complete Fourth Season. Created by Joss Whedon. 1999–2000. 20th Century–Fox, 2003. DVD.
Buffy the Vampire Slayer: The Complete Fifth Season. Created by Joss Whedon. 2000–1. 20th Century–Fox, 2003. DVD.
Buffy the Vampire Slayer: The Complete Sixth Season. Created by Joss Whedon. 2001–2. 20th Century–Fox, 2004. DVD.
Buffy the Vampire Slayer: The Complete Seventh Season. Created by Joss Whedon. 2002–3. 20th Century–Fox, 2004. DVD.
Cinderella. Screenplay by William Peed, et al. 1950. Disney, 2005. DVD.
Ella Enchanted. Screenplay by Laurie Craig, et al. Buena Vista, 2004. DVD.
Enchanted. Screenplay by Bill Kelly. Disney, 2007. DVD.
Grimm: Season One. 2011–12. Universal, 2012. DVD.
Harry Potter and the Chamber of Secrets. Screenplay by Steve Kloves. 2002. Warner Bros., 2003. DVD.
Harry Potter and the Deathly Hallows, Part 1. Screenplay by Steve Kloves. 2010. Warner Bros., 2011. DVD.
Harry Potter and the Deathly Hallows, Part 2. Screenplay by Steve Kloves. Warner Bros., 2011. DVD.
Harry Potter and the Goblet of Fire. Screenplay by Steve Kloves. 2005. Warner Bros., 2006. DVD.
Harry Potter and the Half-Blood Prince. Screenplay by Steve Kloves. Warner Bros., 2009. DVD.
Harry Potter and the Order of the Phoenix. Screenplay by Steve Kloves. Warner Bros., 2007. DVD.
Harry Potter and the Philosopher's Stone. Screenplay by Steve Kloves. 2001. Warner Bros., 2002. DVD.

Harry Potter and the Prisoner of Azkaban. Screenplay by Steve Kloves. Warner Bros., 2004. DVD.
Inkheart. Screenplay by David Lindsay-Abaire. New Line, 2009. DVD.
Lost in Austen. By Guy Andrews. 2008. Granada Television International, 2009. DVD.
The Neverending Story. Screenplay by Wolfgang Petersen and Herman Weigel. 1984. Warner Bros., 2006. DVD.
The Neverending Story II: The Next Chapter. Screenplay by Karin Howard. 1989. Warner Bros., 2006. DVD.
The Neverending Story III: Escape from Fantasia. Screenplay by Jeff Lieberman. 1994. Miramax, 2011. DVD.
The Pagemaster. Screenplay by David Casci, David Kirschner, and Ernie Contreras. 1994. 20th Century–Fox, 2002. DVD.
Percy Jackson & the Olympians: The Lightning Thief. Screenplay by Craig Titley. 20th Century–Fox, 2010. DVD.
"The Quill Is Mightier..." *Xena: Warrior Princess.* By Hilary J. Bader. Episode 3.10. 1998. Universal, 2012. DVD.
The Secret Circle. CW. WKTV-DT2, Utica, 2011–2012. Television.
Shrek. Screenplay by Ted Elliott, et.al. 2001. DreamWorks, 2011. DVD.
Shrek 2. Screenplay by Andrew Adamson. DreamWorks, 2004. DVD.
Sleeping Beauty. Screenplay by Erdman Penner, et al. 1959. Disney, 2008. DVD.
Snow White and the Seven Dwarfs. Screenplay by Ted Sears, et al. 1937. Disney, 2009. DVD.
The Spiderwick Chronicles. Screenplay by Karey Kirkpatrick, David Berenbaum, and John Sayles. Paramount, 2008. DVD.
Stranger Than Fiction. Screenplay by Zach Helm. Columbia, 2006. DVD.
Toy Story. Screenplay by Joss Whedon, et al. 1995. Disney, 2010. DVD.
The Vampire Diaries: The Complete First Season. 2009–10. Warner Bros., 2010. DVD.
The Vampire Diaries: The Complete Second Season. 2010–11. Warner Bros., 2011. DVD.
The Vampire Diaries: The Complete Third Season. 2011–12. Warner Bros., 2012. DVD.

Secondary Sources

Anatol, Giselle Liza, ed. *Reading Harry Potter Again: New Critical Essays.* Santa Barbara: Praeger, 2009. Print.
_____, ed. *Reading Harry Potter: Critical Essays.* Westport, CT: Praeger, 2003. Print. Contributions to the Study of Popular Culture, vol. 78.
Applebaum, Peter. "Harry Potter's World: Magic, Technoculture, and Becoming Human." Heilman, *World* 25–51.
Armitt, Lucy. *Fantasy Fiction: An Introduction.* New York: Continuum, 2005. Print. Continuum Studies in the Literary Genre.
Attebery, Brian. "Fantasy's Roots: Ballads Folktales, and Legends." Mass and Levine 26–34. Excerpt from *The Fantasy Tradition in American Literature: From Irving to Le Guin.* Bloomington: Indiana University Press, 1980.
_____. *Strategies of Fantasy.* Bloomington: Indiana University Press, 1992. Print.
Barone, Diane M. *Children's Literature in the Classroom: Engaging Lifelong Readers.* New York: Guilford, 2011. Print.
Bauerlein, Mark. "The New Bibliophobes." *Educational Horizons* Winter 2010: 84–91. Print.
Bealer, Tracy L. "Militant Literacy: Hermione Granger, Rita Skeeter, Dolores Umbridge, and the (Mis)use of Text." Anatol, *Reading Again* 175–90.
Beckett, Sandra L., and Maria Nikolajeva, eds. *Beyond Babar: The European Tradition in Children's Literature.* Lanham, MD: Scarecrow, 2006. Print.
Benton, Michael. "Readers, Texts, and Contexts: Reader-Response Criticism." Hunt, *Understanding* 86–102.
Birch, Megan L. "Schooling Harry Potter: Teachers and Learning, Power and Knowledge." Heilman, *Critical* 103–20.
Boehm, Beth A. "Feminist Metafiction and Androcentric Reading Strategies: Angela Carter's Reconstructed Reader in *Nights at the Circus.*" *Critique* 37 (1995): 35–49. Print.
Booth, Margaret Zoller, and Grace Marie Booth. "What American Schools Can Learn from Hogwarts School of Witch-

craft and Wizardry." *Phi Delta Kappan* 85.4 (2003): 310–315. *Academic Search Complete.* EBSCO. Web. 4 Jan. 2010.

Bramwell, Peter. "Fantasy, Psychoanalysis and Adolescence: Magic and Maturation in Fantasy." Reynolds 141–55.

Butler, Catherine. "Modern Children's Fantasy." James and Mendlesohn 224–35.

Carnegie, Teena. "Defining the Difference: The Rhetoric of Typography in the Novel." *Textual Studies in Canada* Winter 1998: 81–97. Print.

Cashore, Kristin. "Humor, Simplicity, and Experimentation in the Picture Books of Jon Agee." *Children's Literature in Education* 34 (2003): 147–81. Print.

Chambers, Aidan. "The Reader in the Book." Hunt, *Development* 91–114.

Chappell, Drew. "Sneaking Out After Dark: Resistance, Agency, and the Postmodern Child in JK Rowling's Harry Potter Series." *Children's Literature in Education* 39.4 (2008): 281–293. *Academic Search Complete.* EBSCO. Web. 4 Jan. 2010.

Chen, Fanfan. "From Hypotyposis to Metalepsis: Narrative Devices in Contemporary Fantastic Fiction." *Forum for Modern Language Studies* 44 (2008): 394–411 Print.

Cohn, Dorrit. *Transparent Minds: Narrative Modes for Presenting Consciousness in Fiction.* Princeton: Princeton University Press, 1978. Print.

Coles, Martin, and Christine Hall. "Breaking the Line: New Literacies, Postmodernism and the Teaching of Printed Texts." *Reading* Nov. 2001: 111–4. Print.

Conn, Jennifer J. "What Can Clinical Teachers Learn from *Harry Potter and the Philosopher's Stone*?" *Medical Education* 36.12 (2002): 1176–1181. *Academic Search Complete.* EBSCO. Web. 4 Jan. 2010.

Conn, Jennifer, and Susan Elliott. "Harry Potter and Assessment." *Clinical Teacher* 2.1 (2005): 31–36. *Academic Search Complete.* EBSCO. Web. 4 Jan. 2010.

Crago, Hugh. "Healing Texts: Bibliotherapy and Psychology." Hunt, *Understanding* 180–89.

Croft, Janet Brennan. "The Education of a Witch: Tiffany Aching, Hermione Granger, and Gendered Magic in Discworld and Potterworld." *Mythlore: A Journal of J. R. R. Tolkien, C. S. Lewis, Charles Williams, and Mythopoeic Literature* 27.3–4 [105–106] (2009): 129–142. *MLA International Bibliography.* EBSCO. Web. 6 Jan. 2010.

Dalton, Russell W. "Miraculous Readings: Using Fantasy Novels about Reading to Reflect on Reading the Bible." *Religious Education* 104 (2008): 378–92. Print.

Darigan, Daniel L., Michael O. Tunnell, and James S. Jacobs. *Children's Literature: Engaging Teachers and Children in Good Books.* Upper Saddle River, NJ: Merrill/Prentice Hall, 2002. Print.

Daspit, Toby. "Buffy Goes to College, Adam Murders to Dissect: Education and Knowledge in Postmodernity." *South* 117–30.

DeCandido, Graceanne A. "Bibliographic Good vs. Evil." *American Libraries* Sept. 1999: 44–7. Print.

Demers, Patricia. Preface. *From Instruction to Delight: An Anthology of Children's Literature to 1850.* 2nd ed. Ed. Patricia Demers. New York: Oxford University Press, 2004. xv–xvii. Print.

Dexter, Susan. "The Building Blocks of Fantasy." Mass and Levine 46–51. Rpt. of "Tricks of the Wizard's Trade." *The Writer* Nov. 1997: 7+.

Dickerson, Matthew, and David O'Hara. *From Home to Harry Potter: A Handbook on Myth and Fantasy.* Grand Rapids: Brazos, 2007. Print.

Dickinson, Renée. "Harry Potter Pedagogy." *Clearing House* 79.6 (2006): 240–244. *Academic Search Complete.* EBSCO. Web. 4 Jan. 2010.

Didicher, Nicole E. "The Children in the Story: Metafiction in *Mary Poppins in the Park*." *Children's Literature in Education* 28.3 (1997): 137–49. Print.

Donaher, Patricia, and James M. Okapal. "Causation, Prophetic Visions, and the Free Will Question in Harry Potter." Anatol, *Reading Again* 47–62.

Doughty, Amie A. "Junie B. Jones and the Language Police: Language Attitudes and the Marked Child Narrator." *Barbarians at the Gate: Studies in Language Attitudes.* Ed. Patricia Donaher. Newcastle, UK:

Cambridge Scholars, 2010. 183–203. Print.

———. "'Just a Fairy, His Wits, and Maybe a Touch of Magic': Magic, Technology, and Self-Reliance in Children's Fantasy Fiction." *Children's Literature and Culture*. Ed. Harry Edwin Eiss. Newcastle, UK: Cambridge Scholars, 2007. 53–76. Print.

Doughty, Terri. "Locating Harry Potter in the 'Boys' Book' Market." Whited 243–257.

Duncan, Sarah Parks. "Instilling a Lifelong Love of Reading." *Kappa Delta Pi Record* Winter 2010: 90–3. Print.

Dunne, Michael. "*Stardust Memories*, *The Purple Rose of Cairo*, and the Tradition of Metafiction." *Film Criticism* 12 (1987): 19–27. Print.

Edwards, Kim. "Making Something of Nothing: Emotion, Creation and Reception in *The Neverending Story*." *Screen Education* Spring 2011: 123–7. Print.

Egoff, Sheila A. *Worlds Within: Children's Fantasy from the Middle Ages to Today*. Chicago: ALA, 1988. Print.

Elster, Charles. "The Seeker of Secrets: Images of Learning, Knowing, and Schooling." Heilman, *World* 203–220.

Fairclough, Norman. "Intertextuality in Critical Discourse Analysis." *Linguistics and Education* 4 (1992): 269–93. Print.

Fife, Ernelle. "Reading J.K. Rowling Magically: Creating C.S. Lewis's 'Good Reader.'" Hallett 137–58.

Flaherty, Jennifer. "Harry Potter and the Freedom of Information: Knowledge and Control in Harry Potter and the Order of the Phoenix." *Topic: The Washington and Jefferson College Review* 54 (2004): 93–102. *MLA International Bibliography*. EBSCO. Web. 16 Feb. 2010.

Fludernik, Monika. "Conversational Narration/Oral Narration." *Handbook of Narratology*. Eds. Peter Hühn et al. New York: Gruyter, 2009. *Narratologia/Contributions to Narrative Theory* 19. *Ebrary*. Web. 9 Jan. 2012.

———. *The Fictions of Language and the Languages of Fiction: The Linguistic Representation of Speech and Consciousness*. New York: Routledge, 1993. Print.

———. *An Introduction to Narratology*. Trans. Patricia Häusler-Greenfield and Monika Fludernik. New York: Routledge, 2006. Print.

Fox, Roy F., ed. *Images in Language, Media, and Mind*. Urbana, IL: NCTE, 1994. Print.

Friedman, Leslee. "Militant Literacy: Hermione Granger, Rita Skeeter, Dolores Umbridge, and the (Mis)use of Text." Anatol, *Reading Again* 191–205.

Gallardo C., Ximena, and C. Jason Smith. "Happily Ever After: Harry Potter and the Quest for the Domestic." Anatol, *Reading Again* 91–108.

Gates, Pamela S., Susan B. Steffel, and Francis J. Molson. *Fantasy Literature for Children and Young Adults*. Lanham, MD: Scarecrow, 2003. Print.

Genette, Gerard. *Paratexts: Thresholds of Interpretations*. 1987. Trans. Jane E. Lewin. New York: Cambridge University Press, 1997. Print. Literature, Culture, Theory 20.

Goldstone, Bette P. "Whaz Up with Our Books? Changing Picture Book Codes and Teaching Implications." *The Reading Teacher* 55 (2001–2002): 362–70. Print.

Grieve, Ann. "Metafictional Play in Children's Fiction." *Papers: Explorations into Children's Literature* 8.3 (1998): 5–15. Print.

Gruner, Elisabeth Rose. "Teach the Children: Education and Knowledge in Recent Children's Fantasy." *Children's Literature* 37 (2009): 216–35. Print.

Gutierrez, Peter. "The Right to Be a Fan." *Language Arts* 88 (2011): 226–31. Print.

Hallett, Cynthia Whitney, ed. *Scholarly Studies in Harry Potter: Applying Academic Methods to a Popular Text*. Lewiston, NY: Edwin Mellen, 2005. Print. Studies in British Literature, vol. 99.

Hancock, Marjorie. *A Celebration of Literature and Response: Children, Books, and Teachers in K-8 Classrooms*. 2nd ed. Upper Saddle River, NJ: Pearson, 2004. Print.

Harbin, Leigh. "'You Know You Wanna Dance': *Buffy the Vampire Slayer* as Contemporary Gothic Heroine." *Studies in the Humanities* 32 (2005): 22–37. Print.

Heilman, Elizabeth E. "Blue Wizards and Pink Witches: Representations of Gender Identity and Power." Heilman, *World* 221–39.

_____, ed. *Critical Perspectives on Harry Potter.* 2nd ed. New York: Routledge, 2003. Print.

_____, ed. *Harry Potter's World: Multidisciplinary Perspectives.* New York: Routledge, 2003. Print.

Helfenbein, Robert J. "Conjuring Curriculum, Conjuring Control: A Reading of Resistance in *Harry Potter and the Order of the Phoenix.*" *Curriculum Inquiry* 38.4 (2008): 499–513. *Academic Search Complete.* EBSCO. Web. 4 Jan. 2010.

Hopkins, Lisa. "Harry Potter and the Acquisition of Knowledge." Anatol, *Reading* 25–34.

Hunt, Peter, ed. *Criticism, Theory, & Children's Literature.* Cambridge, MA: Blackwell, 1991. Print

_____. "Introduction: The Expanding World of Children's Literature Studies." Hunt, *Understanding* 1–14.

_____. *Understanding Children's Literature: Key Essays from the Second Edition of* The International Companion Encyclopedia of Children's Literature. 2nd ed. New York: Routledge, 2005. Print.

_____. "What the Authors Tell Us." Hunt, *Understanding* 190–205.

_____. *Children's Literature: The Development of Criticism.* New York: Routledge, 1990. Print.

Hutcheon, Linda. *Narcissistic Narrative: The Metafictional Paradox.* Waterloo, ON: Wilfrid Laurier University Press, 1980. Print. Library of the Canadian Review of Comparative Literature v. 5.

_____. *A Poetics of Postmodernism: History, Theory, Fiction.* New York: Routledge, 1988. Print.

Huszár, Erika. "What Is Transferred from Novel to Film? Some Criticism of Brian McFarlane's Adaptation Analysis Method." *Sino-US English Teaching* 8 (2011): 544–48. Print.

Jacobs, Alan. "Harry Potter's Magic." Review of *Harry Potter and the Sorcerer's Stone. First Things: A Monthly Journal of Religion and Public Life* January 2000: 35–38. Print.

Jakobson, Roman. *Language in Literature.* Cambridge, MA: Belknap-Harvard University Press, 1987. Print.

Jakobson, Roman, and Linda Waugh. *The Sound Shape of Language.* Bloomington: Indiana University Press, 1979. Print

James, Edward, and Farah Mendlesohn, eds. *The Cambridge Companion to Fantasy Literature.* New York: Cambridge University Press, 2012. Print.

Jentsch, Nancy K. "Harry Potter and the Tower of Babel: Translating the Magic." Whited 285–301.

Johnson, Michael K. "Doubling, Transfiguration, and Haunting: The Art of Adapting Harry Potter for Film." Anatol, *Reading Again* 207–221.

Jones, Dudley. "Only Make-Believe? Lies, Fictions, and Metafictions in Geraldine McCaughrean's *A Pack of Lies* and Philip Pullman's *Clockwork.*" *The Lion and the Unicorn* 23.1 (1999): 89–96.

Kaplan, Deborah. "Diana Wynne Jones and the World-Shaping Power of Language." Rosenberg et al. 53–65.

Keenan, Celia. "Who's Afraid of the Bad Little Fowl?" *Children's Literature in Education* 35.3 (2004): 257–70. Print.

Kirk, Joanna. "Challenging Authority: The Metafictional *Story of Tracy Beaker.*" *The Journal of Children's Literature Studies* 3.3 (2006): 25–38. Print.

Klauda, Susan Lutz, and Allan Wigfield. "Relations of Perceived Parent and Friend Support for Recreational Reading with Children's Reading Motivations." *Journal of Literacy Research* 44 (2012): 3–44. Print.

Kurkjian, Catherine. "Worlds of Fantasy." *The Reading Teacher* 59.5 (2006): 492–503. Print.

Langbauer, Laurie. "The Ethics and Practice of Lemony Snicket: Adolescence and Generation X." *PMLA* 122 (2007): 502–21. Print.

Larsen, Svend Erik. "Self-Reference: Theory and Didactics between Language and Literature." *Journal of Aesthetic Education* 39.1 (2005): 13–30. Print.

Lavoie, Chantel M. "The Good, the Bad, and the Ugly: Lies in Harry Potter." Anatol, *Reading Again* 77–87.

Lehr, Susan. "Fantasy: Inner Journeys for

Today's Child." *Publishing Research Quarterly* 7.3 (1991): 91–101. *Academic Search Complete.* Web. 20 Nov. 2012.

Lehr, Susan S. *Beauty, Brains, and Brawn: The Construction of Gender in Children's Literature.* Portsmouth, NH: Heinemann, 2001. Print.

Le Lievre, Kerrie Anne. "Wizards and Wainscots: Generic Structures and Genre Themes in the Harry Potter Series." *Mythlore* 24.1 (2003): 25–36. *Literature Resource Center.* Gale. Web. 16 Feb. 2010.

Levin, Harry, Carole A. Schaffer, and Catherine Snow. "The Prosodic and Paralinguistic Features of Reading and Telling Stories." *Language and Speech* 25.1 (1982): 43–54. *Academic Search Complete.* Web. 3 Jan. 2012.

Lewis, David. "The Constructedness of Texts: Picture Books and the Metafictive." *Signal* 62 (1990): 131–46. Print.

Little, Edmund. "Re-Evaluating Some Definitions of Fantasy." Mass and Levine 52–62. Excerpt from *The Fantasts.* Amersham, UK: Avebury, 1984.

Little, Tracy. "High School Is Hell: Metaphor Made Literal in *Buffy the Vampire Slayer.*" South 282–93.

Lukens, Rebecca J. *A Critical Handbook of Children's Literature.* 8th ed. New York: Pearson, 2007. Print.

Lurie, Alison. *Don't Tell the Grown-Ups: The Subversive Power of Children's Literature.* New York: Back Bay-Little, Brown, 1990. Print.

_____. "Not for Muggles." *The New York Times Review of Books* 46.20 (1999): 6+. Print.

MacRae, Cathi Dunn. *Presenting Young Adult Fantasy.* New York: Twayne-Simon & Schuster, 1998. Print. Twayne's United States Authors Series No. 699.

Maier, Sarah E. "Educating Harry Potter: A Muggle's Perspective on Magic and Knowledge in the Wizard World of J.K. Rowling." Hallett 7–27.

Mass, Wendy, and Stuart P. Levine, eds. *Fantasy.* San Diego: Greenhaven, 2002. Print. Companion to Literature Movements and Genres.

_____. "What Is Fantasy?" Mass and Levine 12–24.

Mathews, Richard. *Fantasy: The Liberation of Imagination.* New York: Routledge, 2002. Print. Genres in Context.

Mayes-Elma, Ruthann. *Females and Harry Potter: Not All That Empowering.* New York: Rowman, 2006. Print.

McGillis, Roderick. "Learning to Read, Reading to Learn; or Engaging in Critical Pedagogy." *Children's Literature Association Quarterly* 22.3 (1997): 126–132. Print.

McHale, Brian. *Postmodernist Fiction.* New York: Methuen, 1987. Print.

McMillan, Cheryl. "Metafiction and Humor in *The Great Escape from City Zoo.*" *Papers: Explorations into Children's Literature* 10.2 (2000): 4–11. Print.

Meek, Margaret. *How Texts Teach What Readers Learn.* Stroud, UK: Thimble, 1988. Print.

Mendlesohn, Farah. *Rhetorics of Fantasy.* Middletown, CT: Wesleyan University Press, 2008. Print.

Mol, Suzanne E., and Adriana G. Bus. "To Read or Not to Read: A Meta-Analysis of Print Exposure from Infancy to Early Adulthood." *Psychological Bulletin* 137 (2011): 267–96. Print.

Moss, Anita. "Varieties of Children's Metafiction." *Studies in the Literary Imagination* 18.2 (1985): 79–92. Print.

Moss, Geoff. "Metafiction and the Poetics of Children's Literature." *Children's Literature Association Quarterly* 15.2 (1990): 50–2. Print.

Muntersbjorn, Madeline. "Pluralism, Pragmatism, and Pals: The Slayer Subverts the Science Wars." South 91–102.

Musić, Rusmir, and Lyndsay J. Agans. "Five Lessons of a Dumbledore Education: What Harry Potter's Mentor Knows." *About Campus* Nov.-Dec. 2007: 21–3. Print.

Nel, Philip. "You Say 'Jelly,' I Say 'Jell-O'?: Harry Potter and the Transfiguration of Language." Whited 261–284.

Nelson, Claudia. "Writing the Reader: The Literary Child in and beyond the Book." *Children's Literature Association Quarterly* 31.3 (2006): 222–36. Print.

Niemelä, Maarit. "The Reporting Space in Conversational Storytelling: Orchestrating All Semiotic Channels for Taking a Stance." *Journal of Pragmatics* 42 (2010): 3258–70. *Academic Search Complete*. Web. 3 Jan. 2012.

Nikolajeva, Maria. *Children's Literature Comes of Age: Toward a New Aesthetic*. New York: Garland, 1996. Print. Children's Literature and Culture, Vol. 1.

———. "The Development of Children's Fantasy." James and Mendlesohn 50–61.

———. "Exit Children's Literature?" *The Lion and the Unicorn* 22 (1998): 221–36. Print.

———. "Heterotopia as a Reflection of Postmodern Consciousness in the Works of Diana Wynne Jones." Rosenberg et al. 25–39.

———. "How Fantasy Is Made: Patterns and Structures in *The Neverending Story* by Michael Ende." *Merveilles & Contes* 4 (1990): 34–42. Print.

———. "'I Spy Rumpelstiltskin': Playing Games with the Reader in *The Witch's Boy*." *Marvels & Tales* 25 (2011): 316–28. Print.

———. *The Magic Code: The Use of Magical Patterns in Fantasy for Children*. Stockholm: Almqvist, 1988. Print.

Nodelman, Perry. *The Hidden Adult: Defining Children's Literature*. Baltimore: Johns Hopkins University Press, 2008. Print.

Norrick, Neal R. "Using Large Corpora of Conversation to Investigate Narrative: The Case of Interjections in Conversational Storytelling Performance." *International Journal of Corpus Linguistics* 13.4 (2008): 438–64. *Academic Search Complete*. Web. 3 Jan. 2012.

Oakes, Margaret J. "Flying Cars, Floo Powder, and Flaming Torches: The Hi-Tech, Low-Tech World of Wizardry." Anatol, *Reading* 117–28.

Pantaleo, Sylvia. "An Ecological Perspective on the Socially Embedded Nature of Reading and Writing." *Journal of Early Childhood Literacy* 9 (2009): 75–99. Print.

———. "Exploring the Metafictive in Elementary Students' Writing." *Changing English* 14 (2007): 61–76. Print.

———. "The Long, Long Way: Young Children Explore the Fabula and Syuzhet of *Shortcut*." *Children's Literature in Education* 35 (2004): 1–20. Print.

———. "Postmodernism, Metafiction, and Who's Afraid of the Big Bad Book?" *Journal of Children's Literature Studies* 3.1 (2006): 26–39. Print.

———. "Scieszka's *The Stinky Cheese Man*: A Tossed Salad of Parodic Re-versions." *Children's Literature in Education* 38 (2007): 277–95. Print.

———. "What Do Four Voices, a Shortcut, and Three Pigs Have in Common? Metafiction!" *Bookbird* 42.1 (2004): 4–12. Print.

———. "Young Children Engage with the Metafictive in Picture Books." *Australian Journal of Language and Literacy* 28 (2005): 19–37. Print.

———. "Young Children Interpret the Metafictive in Anthony Browne's *Voices in the Park*." *Journal of Early Childhood Literacy* 4 (2004): 211–33. Print.

Pennington, John. "Alice at the Back of the North Wind, Or the Metafictions of Lewis Carroll and George MacDonald." *Extrapolation* 33 (1992): 59–72. Print.

———. "From Elfland to Hogwarts, or the Aesthetic Trouble with Harry Potter." *The Lion and the Unicorn* 26.1 (2002): 78–97. *MLA International Bibliography*. EBSCO. Web. 6 Jan. 2010.

———. "Phantastes as Metafiction: George MacDonald's Self-Reflexive Myth." *Mythlore* 14.3 (1988): 26–9. Print.

Perry, Evelyn M. "Metaphor and MetaFantasy: Questing for Literary Inheritance in J.K. Rowling's *Harry Potter and the Sorcerer's Stone*." Hallett 241–75.

Petzold, Dieter. "A Neverending Success Story?: Michael Ende's Return Trip to Fantastica." Beckett and Nikolajeva 209–40.

Philpot, Don K. "Children's Metafiction, Readers, and Reading: Building Thematic Models of Narrative Comprehension." *Children's Literature in Education* 36 (2005): 141–59. Print.

Pierce, Tamora. "Fantasy Books for Adolescents Inspire and Empower." Mass and Levine 63–8. Rpt. of "Fantasy: Why Kids Read It, Why Kids Need It." *School Library Journal* Oct. 1993: 50–1.

Pinsent, Pat. "The Education of a Wizard:

Harry Potter and His Predecessors." Whited 27–50.

Pond, Julia. "A Story of the Exceptional: Fate and Free Will in the Harry Potter Series." *Children's Literature* 38 (2010): 181–206. Print.

Prince, Gerald. *Narratology*. New York: Mouton, 1982. Print.

Pugh, Tison, and David L. Wallace. "Heteronormative Heroism and Queering the School Story in J.K. Rowling's *Harry Potter* series." *Children's Literature Association Quarterly* 31.3 (2006): 260–81. Print.

Reynolds, Kimberley, ed. *Modern Children's Literature: An Introduction*. New York: Palgrave Macmillan, 2005. Print.

Richardson, J. Michael, and J. Douglas Rabb. *The Existential Joss Whedon: Evil and Human Freedom in* Buffy the Vampire Slayer, Angel, Firefly *and* Serenity. Jefferson, NC: McFarland, 2007. Print.

Ringrose, Christopher. "A Journey Backwards: History Through Style in Children's Fiction." *Children's Literature in Education* 38 (2007): 207–18. Print.

Rosenberg, Teya, et al. *Diana Wynne Jones: An Exciting and Exacting Wisdom*. New York: Lang, 2002. Print. Studies in Children's Literature Vol. 1.

Rosenblatt, Louise M. *The Reader, the Text, the Poem: The Transactional Theory of the Literary Work*. Carbondale: Southern Illinois University Press, 1978. Print.

Rotruck, Amie Rose. "Where Have All the Tomboys Gone? Female Figures in British Children's Fantasy Series." *Foundation* 88 (2003): 54–67. Print.

Rudd, David. "Theorising and Theories: How Does Children's Literature Exist?" Hunt, *Understanding* 15–29.

Sanders, Joe Sutliff. "The Critical Reader in Children's Metafiction." *The Lion and the Unicorn* 33(2009): 349–361. Print.

Sarland, Charles. "Critical Tradition and Ideological Positioning." Hunt, *Understanding* 30–49.

Schanoes, Veronica L. "Cruel Heroes and Treacherous Texts: Educating the Reader in Moral Complexity and Critical Reading in J.K. Rowling's Harry Potter Books." Anatol, *Reading* 131–145.

Schiffrin, Deborah. *Discourse Markers*. New York: Cambridge University Press, 1987. Print. Studies in International Sociolinguistics 5.

Scholes, Robert. *Fabulation and Metafiction*. Chicago: University of Illinois Press, 1979. Print.

Skulnick, Rebecca, and Jesse Goodman. "The Civic Leadership of *Harry Potter*: Agency, Ritual, and Schooling." Heilman, *World* 261–277.

Smith, Karen Manners. "Harry Potter's Schooldays: J.K. Rowling and the British Boarding School Novel." Anatol, *Reading* 69–87.

South, James B. "'All Torment, Trouble, Wonder, and Amazement Inhabits Here': The Vicissitudes of Technology in *Buffy the Vampire Slayer*." *Journal of American & Comparative Cultures* 24 (2001): 93–102. Print.

South, James B., ed. *Buffy the Vampire Slayer and Philosophy: Fear and Trembling in Sunnydale*. Chicago: Open Court, 2003. Print.

South, James B. "'My God, It's Like a Greek Tragedy': Willow Rosenberg and Human Irrationality." South 131–45.

Steege, David K. "Harry Potter, Tom Brown, and the British School Story: Lost in Transit?" Whited 140–56.

Stephens, John. "Analysing Texts: Linguistics and Stylistics." Hunt, *Understanding* 73–85.

_____. *Language and Ideology in Children's Fiction*. New York: Longman, 1992. Print.

_____. "Metafiction and Interpretation: William Mayne's *Salt River Times, Winter Quarters*, and *Drift*." *Children's Literature* 21 (1993): 101–17. Print.

Stephens, John, and Robyn McCallum. *Retelling Stories, Framing Culture: Traditional Story and Metanarratives in Children's Literature*. New York: Garland, 1998. Print.

Stephens, Rebecca. "Harry and Hierarchy: Book Banning as a Reaction to the Subversion of Authority." Anatol, *Reading* 51–65.

Stoodt-Hill, Barbara D., and Linda B. Amspaugh-Carson. *Children's Literature: Discovery for a Lifetime*. 2nd ed. Upper

Saddle River, NJ: Merrill-Prentice Hall, 2001. Print.

Stonehill, Brian. *The Self-Conscious Novel: Artifice in Fiction from Joyce to Pynchon.* Philadelphia: University of Pennsylvania Press, 1988. Print. Penn Studies in Contemporary American Fiction.

Suleiman, Susan R., and Inge Crosman, eds. *The Reader in the Text: Essays on Audience and Interpretation.* Princeton: Princeton University Press, 1980. Print.

Sunderland, Jane. *Language, Gender, and Children's Fiction.* New York: Continuum, 2011. Print.

Sutton, Roger. "Metafiction for Beginners." Rev. of *The Red Book* by Barbara Lehman and *Into the Forest* by Anthony Browne. *The New York Times Book Review* 14 Nov. 2004: 22. Print.

Tatsumi, Takayuki. "Comparative Metafiction: Somewhere between Ideology and Rhetoric." *Critique* 39 (1997): 2–17. Print.

Teare, Elizabeth. "Harry Potter and the Technology of Magic." Whited 329–42.

Thompson, Deborah L. "Deconstructing Harry: Casting a Critical Eye on the Witches and Wizards of Hogwarts." Lehr 42–50.

Tiffin, Jessica. "Ice, Glass, Snow: Fairy Tale as Art and Metafiction in the Writing of A. S. Byatt." *Marvels & Tales* 20 (2006): 47–66. Print.

———. *Marvelous Geometry: Narrative and Metafiction in Modern Fairy Tale.* Detroit: Wayne State University Press, 2009. Print. Series in Fairy-Tale Studies.

Tolan, Fiona. "'Everyone has left something here': The Storyteller-Historian in Kate Atkinson's *Behind the Scenes at the Museum.*" *Critique* 50 (2009): 275–90. Print.

Tomashevsky, Boris. "Thematics." *Russian Formalist Criticism: Four Essays.* Trans. Lee T. Lemon and Marion J. Reis. Lincoln: University of Nebraska Press, 1965. 61–95. Print.

Trites, Roberta Seelinger. "Manifold Narratives: Metafiction and Ideology in Picture Books." *Children's Literature in Education* 25 (1994): 225–42. Print.

Van Praagh, Shauna. "Adolescence, Autonomy, and Harry Potter: The Child as Decision-Maker." *International Journal of Law in Context* 1.4 (2005): 335–73. Print.

Walker, Jeanne Murray. "Fantasy Allows Children to Question the Status Quo." Mass and Levine 69–77. Excerpt from "Critical Issues and Approaches." *Teaching Children's Literature: Issues, Pedagogy, Resources.* Ed. Glenn Edward Sadler. New York: MLA, 1992.

Wall, Barbara. *The Narrator's Voice: The Dilemma of Children's Fiction.* New York: St. Martin's, 1991. Print.

Waller, Alison. *Constructing Adolescence in Fantastic Realism.* New York: Routledge, 2009. Print. Children's Literature and Culture series.

Waugh, Patricia. *Metafiction: The Theory and Practice of Self-Conscious Fiction.* New York: Routledge, 1984. Print. New Accents series.

Whited, Lana A., ed. *The Ivory Tower and Harry Potter: Perspectives on a Literary Phenomenon.* Columbia: University of Missouri Press, 2002. Print.

Widdowson, Peter. "'Writing Back': Contemporary Re-visionary Fiction." *Textual Practice* 20 (2006): 491–507. Print.

Wilcox, Rhonda. "In 'The Demon Section of the Card Catalog': *Buffy* Studies and Television Studies." *Critical Studies in Television* 1 (2006): 37–48. Print.

Wilkey-Stibbs, Christine. "Intertextuality and the Child Reader." Hunt, *Understanding* 168–79.

Wolfe, Gary K. *Critical Terms for Science Fiction and Fantasy: A Glossary and Guide to Scholarship.* New York: Greenwood, 1986. Print.

Wu, Yung-Hsing. "The Magical Matter of Books: Amazon.com and *The Tales of Beetle the Bard.*" *Children's Literature Association Quarterly* 35 (2010): 190–207. Print.

Wyile, Andrea Schwenke. "The Drama of Potentiality in Metafictive Picture Books: Engaging Pictorialization in *Shortcut, Ooh-la-la,* and *Voices in the Park* (with Occasional Assistance from A. Wolf's *True Story*)." *Children's Literature Association Quarterly* 31 (2006): 176–96. Print.

Yates, Sally. "Understanding Reading and Literacy." Hunt, *Understanding* 159–67.

Yearwood, Stephanie. "Popular Postmodernism for Young Adult Readers: *Walk Two Moons*, *Holes*, and *Monster*." *The ALAN Review* Spring/Summer 2002: 50–3. Print.

Zanger, Jules. "Fantasy Literature Both Reflects and Defies Reality." Mass and Levine 35–45. Rpt. of "Heroic Fantasy and Social Reality: *Ex nihilo nihil fit*." *The Aesthetics of Fantasy Literature and Art*. Ed. Roger C. Schlobin. Notre Dame: University of Notre Dame Press, 1982.

Zimmerman, Virginia. "Harry Potter and the Gift of Time." *Children's Literature* 37 (2009): 194–215. Print.

Zipes, Jack. *Relentless Progress: The Reconfiguration of Children's Literature, Fairy Tales, and Storytelling*. New York: Routledge, 2009. Print.

_____. *Sticks and Stones: The Troublesome Success of Children's Liteature from Slovenly Peter to Harry Potter*. New York: Routledge, 2001. Print.

Index

Abbott, Tony 2, 6, 7, 51, 56–88, 63, 167
Abhorsen trilogy 2, 28–30, 31, 34, 42
The Absolutely True Diary of a Part-Time Indian 25
The Adventures of Tom Sawyer 5, 13, 14
Alice's Adventures in Wonderland 14, 18
Andersen, Hans Christian 19
Arabian Nights 51
Armitt, Lucie 15, 16, 18, 19
Around the World in Eighty Days 57, 58
Artemis Fowl 2, 11, 34–36, 37, 45, 168
Attack of the Mutant 51, 58–60
authority 1, 3, 5, 6, 7, 8, 12–14, 25, 26, 27, 28, 34, 35, 37, 39, 43, 44, 45, 46, 47, 49, 59, 65, 86, 91, 92, 112, 113, 121, 123, 128, 129, 132, 133, 135, 139, 148, 167, 168

Barone, Diane M. 9, 10
Bealer, Tracy L. 120, 121, 127
Bedtime Stories 107–110
Beware of Storybook Wolves 2, 6, 50, 52–53, 54
Beyond the Spiderwick Chronicles series 39–41, 168
Black, Holly 2, 37–41, 43, 44, 47, 82, 83, 84, 102, 116, 167, 168
Blume, Judy 13
book learning 2, 8, 14, 27, 30, 43, 47, 87, 88, 111, 112, 116, 118, 121, 122
The Book Thief 25
Bosch, Pseudonymous 7, 15, 64–66, 67, 68, 77, 80
Bramwell, Peter 24
Brennan, Herbie 2, 6, 35–37, 167
Buffy the Vampire Slayer 87–92, 105
Butler, Catherine 19

Caine, Rachel 2, 7, 44–47, 167
Captain Underpants series 3, 7, 8, 77–80, 168
Carroll, Lewis 18, 19

Casci, David 92
Chen, Fanfan 55
Child, Lauren 2, 6, 50, 52–54, 55, 58, 63
A Christmas Carol 57, 58
The Chronicles of Narnia 18, 20
"Cinderella" 27, 54, 100
Cleary, Beverly 13
Cohn, Dorritt 68
Colfer, Eoin 2, 11, 34–36, 37, 45, 168
Contreras, Ernie 50, 51–52, 53, 54, 55, 56, 60, 63, 92, 93, 168
Cormier, Robert 64
Cracked Classics series 2, 6, 7, 51, 56–58, 167
Crago, Hugh 12
critical reading 25, 85, 112, 113, 123, 131

Darigan, Daniel L. 59
Demers, Patricia 9
diaries 2, 31, 33, 65, 101, 105, 113–114, 132–133, 136; *see also* journals
didacticism 1, 5–6, 7, 9–12, 14, 19, 21, 23, 24, 25, 26, 27, 50, 51, 54, 56, 58, 92, 94, 167, 168
Didicher, Nicole 17
DiTerlizzi, Tony 2, 37–41, 43, 44, 47, 82, 83, 84, 102, 116, 167, 168
Don Quixote 21
Dracula 58

Ella Enchanted (book) 2, 6, 27–28, 81, 82, 167
Ella Enchanted (film) 81–82
Enchanted 98–100, 107, 110
Ende, Michael 7, 50, 54–56, 58, 63, 94, 95, 96, 165, 168
The Epic of Gilgamesh 14
experiential learning 27, 111

Fade 64
Faerie Wars 2, 6, 36–37, 167

195

Fludernik, Monika 67–8
Freaky Friday 64
Friedman, Leslee 120, 126, 129, 134
Funke, Cornelia 2, 6, 8, 140–154, 155, 159, 162, 167

Gates, Pamela S. 15, 17, 19
"Goldilocks" 53, 54
Goldstone, Bette P. 23
Grieve, Ann 23
Groosham Grange series 13
Gulliver's Travels 51

Harry Potter series 2, 5, 8, 10, 13, 14, 16, 17–18, 111–139, 140, 159, 167, 168
The Hobbit 18
Hollindale, Peter 11
Horowitz, Anthony 13
hostile readers 162–164
Hughes, Thomas 13
The Hunger Games series 16
Hunt, Peter 10, 13, 14, 15, 19
Hutcheon, Linda 21, 22

ideology 1, 6, 7, 11, 13, 20, 23, 25
imaginative readers 96, 162–164
The Immortals series 20
implied author 64, 65, 66, 69–72, 74, 76, 77, 78, 79
implied reader 66, 67, 68, 69, 78
Inkheart series 2, 6, 8, 140–154, 155, 159, 162, 167
intertext 22, 98
intrusion fantasy 17, 18, 37, 101, 107

"Jack and the Beanstalk" 51, 93
Jacobs, James S. 59
Jakobson, Roman 10
journals 101–103, 104, 105, 106, 107; *see also* diaries
Junie B. Jones series 13

The Kane Chronicles 2, 7, 8, 66, 67, 68, 69–77, 80
Kipling, Rudyard 13
Kirschner, David 50, 51–52, 53, 54, 55, 56, 60, 63, 92, 93, 168

Lang, Andrew 18
The Last of the Mohicans 94
Lavoie, Chantel M. 128, 138
Lehr, Susan 17
Levine, Gail Carson 2, 6, 27–28, 81, 82, 167
Levine, Stuart P. 16, 17, 18, 19
Lewis, David 50, 141
Libyrinth 6, 47–49, 168
The Lioness Quartet 20

literacy 1, 2, 7, 8, 47, 48, 141, 146, 148, 149, 150, 154, 164
Little House series 13
"Little Red Riding Hood" 53
Little Women 1, 14
Lord of the Rings series 17, 94
Lurie, Alison 1, 14, 24

MacDonald, George 18
The Mahabharata 15
Malice series 7, 51, 58, 60–63, 67, 154, 167–168
Mass, Wendy 16, 17, 18, 19
Mathews, Richard 14, 15, 16, 18
McCaughrean, Geraldine 64
Mendlesohn, Farah 8, 17–18, 37, 107, 155, 158, 162
metafiction 3, 7, 8, 21–26, 50, 54, 63, 64–65, 66, 67, 69, 71, 76, 78–79, 80, 100, 112, 141
Miéville, China 24
Moby Dick 51, 52
Molson, Francis J. 15, 17, 19
The Morganville Vampires 2, 7, 44–47, 167
Moss, Anita 21
Moss, Geoff 22–23
Mrs. Frisby and the Rats of NIMH 25
The Mysteries of Harris Burdick 5, 6

The Name of This Book Is Secret 7, 15, 64–66, 67, 68, 77, 80
Nelson, Claudia 50, 58, 63, 140–141, 162–163
The Neverending Story (book) 7, 50, 54–56, 58, 63, 94, 95, 96, 165, 168
The Neverending Story (film) 94–96, 97, 98, 100
The Neverending Story II: The Next Chapter 94, 96–97
The Neverending Story III: Escape from Fantasia 94, 97–98
Newbery, John 9
Nikolajeva, Maria 19, 22, 24, 64, 65, 66, 69, 77, 80
Nix, Garth 2, 28–30, 31, 34, 42
Nodelman, Perry 1, 6, 11, 12, 13, 14, 20, 24, 25, 26, 63, 167
North, Pearl 6, 47–49, 168

The Odyssey 15

A Pack of Lies 64
The Pagemaster (book) 50, 51–52, 53, 54, 55, 56, 60, 63, 92, 93, 168
The Pagemaster (film) 92–94, 98, 100
Pantaleo, Sylvia 23, 54
Park, Barbara 13

parody 7, 8, 79, 80
pedagogy 112, 120, 121
Percy Jackson & the Olympians 2, 7, 8, 66–69, 70, 71, 72–73, 75, 76, 77, 80
Perrault, Charles 9
Petzold, Dieter 94
Pierce, Tamora 20–21
Pilkey, Dav 3, 7, 8, 77–80, 168
Pippi Longstocking 5, 13
The Princess and the Goblin 18

Ramona series 13
realism 1, 6, 8, 13, 15–16, 17, 21–22, 23, 24, 27, 28, 50, 64
realistic fiction *see* realism
rebellion 14, 121, 129, 132–138
reluctant readers 1, 2, 13, 56, 57, 140, 167
Riordan, Rick 2, 7, 8, 66–77, 80
Rodgers, Mary 64
Romeo and Juliet 57
Rowling, J.K. 2, 5, 8, 10, 13, 14, 16, 17–18, 111–139, 140, 159, 167, 168
Rudd, David 12

Sage, Angie 7, 15, 30–34, 37, 43, 59, 67, 168
Sanders, Joe Sutliff 3, 24–26, 27, 50, 63, 112, 167
Sarland, Charles 1, 6, 11, 12, 13, 16, 23
Schanoes, Veronica L. 112–113, 122
Scott, Michael 6, 7, 41–44, 47, 167, 168
The Secret Circle 84–87, 88, 89, 168
The Secrets of the Immortal Nicholas Flamel series 6, 7, 41–44, 47, 167, 168
self-reliance 8, 40, 112, 121, 123, 139
self-sufficiency 3, 86, 87, 91, 168
Septimus Heap series 7, 15, 30–34, 37, 43, 59, 67, 168
"Sleeping Beauty" 53
Smith, L.J. 84, 101
"Snow White" 99
The Spiderwick Chronicles (books) 2, 37–39, 40, 41, 43, 44, 47, 82, 83, 84, 102, 116, 167, 168

The Spiderwick Chronicles (film) 82–84, 85, 91, 106
Stalky & Co. 13
Steffel, Susan B. 15, 17, 19
Stephens, John 1, 6, 11, 19, 20, 24, 25
Stine, R.L. 51, 58–60, 63
Stonehill, Brian 21, 22, 24
The Strange Case of Dr. Jekyll and Mr. Hyde 51, 52
subversiveness 1, 5, 7, 14, 20, 24, 25, 34, 35, 50, 58, 79, 132, 133, 135, 167, 168
The Sylvie Cycle 3, 8, 155–165

Tales from the Thousand and One Nights 147
Tales of a Fourth Grade Nothing 13
Tolkien, J.R.R. 17
Tom Brown's School Days 12
Townley, Roderick 3, 8, 155–165
Toy Story 165
Treasure Island 2, 51, 94, 147, 157
Tristram Shandy 21
Trubetzkoy, Nikolai 10
Tunnell, Michael O. 59
Twilight series 16

Un Lun Dun 24, 25

The Vampire Diaries 91, 101–107, 108
Van Allsburg, Chris 5, 6

Walker, Jeanne Murray 19, 20, 21, 168
Waugh, Patricia 21, 22, 80
Who's Afraid of the Big Bad Book? 6, 50, 52, 53–54, 55, 58
The Wind in the Willows 18
A Wizard of Earthsea 20
The Wonderful Wizard of Oz 157
Wooding, Chris 7, 51, 58, 60–63, 67, 154, 167–168

Zanger, Jules 24
Zipes, Jack 10